HIDDEN GEMS

'A word is a bridge thrown between myself and another.'
M M Bakhtin / V N Volosinov (1986)

hidden gems

EDITED BY DEIRDRE OSBORNE

OBERON BOOKS

This collection first published in 2008 by Oberon Books Ltd
521 Caledonian Road
London N7 9RH
Tel: 020 7607 3637
Fax: 020 7607 3629
info@oberonbooks.com
www.oberonbooks.com

Table of Contents

Acknowledgements

My sincerest thanks: to James Hogan for enabling this project to take place, to Stephen Watson for his editing work and to Edith Frampton. My gratitude to Mojisola, Valerie, Courttia, Lennie, Lemn and Paul for trusting me with their precious plays and to Gabriele, Suzanne, Valerie, Robert and Lynette for their critical commentaries at such short notice! I could not have put this together without the ongoing personal support in the UK from Lara, Tom, Kate, Gotti, Utibe, Maria, Kadija and Karen. For this, I am immensely grateful.

For Isabella

Introduction

By Dr Deirdre Osborne

(Goldsmiths, University of London)

The year 2003 marks the beginning of a significant phase in British theatre history. In that year, eleven plays by black British dramatists were staged in mainstream London theatres,[1] creating an unprecedented profile for work that historically had not experienced continuous visibility in the British theatrescape. The phenomenon was greeted by black artists in a variety of ways, ranging from claims for a renaissance in black British drama, to guarded responses that this might not necessarily signal a permanent situation.[2]

In both marginal and mainstream socio-cultural contexts, the changing profile of drama by indigenous black British writers illustrates how identity is fluid, affected by political, economic, and social processes, as Rahier observes,

---

1   The venues and plays were: **Royal Court Theatre**: *crazyblackmuthaf***in'self* by DeObia Oparei (January 2003) and *Fallout* by Roy Williams (June 2003), **Hampstead Theatre**: *born bad* by debbie tucker green (April 2003), **Royal National Theatre**: *Elmina's Kitchen* by Kwame Kwei-Armah (May 2003), **Soho Theatre**: *dirty butterfly* by debbie tucker green (February 2003) and *Wrong Place* by Mark Norfolk (October 2003), **Theatre Royal Stratford East**: *Urban Afro Saxons* by Kofi Agyemang and Patricia Elcock (November 2003). This continued into 2004 with the Royal Court Theatre staging *The Sons of Charlie Paora* by Lennie James (February 2004) – published for the first time in this volume – and *Blest Be the Tie* by Dona Daley (April 2004), Theatre Royal Stratford East's *The Big Life* by Paul Sirett and Paul Joseph (April 2004) and Royal National Theatre's *Sing Yer Heart Out for the Lads* by Roy Williams (April 2004) and Kwei-Armah's *Fix Up* (December 2004). Rhashan Stone's *Two Step* premiered at the Almeida as part of the September PUSH 04 season of black-led arts.

2   In response to Andrea Enisuoh's statement about 'a huge frenzy of activity […] a renaissance in black theatre', the director Paulette Randall linked her misgivings – 'that was just a fluke' – to the politics of subsidy: 'everyone's got to do something culturally diverse now otherwise, you ain't going to get your money basically […] the only difference is that we had plays that were in fairly, I mean incredibly established buildings'. In contrast, the playwright Kwame Kwei-Armah responded 'that we could have during that period of fourteen months, eleven plays on, that come from our cultural perspective, for me is a wonderful thing […] it is a signal not just to the community from which I herald, to say, that we are beginning to allow you to tell stories from your own perspective and your own lens and allow it to go into the mainstream.' *Theatre Voice* recorded 22/10/2004. Transcript 3. Black British Theatre.

> Identities, whatever they may be, cannot be defined once and for all, in fixed or essentialist terms, as if they were unchanging, frozen, as it were, in time and space. [...] they are constantly enacted and re-enacted, performed and performed anew, within specific situations [...] that provide sites for their negotiations and renegotiations, their definitions and redefinitions. (Rahier 1999: xv)

In the mid-nineties, Amina Mama had concluded that an irresolvable tension operated in the pairing of terms Black British: '[t]he black British subject is therefore born out of an imposed contradiction between blackness and British-ness, British-ness being equated with whiteness in the dominant symbolic order'. (Mama 1995: 114) However, by the new millennium, a shift in the process of terming is detectable, when Mike Phillips notes, '[a]t its most basic, and incidentally, its most meaningful level, to be black British implies a history of interaction and negotiation with the white British over the routine features of everyday life in Britain'. (Phillips 2002: 62) A case might well be made for a used-by-date for certain terminology, indicating the shifts and dissociations that are traceable. Certainly it remains necessary to 'read the label carefully before use'. For, as Heidi Safia Mirza has pointed out, '[t]erminology constructs boundaries and meaning. [...] The organic nature of terming means that a word must come from its value to those who use it.' (Mirza 1997: 19)

An example of this can be seen when, at the commemorative celebration of Ken Saro-Wiwa, *Dance the Guns to Silence* (London South Bank, 2005), the poet and playwright Lemn Sissay, as Master of Ceremonies, emphasised, 'Everything I do, I do as a black man' because, as he later explained,

> Throughout my career, I've seen the wider media and audiences believe you're talking about being black *only* when you tell them you are and when you say you're proud to be black, there's always somebody who'll say 'no, no, you're a human being, we're all human beings'. Does that assume that when you say you're a black man, you feel you're either: less of a human being, or different? Every now and then I want to remind people that if I write [for example] a love poem, I do it in the context of being a black man.[3]

3   Lemn Sissay. Personal interview with Deirdre Osborne, September 2006.

(I) dentity politics have been a key characteristic in asserting the right to write for people who have experienced marginalisation. The term is not used here to indicate a special route to authenticity achieved by multiple oppressive subjecthoods – one privileged over the other – but to emphasise the fashioning of a creative voice that reveals (as Mirza identifies in relation to Black British Feminism), '*other ways of knowing*' and 'functions as a challenge to the taken-for-granted normative assumptions of prevailing discourse'. (Mirza 1997: 5) The playwrights in this anthology certainly strive to represent the alternatives of knowing to which Mirza refers. They may draw upon strong links to English literary and theatrical traditions, but their work also asserts a counter-narrativity, in which – as Lauri Ramey observes of Black British poets – 'art as a site for reclaiming the powers of identity and belonging that reinforce self and culture, past and present' is evident. (Ramey 2004: 120) In advocating the counter-story as a means of developing full moral agency and self-worth, Hilde Lindemann Nelson describes the evolution of one's personal identity:

> [It] embodies an understanding. Through one's own and others' selective, interpretive, and connective representations of the char-acteristics, acts, experiences, roles, relationships, and commitments that contribute importantly to one's life over time, an identity makes a certain sort of sense of who one is. (Nelson 2001: 15)

The intricacies of carving out access to cultural citizenship frequently go hand-in-hand with political gains and these reverberate across imaginary and national landscapes. Proclaiming a positive identity through the term black counters the historical and political distortions effected by white supremacy which have become socially enshrined as institutionalised racism. Learning to love blackness (as bell hooks articulates from an American context[4]) is an act of resistance and retrieval in a white-dominated cultural arena. It requires the recognising of overt and systematic prejudice as well as domination through more subtle forms. It involves a mental and emotional decolonisation, a

---

4   hooks, bell. *Black Looks: Race and Representation* Boston, MA: South End Press, 1992.

recalibration of attitudes and beliefs about black people – held by both black and white folk – that position and represent black people unfavourably against the monolithic norm of whiteness.[5]

Ideological and social reliance upon the binary of black and white as a basis for hierarchical distinctions has become increasingly untenable, in the face of the heterogeneity of members of the British population, at the ex-imperial centre and in the multiplicity of indigenous identities[6] – and not only from within the borders of the British Isles. As Jantjes argues, the post-1993 opening up of European borders has further destabilised cultural fixtures:

> The myth of British culture being insular and racially specific was slowly crumbling under the evidence of cross-cultural mixing with both European and extra-European cultures. (Jantjes 2000: 267)

Historically, black dramatists working in British theatre have not experienced a playing field comparable to their white counterparts. In addition, black British artists have contended with an antecedence of displacement by African-American artists. 'Opportunities for experimentation, failure, and refinement have not habitually accompanied the genesis of black theatre in Britain as black theatre practitioners in all spheres of expertise have encountered establishment roadblocks on their routes to development and practice.' (Osborne 2007: 223) There are also further inhibitors to the scope and artistic ambitions of writers. In Bonnie Greer's article, 'The Great Black Hope', Baroness (Professor) Lola Young refers to 'complicity on the part of black people too, who view anything that isn't "street" to be "inauthentic" and not "really black"'. Another interviewee, Christopher Rodriguez,

---

5   Lorna Laidlaw, one of the first two black actresses in the Birmingham-based company, Women and Theatre, commented on the restrictive expectations she faced in performing. 'You can't help but be aware of your colour when you perform. In a production I did with another company, I played the part of a young girl of seventeen who started a relationship with a young boy which culminated in teenage pregnancy. The discussion that followed after the performance highlighted the audience view of "Oh well, Black people always do that, they always have babies really young".' (Aston 1997: 132).

6   For examples of social commentators who draw attention to this, see: Rose and Rose who refer to, 'complex identifiers such as "black English" or "Brummie Punjabi British" or "British Sikh"' (Rose and Rose 2005:21) and Alibhai-Brown, who describes 'a large number of bi-racial and combined ethnicity people, as well as all kinds of ethnic and religious groups including the English, Scottish, Welsh, Irish, Polish, Turkish, Jewish, Chinese, and a host of other people.' (Alibhai-Brown 2001: viii).

describes the influential filtering process that occurs when a venue (with a majority white audience profile) commissions and stages work by black dramatists: '[i]t could create a situation in which the work may be limited to sensationalism, or easy narratives that compound what the audiences believe of non-whites anyway'. Greer herself recounts a young black director's words, 'there are black people out there right now who start out far more qualified to run British cultural institutions [than their white peers.] But for many boards we still represent a risk [...] that somehow a black person would lead their institution down some monocultural route that is race specific.' (Greer 2006: 23)

British theatre's white-male dominated critical coterie is hugely influential as a filter to public perception. Although the vast multi-generic, polyphonic, ritual-based African theatre traditions have influenced many black dramatists, the critical judgements of the work have been dominated by Euro-centric and Western aesthetic models as definitive indicators of merit. This has led to disparaging and dismissive critical responses to much black-led work or, in turn, over-compensatory praise for work that is culturally unfamiliar.[7] As Lynette Goddard writes in relation to black women dramatists, '[t]he whole aesthetic structure of Western critical taste and judgement exists to support the white/male status quo, so the black woman playwright necessarily has to transgress some Western aesthetic principles to make her point'. This subsequently leaves a playwright open 'to being criticised for not sticking to the rules of the theatrical discourse that she is attempting to enter'. (Goddard 2007: 98). White male critics' inability to register the inappropriateness and irrelevance of their dominant aesthetic standards to work that operates with different aesthetic principles and political agendas continues to be prevalent in a theatre history which has been beset by invisibility and archival neglect.[8] This, in turn, renders problematic identifying a uniquely black British theatre aesthetic.

7   Alibhai-Brown, Yasmin. 'Black art can be just as bad as art by whites' *The Independent* 5 February, 2005.

8   In response to issues around the perpetuity of black theatre, the Arts Council of England commissioned a sustained theatre consultation about the infrastructural and developmental needs of 'The Sector'. This term, coined by SuAndi and adopted by the report aimed to 'place to one side all of the heritage-based ways of naming practitioners'. As the report noted, '[i]f progress is to be made, it is vital that artists and art – and those who contribute to its making and distribution – must be considered on the basis of quality of work'. (*Whose Theatre?: Report on the Sustained Theatre Consultation* 2006:

The longevity of plays (measured through publication and revival in performance) is dependent upon the intimate connection between critical attention and the cultural legitimation this can provide. The impetus behind *Hidden Gems* is two-fold: (i) to centralise plays whose distinctive subject-matter and experiments with form and genre position the experiences of black people in local, national and international contexts of culture, politics and performance; and (ii) to urge the development of inter-disciplinary critical practices, interactions between people who champion the work and people who produce, perform and explain the intentions behind it. The plays in this volume testify to their writers reaching out beyond the conditions and constraints around subject matter which many black dramatists have faced in seeking to have their work commissioned and staged. The essayists who critically introduce the plays have long been committed to teaching and critically engaging with writing and performance which centralises black experiences in Britain.

Playwrights Paul Anthony Morris and Courttia Newland implicitly critique the agency of powerful institutions – the International Monetary Fund (*35 Cents*) and the Arts Council (*B is for Black*) – in perpetuating disenfranchisement and impoverishment, economically and culturally, through applications of fiscal control and subsidy redolent of imperialist ideology. As Suzanne Scafe writes in her critical introduction to *B is for Black*, Newland presents the 'difficult issue of public funding for the arts in a society where muted but damaging forms of racism continue to undermine its multicultural aspirations'. (19) In highlighting a history of injustice and oppression, an agit-prop influence is apparent in Morris' play. Robert Beckford's discussion, 'Slave Trade to Trade Slaves' historicises the goods-driven profiteering and its human toll:

> Slavery and then colonisation in Jamaica established and indeed normalised harsh working conditions, a near-psychotic drive for cheap produce, unequal social relations and foreign domination of social

---

13) There have been recent significant advances made organisationally with partnerships between the Victoria and Albert Museum's Theatre collection, Talawa and Future Histories, as an attempt to redress the chronic disappearance of legacies of black theatre and performance in Britain. Jo Melville's living archive of posters and ephemera dating back to Ira Aldridge in the nineteenth century is an example of a non-subsidised archive which tours regional Britain. (Eye to Eye Productions)

and political affairs. The latest wave builds on the old – the whips and chains being replaced by financial burdens of equal restriction and brutality. (353)

Like Morris, whose play is set in Jamaica, Lennie James' *The Sons of Charlie Paora* also uses an ex-colonial context, New Zealand, as the location for his drama. The ongoing destructive repercussions of colonisation upon the indigenous Maori people and their traditions, exposes the fallacy of any notion of a post-colonial world. The fissure between cultures seems irreparable; the rise of the introduced Europeans continues to correspond to the demise of the original race – all viewed through what Valerie Kaneko Lucas refers to as 'the prism of a complex intercultural lens' (192) where,

> the play explores the tensions of dual heritage. Although Paora was only one-eighth Maori, 'his soul was brown' [...] and the boys claim him as one of their own, according him the same respect they might to a Maori chieftain. Yet Paora's children claim him as white, and his marriage to a white woman as his attempt to transcend a Maori heritage which they associate with the underclass. (194)

James' own experience reveals the complexity of vantage points in viewing the colonial legacy. When working on the play in New Zealand in 2001, he recalls his shock of inclusion in British theatre heritage. 'In New Zealand I became an Englishman [...] in New Zealand, all the history of England was my history. When people interviewing me spoke of the long history of British theatre, it was all mine. I was allowed to own it... I can't tell you how strange that sensation was.' (James 2004: 12) A further disarming reading of him occurred in a social situation, at a bar, when he was blamed, as a British citizen, for imperial Britain's misdeeds towards the indigenous Maori people. Thus, the narrative of decolonising accountability supplanted any shared experiences of racial oppression that might be forged between a Maori and a black Briton. James' origins in the centre of the ex-empire ratified him as a beneficiary of its history when viewed from this ex-colonial context – an irony that did not escape him.

The three monodramatists in this anthology, Mojisola Adebayo, Valerie Mason-John and Lemn Sissay, write and then perform themselves into being, through trans-generic methodologies. The forms they choose are dynamic – not fixed – resistant to the abstract logic of Western thought. The body of their texts (written down first) is transmitted through their own bodies, thereby allowing personal and specific evolutions of their texts into performance. In performing their monodramas, they represent a synthesis of their physical body as a tool for articulating the text (visually and verbally), the social, gendered, racialised bodies that have been attributed to them and the theatre and performance sign-systems in which it all takes place. The body politic, which inscribes their social identities in racial and gendered ways, is de-scribed and re-written, in their creative renderings, via these monodramas.

I use the term monodrama rather than solo performance or autobiography in performance. The difficulties in terminology can be seen in specific examples. Mason-John's 'Queen' in *Brown Girl in the Ring* does not refer to Mason-John's actual name, although her costume of platinum wig and white evening gown and gloves is reminiscent of her MC persona, Queenie. Adebayo, who cross-dresses as a white man to play the disguised Ellen Craft, and Sissay, who wears his own everyday clothes in performing *Something Dark,* are explicitly self-referential, to varying degrees in using their own names as speakers of the text, but all three performers play characters as well. This produces a complex fusion of speaking positions and subjectivities. It also elicits the question of whether or not these monodramas could be performed credibly by other people – and if not, what effect does this have upon the longevity of the pieces?

An approach to analysing monodrama promises considerable overlap of literary criticism and performance analysis. Laura Severin employs John Pearson's notion of intracompositional framing (Pearson 1990: 16), in her analysis of four modern women poets noteworthy for their live performances and suggests multiple 'interartistic' frames work together. (Severin 2004: 4) For Severin, the legacy of the Victorian dramatic monologue establishes a springboard which launches these women's performances of their poetry. Firstly, the double disclaimer of what *might* be the female poet's views – use of first-person pronoun – is made ambiguous by the artistic vehicle of the poetic voice. The speaker frames the poet's voice, which is then theatricalised through performance.

Valerie Mason-John's *Brown Girl in the Ring* actually collapses the royal body and the body politic into a regal everywoman who testifies to the ongoing effects of the racialising colonial enterprise and its stranglehold on history in which, as Gabriele Griffin identifies in her essay, 'the conjunction of race and class figures as a violent terrain in which only certain permutations and heritages are acknowledged'. (283) Griffin draws upon Judith Butler's model of relationality in accounting for oneself, the constructing of 'I' and the tenacity required when – Sissay's *Something Dark* also attests to this – '[t]hat experience is one where connection, lineage, belonging and identity are denied. And that denial requires a constant effort from the self both to construct and maintain itself.' (281) Likewise, *Moj of the Antarctic*, by Mojisola Adebayo, is a project of retrieval and archiving through dramatising 'untold stories from black history' (Lynette Goddard, 143). Adebayo's monodrama functions as a poignant commemoration of the ingenuities of survival for an Afri-queer ancestor in a white-male dominated world that traded in human beings. As Goddard notes, 'The show connects the past with the present and links a range of different themes such as race, gender, and sexuality with big global issues such as climate change.' (143) Adebayo encapsulates her project as an:

> [e]xploration of climate change and the impact on Antarctica and Africa, the legacies of the industrial revolution and the slave trade, whiteness, racism, the binary and what it means to be 'Queer' and Black, *Moj of the Antarctic: An African Odyssey* is, in a sense, in Foucault's terms, a history / herstory of the present. (Adebayo March 2007: n.p.)

There is no doubt that since 2003 there have been opportunities to see plays by indigenous black dramatists, in mainstream British theatres, on a scale not previously possible. However, whilst this suggests a cultural inclusiveness that was historically only sporadically achieved, the West End, with its dictate of commercial viability, has to date risked housing only one play – a transfer of the Royal National Theatre's *Elmina's Kitchen* by Kwame Kwei-Armah which was contingent upon his playing the lead role, due to his high profile in the television soap opera, *Casualty* (BBC). That said, since the (2003–2004) season (noted above), the uninterrupted staging of black dramatists' work across a range of venues suggests, tantalisingly, that an important shift has occurred in what theatres will offer, what audiences want to see and what playwrights (albeit still a male majority) can produce in response to their own creative needs.[9]

9   The following London theatres staged these plays between 2005 and 2008 (notably there are some revivals): **The Tricycle:** *One Under* by Winsome Pinnock (February – March 2005), *Let There Be Love* by Kwame Kwei-Armah (January – February 2008), *Days of Significance* by Roy Williams (transfer of RSC production, March 2008), **Soho Theatre:** *trade* by debbie tucker green (March 2006), *White Open Spaces* by Francesca Beard, Richard Rai O'Neill, Rommi Smith, Ian Marchant, Sonali Bhattacharyya, Courttia Newland, Kara Miller (September – October 2006), *The Christ of Coldharbour Lane* by Oladipo Agboluaje (May – June 2007), *Pure Gold* by Michael Bhim (September – October 2007), *Joe Guy* by Roy Williams (January – February 2008), **Theatre Royal Stratford East:** *High Heel Parrotfish* by Christopher Rodriguez (April – May 2005), *Bashment* by Rikki Beadle-Blair (May – October 2005), *The Harder They Come* by Perry Henzell (May – June 2006, revived February – March 2007 and for the Barbican Theatre, March 2008), *Marilyn and Ella* by Bonnie Greer (February – March 2008), *FaddaMuddaSistaBrudda* by Rikki Beadle-Blair (May 2008), **Royal Court Theatre:** *stoning mary* by debbie tucker green (April 2005), *93.2 FM* by Levi David Addai (August 2005), *11 Josephine House* by Alfred Fagon (revival, 29 November 2006), *random* by debbie tucker green (March – April 2008), *Oxford Street* by Levi David Addai (May 2008), **The Young Vic:** *generations* by debbie tucker green (February 2007), *dirty butterfly* by debbie tucker green (revival February 2008), *Mules* by Winsome Pinnock (revival, March 2008), **Royal National Theatre:** *Statement of Regret* by Kwame Kwei-Armah (January – April 2008), **Lyric Theatre, Hammersmith:** *Sweet Yam Kisses* by Pat Cumper and Courttia Newland (February – March 2006), *Absolute Beginners* by Roy Williams (April – May 2007), *Rough Crossings* by Simon Schama, adapted by Caryl Phillips (September – October 2007), **Hackney Empire:** *De Botty Business* by Benjamin Zephaniah (5 March 2008), *Noughts and Crosses* by Malorie Blackman, adapted by Dominic Cooke (March – April 2008), *Revenge of a Black Woman* by the Blue Mountain Theatre Company (April 2008).

B IS FOR BLACK

Politics, Multiculturalism and Performance: Courttia Newland's *B is for Black*

By Dr Suzanne Scafe
(London South Bank University)

ourttia Newland, the author of *B is for Black*, is an accomplished novelist and playwright. His first two novels, *The Scholar* (1997) and *The Society Within* (1999) are both popular – they have been reprinted several times – and critically acclaimed. These novels, set on the fictional Greenside Estate, West London, are gritty portraits of the culture and lives of their young, mostly black characters. Described variously as the new Irving Welsh, 'the rising star of Brit-lit and chronicler of inner city life' and 'purveyor of urban realism',[1] Newland has consciously tried to move out of the '"ghetto-writing" niche I have been deposited in'.[2] Not content with returning to the same successful formula and genre, he has written a series of well-received detective novels and more recently, a collection of short stories that experiment with the uncanny, entitled *Music for the Off-Key: Twelve Macabre Short Stories* (2006). Newland has also edited an anthology of black British writing, *IC3: The Penguin Book of New Black Writing in Britain* (2000) and is currently working on a film adaptation of his first novel. His career as a playwright began in 1997 with the production of *Estate of Mind* by The Post Office Theatre Company. After its successful first run at the Portobello Festival, London, Newland was confirmed as the company's in-house writer and The Post Office Theatre Company, with Riggs O'Hara as its director, was formally established.

B is for Black is Newland's fifth play: it continues to reflect and develop his preoccupation with the fraught and complex relationships between individual, cultural and class identities, but in this work these issues are represented through its main character Ben, a black Oxford graduate who grew up in Barnes, a cultural world away from the mean streets and walkways of the Greenside estate. Despite the dominant theme of cultural conflict, however, there are several moments of caring and affectionate interaction between the characters and Newland

---

1 www.britishcouncil.org/usa-arts-literature-uk.

2 'Courttia Newland on Himself' in *Shots: The Crime and Mystery Magazine* http://www.shotsmagazine.co.uk.

seems concerned to demonstrate, as he has in his later play *Sweet Yam Kisses* (2006) – co-written with Patricia Cumper – that there is the potential for positive, supportive relations across cultural divides and within the black community. This play is also about writing, performance and the difficult issue of public funding for the arts in a society where muted but damaging forms of racism continue to undermine its multicultural aspirations. Each scene is framed by introductions and commentary from a chorus of young actors, Jones, Lamming and Spencer, whose marginalised position in relation to the main drama is used to represent the often fraught relationship between small community theatres such as The Post Office, whose innovative work is often hidden or ignored, and the powerful interest groups that dominate the world of arts management and funding. Humorous asides are directed at O'Hara and 'Courts' (Newland); their interactions, suggesting a Brechtian influence, mirror the improvisation-led theatre for which The Post Office is known and emphasise the self-reflexive character of the play. The characters signal the use of dramatic irony and speak to its Shakespearean echoes: they debate the play's concerns, one of which is to critique the rhetoric that frames the formal discourses of arts, culture, the media and public funding. Spencer's comment, 'It'll be alright – Cultural diversity is in right now you know... There's loads of award schemes and lottery money and initiatives set up to help people like us get a foothold in the market place! You have to believe it!' is met with silence, before Lamming retorts: 'You didn't read the script did you?' (29–30) This conversation serves as a preface to the play and provides an informed context for the action that unfolds.

Ben is introduced in the next scene, the first scene of the 'main' play, by his opposite, Imani, described as 'your typical conscious sister [who has] modified her dress slightly in order to appear funky and not too militant'. (31) She is an administrative assistant in the local authority arts office and Ben is the newly employed, first black Senior Arts Officer. The drama is built around the interaction between these two characters and the tension that arises from the hints about their sexual attraction, their cultural difference and similarities and finally, their conflicting ambitions. Imani is intelligent and sexually attractive; she is also playful and outgoing and uses all these characteristics to manipulate and attempt to destroy Ben. She introduces him to 'Children of Tamana' (COT), the group that she and her boyfriend

Don are involved with, and she exposes him to information and ideas about black civilisations and culture. She explains the origins of the word 'Tamara' and the aims of the group: 'Tamara, a place in Ancient Kamit where many people believe the Black Civilisation grew to maturity. The project I'm involved in has vowed to continue that task, bringing positive teachings, spirituality and healing to sons and daughters of Kamit'. (61) In an ironic reversal of her name's meaning – 'faith' in Swahili – she exercises bad faith, creating rifts and divisions where she could have enabled healing and nurturing.

Initially she is represented as both the conduit and an obstacle to his cultural growth and development. She encourages him to read but is also a reminder of who he is not and how far he has travelled from his cultural 'roots'. As he learns more and more about African history and culture, he moves further away from his white father-in-law, who employed Ben to 'enforce the Status Quo' and his wife, who feels increasingly alienated by his preoccupation with what she perceives as his militancy. Ben's increased consciousness of his cultural identity and the achievements of African culture are represented as positive and enriching. What the play seems to suggest, however, is that not everyone who is politically and culturally 'conscious' has Ben's integrity, his kindness and his good nature. Although the information that Imani has is vital to the promotion of black cultural pride – and to any concept of multiculturalism and diversity – she uses what she knows in a project of self-aggrandisement rather than for the betterment of her community. By the end of the play Don's successful theatre group, which has struggled without funding for eight years, is no nearer to being funded. The local authority could have been encouraged by Ben's influence to take its commitment to diversity seriously but Raymond, the leader of the council and his father-in-law, is alienated by the politically ill-judged rhetoric of Ben's first speech at the COT meeting. The distance between the centres of money and power and culturally and socially marginalised groups such as COT remains intact and Ben, the potential bridge between the two, is about to be destroyed.

One theatre critic has described the play as 'Othello with three Iagos'[3] and as the characters in the chorus suggest, there is an intentional use of elements of Shakespearean tragedy. Ben is described by Imani as the 'token' minority in a white world but he is also an

3   Review of 'B is for Black' Kieron Quirke *Time Out* 8 October 2003.

outsider in the black inner-city world to which he is recruited. He is not an orator of Othello's stature but he is a gifted public speaker and it is his final speech and its powerful effect on his audience that brings about his final demise. Imani, like Iago, is manipulative almost without motive: she enjoys his entrapment and the power she is able to wield over him. Raymond and Michael, who are also interested in driving a wedge between Ben and his wife Kate, simply support her machinations. In the end, however, Ben neither kills nor dies and the tragedy that unfolds is one of lost hopes and aspirations. The future for the children of Africa, or 'Ancient Kamit' as defined by Imani, is blighted by hatred and conflict.

In an essay entitled 'Courttia Newland's Psychological Realism and Consequential Ethics', R. Victoria Arana argues that all his work demonstrates the importance of 'ethical behaviour' but that this is made emphatic in *B is for Black*. She writes: 'sound societies call for ethical behaviour on the part of their members and ethical behaviour entails caring for the true happiness of others, over and above racial, class and ethnic or gender differences'. In addition she adds that Newland stresses the importance of ethical behaviour 'at home' or with 'one's closest kin'.[4] Almost at the end of the play Ben says: 'You know Imani... You know when I first met you I used to think that in other times...; you know, in another life, if things were different and we were different people, maybe we'd...'. And he continues, 'But that could never happen here and now, in our time could it?' (139) These lines underline the play's pessimistic ending and its suggestion that before multiculturalism, however it is defined, is achieved, the 'children of Africa/Kamit' need to be able to work in harmony in order to achieve a shared goal of greater cultural and political awareness.

4   Arana, R. Victoria. 'Courttia Newland's Psychological Realism and Consequential Ethics' in Kadija Sesay ed. *Write Black, Write British: From Post Colonial to Black British Literature* Hertford, Hansib 2005 pp 86-106.

B is for Black

by

Courttia Newland

Characters

IMANI SHAW

BEN NELSON

KATE NELSON

RAYMOND ARMITAGE

MICHAEL CERWIN

DON KENWORTHY

JONES

LAMMING

SPENCER

B is for Black was first performed on 1 October 2003 at Oval House Theatre in a production by The Post Office Theatre Company, with the following cast:

IMANI SHAW, Carol Moses

BEN NELSON, Joel Trill

KATE NELSON, Emma Rand

RAYMOND ARMITAGE, Ronald Markham

MICHAEL CERWIN, Dominik Golding

DON KENWORTHY, Akpome Macaulay

JONES, Daniel Booth

LAMMING, Leon Barr

SPENCER, Veronica Isabel

Director Riggs O'Hara
Set & Costume Design Clara Cormack
Lighting Design Riggs O'Hara

Act One

SCENE 1

House lights dim. LAMMING and JONES enter the stage from opposite sides – LAMMING on the left, JONES on the right. They move hurriedly, as if there is no time to waste and spare none letting the audience get settled in. JONES approaches the audience with a friendly ringmaster's grin.

JONES: Laaadies and gentlemen, girls and boys, we The Post Office Theatre Company welcome you; one and all –

LAMMING: (*Bored.*) All and one –

JONES shoots LAMMING a look but doesn't let him stop his flow.

JONES: – To *The Multicultural Theme Show*!

JONES pauses to allow time for him to take a bow and collect his appreciation from the audience. Beside him, LAMMING hasn't bowed and is shaking his head painfully.

LAMMING: Now look what you've done.

JONES: (*Irritated.*) What?

LAMMING: You messed it all up man. At the beginning. We've only just started and you messed it all up. Riggs is gonna go mad. Court's is gonna turf you out the company. You're gonna get it.

JONES: How? What did I do?

LAMMING: I bet Riggs is sitting in the dressing room right now wiv the knives out for you. You're gonna get it man.

JONES: So d'you mind telling me what I supposedly did wrong?

LAMMING grins. It's clear that he's enjoying this little moment of his.

LAMMING: You said the wrong play. You said – 'Ladies and Gentleman, blah, blah, blah, welcome one and all, all and one to *The Multicultural Theme Show*!' That's wrong! That's next year's play! This year's play is –

27

They say this next line together.

BOTH: *B is for Black!*

LAMMING: (*Casual.*) You kept doing it in rehearsal too. I thought you woulda learnt the line by now.

JONES reaches into his back pocket and pulls out an A4 sheet of paper, stabbing at it with a finger.

JONES: It's in the script!

LAMMING: All right, so now we've done that bit don't you reckon we should set the people straight before we lose our jobs?

JONES: (*Putting away his script.*) Don't you need to get paid for work to constitute a job? Otherwise it's slavery, right?

LAMMING: Don't worry, you're doing this for love.

JONES: Am I?

LAMMING: That's what Riggs and Courts told me.

JONES: Oh okay.

Silence.

LAMMING: Go on then!

JONES: Oh! Oh yeah, all right then. Laaadies and gentlemen, girls and boys, we The Post Office Theatre Company welcome you, one and all, all and one, to our premier run of our all-star play – *B IS FOR BLACK*!!

JONES really attempts to work the audience, moving close up to them, shaking someone by the shoulder or knee, trying to instill some excitement into them. Behind him, LAMMING is shaking his head.

LAMMING: (*Bored.*) Tonight you will see a tale of one man's quest, a tale of betrayal, love and misplaced trust –

JONES is staring at him.

Yes?

JONES: You think *I'm* messin' it up? Put some welly into it will you? I've seen more life in a morgue.

LAMMING: It doesn't work. The intro. I said it already. It's old skool man.

JONES: (*Laughing.*) I'd like to see you tell our writer that!

LAMMING: (*Looks into the audience for me.*) It doesn't work!

JONES: (*Hisses.*) Ay; will you stop that! There's a woman casting for *Hollyoaks* in the third row and if you mess this up for me I'm gonna stone you to death, I swear I will.

LAMMING: (*Grins.*) It don't matter, you ain' gettin a part. Not when you're with this company mate. You're too street now.

JONES: Oh, and you're not?

LAMMING: Nah mate, I'm urban! Dat's a whole different ting. Urban means I can be the token Black guy in an all-white cast and have a five-year run in any soap I choose.

LAMMING looks pleased at this prospect.

JONES: An dat's a good thing?

LAMMING: It's a career! An it's much better than being white in a majority black company, believe me.

JONES: You think so?

LAMMING: I know so man...

SPENCER is pushed from stage left by KATE and RAYMOND. They take a quick peek at the audience and then disappear, leaving SPENCER looking awkward.

SPENCER: (*To LAMMING and JONES.*) Hey, wha' you doin?

BOTH: Nothin.

SPENCER: Well start the bloody show will you?

The boys look hurt. They sit on the side of the stage dejectedly, as if SPENCER's speech took the wind out of both their sails.

Oh for crying out loud!

She walks over to the boys and sits between them, putting an arm around each shoulder.

It'll be all right... Cultural Diversity is in right now you know... There's loads of award schemes and lottery money and initiatives set up to help people like us get a foothold in the marketplace! You have to believe it!

More silence.

LAMMING: You didn't read your script did you?

SPENCER: (*Slightly ashamed.*) I read my part.

JONES: You should have a look at the rest.

SPENCER: I tell you what, I'll do the intro!

JONES: Thanks Spencer. You're a star.

SPENCER gets to her feet.

Laaadies and gentlemen, girls and boys, we The Post Office Theatre Company welcome you, one and all, all and one, to the premier run of our all-star play –

JONES: We've done that bit.

SPENCER: Huh?

JONES: We did that bit already.

LAMMING: Twice.

SPENCER: Oh. So where shall I take it from?

JONES: '… Love and misplaced trust…'

LAMMING: I still think that's way too dramatic…

SPENCER: Sssh! It's too late now innit? (*She false-smiles into the audience.*) … A tale of betrayal, love and misplaced trust. You will laugh, cry, be moved to anger then want to laugh once again. Ladies and gentlemen, tonight we give you – B IS FOR BLACK!

Front lights dim and rear lights go up. LAMMING, SPENCER and JONES leave the stage.

SCENE 2

Rear lights reveal the office, with computers, tables and chairs. A lone woman, IMANI, sits at one of the computers talking on the phone. She looks like your typical conscious sister, though she has modified her dress slightly in order to appear funky and not too militant.

IMANI: Uh huh… Mmmmm… Yeah…. Exactly! Mmmm…. Uh huh… (*She laughs.*) You're so sweet! Well thank you darling but I'm really not that bothered, truthfully I'm not. I'm just happy they got a Black man an' not one of these kids straight outta college all bright-eyed and bushy-tailed, you know? Mmmm… That's what I'm saying! Well, I caught sight of his CV last week… Very impressive I must say… Oxford graduate… Yeah! Uh, English Lit, Economics… He even put skiing as one of his hobbies… I know! Maybe he's the brother from another planet…

The door opens and BEN walks into the office. He's a tall clean-cut-looking Black man with an air of self importance around him. IMANI spies him and unconsciously sits up a little straighter. BEN gives her a friendly nod and waits by the door.

Yeah, tell me about it… I'm looking forward to it though. I've got a feeling big things are going to happen in this department… Yeah… Yeah… All right Jean, I betta be off yeah? See you darling.

She puts the phone down and smiles at BEN, then gets to her feet and sticks out a hand.

Sorry about that, it was Jean Withers from Pulse Theatre, you know down in North Chamberlayne? She's such a chatterbox I can hardly get her off the phone.

BEN smiles politely but says nothing.

I'm Imani Shaw, pleased to meet you. You are Ben Nelson aren't you?

BEN: Yes. Yes, I am.

IMANI: Welcome to West Chamberlayne Arts. And congratulations by the way.

BEN: Thank you.

BEN moves over to the only empty desk in the small office. IMANI watches him like a mother witnessing her child's first steps. BEN walks to the desk and stands silently for a moment, then picks up a small plastic bag left there.

IMANI: To welcome you into the fold.

BEN: Ah! Thank you… I wasn't expecting anything –

IMANI: Of course you weren't. Would you like a cup of tea?

BEN: Yes. Yes please.

IMANI leaves the office. BEN sits down and looks around at everything. He seems contemplative and confident, yet wary. He opens the plastic bag. Inside is an African carving, which he looks over with a faint smile on his lips. There is a greetings card with the present, another African offering. BEN reads the message. His smile gets wider. He switches on his computer and taps the desk. IMANI comes back with two steaming mugs. She hands one to BEN and sits at her desk.

IMANI: There you are. Sugar's in the little packets by the side of your computer.

BEN: Thank you.

IMANI: You're welcome. *(Pause.)* Like it?

BEN: Well, I've only just got here… Oh, you mean the carving. Yes, it's beautiful. Thank you very much.

IMANI: No worries. I want you to feel at home here B. There's never been two Black people in this department at the same time.

BEN: Really? That's novel. How long have you been here?

IMANI: Two years, on and off.

She turns to her desk and begins typing into her computer. BEN watches her for a long while.

BEN: Uhh… Do you have any idea what I should be getting on with today? No one's really told me anything.

IMANI: *(Turns to face him.)* Oh sorry, I forgot to tell you that Mr. Tompkins left your itinerary by your in-tray. He said to call him if you have any problems or queries.

BEN: Oh. Oh, okay.

IMANI turns her back on him once more and keeps typing. BEN, looking lost, sips his tea and looks over his in tray. Grabbing a sheet of A4, he reads, then puts down his tea and begins to type. IMANI looks over her shoulder briefly, smiles, then continues on. Lights dim.

SCENE 3

KATE walks on stage holding a large box and struggling with the load. We can see from the pictures and writing that this box contains a brand new computer. She eases it down, then straightens up slowly, holding her back and sighing. She's just about to go back out of the living room door when a man comes in, holding another box – this one containing speakers. They stop and stare at each other for a long time. The man is MICHAEL.

KATE: What are you doing here?

MICHAEL: You don't know do you? You honestly don't know how much it hurts to hear you talk like that Katie. Otherwise you wouldn't do it. Would you?

KATE: *(Ashamed.)* Look, you know I don't mean any harm. I'd just like to know what you're doing in my house. I think that's a legitimate question.

MICHAEL: The front door was open. You can't leave your front door open even if you do live in North Chamberlayne, and you definitely can't go off and leave your car unlocked. You're asking for trouble Katie.

KATE: Thanks. You're right. And will you please stop calling me Katie? My name is Kate.

MICHAEL: Fair enough. Where shall I put this?

KATE: Just wherever. I'll move it later.

MICHAEL does as he's told then stands up, looking steadily at KATE. She doesn't hold his gaze, but doesn't move either.

MICHAEL: Can I sit down?

KATE: (*Sighs.*) Go on then.

He does. She stares for a moment, then sits on the other side of the sofa, far away from MICHAEL.

MICHAEL: So how have you been?

KATE bursts out laughing. MICHAEL looks hurt again.

What?

KATE: Nothing Michael. Nothing. I've been fine actually. Trying to do this old house up for the most part. Stripping, sanding, painting, buying bits and pieces, making the place ours. It's taken a while but it's getting there.

MICHAEL: It looks good. You're doing a great job.

KATE: Well, the living room isn't quite finished, or the hallway... And I have had some help...

MICHAEL: (*Smarting.*) I know that... I know...

KATE: Of course... (*Big sigh.*) So, how have you been?

MICHAEL: Not bad at all actually. Sold a couple of paintings last month.

KATE: Did you?

MICHAEL: I certainly did! You know that purple and blue one on the massive canvas, the one with the splashes you said reminded you of a bad trip.

KATE: How could I forget? You sold it?

MICHAEL: Only for a grand!

KATE: No! Michael, that's wonderful, it really is!

MICHAEL: Yeah, I've spent the money but at least I'm getting my name out there. All I need is a magazine feature or a full exhibition and I'll sell the others, I know I can. I love my work now Kate.

MICHAEL: You always loved your work. You just went through a bad patch that's all. It can happen to the best of us.

MICHAEL: Could say the same for us I suppose. Couldn't you?

KATE looks at her feet.

KATE: How did you find me?

MICHAEL: I saw your father in town. He told me you wouldn't mind my coming over. It's been so long.

KATE: He should've given you the number here if he really wanted to be helpful. Father always thinks of me last when he's carrying out his kind deeds.

MICHAEL: If you must know, I think he felt rather sorry for me. He was being helpful Katie.

KATE gets to her feet. She grabs a pen and scribbles onto a piece of paper. MICHAEL's eyes never leave her. She hands him the paper.

KATE: I think you should go now. There's my phone number so you can call and pop around when I've had a chance to tidy up, or maybe when my husband's home. I'd like you to meet him. I think you'd get on. Anyhow, give me a call in a week or so when I'm less busy and we'll catch up properly. I'd love to talk but I really must get to work, all right?

MICHAEL is a bit taken aback but manages to maintain composure.

MICHAEL: Fine. I'll call you next week.

KATE: Fine. Nice to see you again.

MICHAEL: (*Smiles.*) Really good to see you Katie, it truly is. Don't worry, I'll see myself out.

MICHAEL leaves. KATE goes over to her drinks table and pours a glass of brandy. She downs it in one, then goes back to the sofa and sits there gazing at nothing. Lights dim.

SCENE 4

Lights up. BEN is standing by his desk facing IMANI, who has turned her chair around and is watching him with great interest. There is a jovial feel in the office now.

BEN: ... So, there's me full of pride and confidence walking into the club, through the front mind, just so everyone can see me. All me mates, my girlfriend of the time, the talent scout... And even though none of them were looking at me, I still felt good about the night's performance, still felt like I could make my mark. So I get to the backstage dressing room, open the door; and Imani (*Laughs.*) I can't overstate how much like a jury those guys looked. They were silent. They stared into my face like they wanted to tell me what was wrong through mental telepathy, only they couldn't work up the power. Me being the bright spark of the group, I could tell something was up right away, so I say; 'Guys. Guys, what's goin' on?' And the only one of them with any self respect – Grant, I'll never forget that man – says to me: 'You can't play guitar, you can't dance and you definitely can't sing Ben Nelson. So you tell us. Why the hell are you leading this band?'

They collapse into belly-hugging, thigh-slapping laughter.

IMANI: You poor thing! So what did you say?

BEN: All I could do was look him straight in the eye and tell the truth. They were my best friends for Christ sake! So I say, 'Cos you're all too kind to tell me that I stink?' They laugh, I laugh, Grant sings lead in my place and they get the bloody recording contract. They wouldn't have if I'd sung that night.

IMANI: But what about you though? I thought you had dreams of being the UK's answer to Jimmy Hendrix, Lenny Kravitz? What did you do?

BEN: Ah, I knew I didn't have it really. I'd been running around for a long time trying to convince myself and the world, but I didn't have what it took and it showed. I went off to Uni and the guys let me look over their contracts from time to time; theirs was the first contract I successfully negotiated. It was a good one too, but the record biz didn't work out for them. By then I'd realised I didn't have to be an artist to be involved in the arts.

IMANI: At least you realised. Some people never do.

BEN: Yes, but what's really needed is some kind of infrastructure put in place to nurture some of those people. Not all of them, just some. I've seen it so many times: an average talent through hard work, perseverance and guidance, becomes outstanding within a very short space of time. What's missing from most funding bodies is patience and a desire to build a working relationship with the artists around them. You know how it goes. For the most part the arts are just another business run on a who-you-know basis, when most of the true talent – the street-level artists – never get a look in. It's unfair, and it's got to stop.

IMANI: (*Smiling.*) Yes well, you're right – you know you're right. But what do you intend to do about it now you run the show?

BEN: That's a good question and one that I've thought about for a long time. How do I make things better? Do you know that I told myself I wouldn't apply for this job if I couldn't find an answer? (*Laughs.*) Course you don't, how would you know that? The way I see it, I've got to be the conduit between what's going on out there and the decisions being made beyond here. I've got to make sure useful information is passed to artists regardless of their relations with arts officers, in the hope of building new alliances with a wider range of practitioners. Then, and only then, will the artistic climate in Chamberlayne change, and change for the better.

IMANI: (*Clapping.*) Bravo! I like that! Well said!

BEN: Now I'm going to get off my soapbox if you don't mind. More tea?

IMANI: Yes thank you.

BEN leaves the office. IMANI is smiling to herself like a teenager in love. The phone rings and she answers.

West Chamberlayne Arts… Hey, how you doing? I'm fine, not bad at all… Yeah, I'll be there, of course I will. Do you need anything? Uh huh… Sure, no problem. Actually, I was thinking that I might bring somebody with me. Yeah… The guy that started at my work, remember I told you about him? I think so… Anyway, I'll be there for sure even if I come on my own… Yeah…

BEN comes back into the office.

Okay babe, that sounds great! See you tomorrow. Bye…

BEN: No sugar, right?

IMANI: Right. I'm trying to lose these thighs and while I admit that I'm not trying very hard, every mickle makes a mockle as my Gran used to say.

BEN: Well don't try too hard. Women are so weight conscious these days it's hard to believe that men actually prefer you with a bit of surplus; but we do.

IMANI: That would make me feel better if I was even remotely worried about what men thought.

BEN: What? You're one of those lot saying you want to lose the weight for you, all that lark?

IMANI: (*Smiles.*) 'That lark', is exactly what I'm saying!

BEN: Okay… I'll shut my mouth then shall I?

IMANI: You are a smart man… Did they teach diplomacy at Oxford then?

BEN: Oh no! My mother taught me that!

They are smiling, enjoying the light-hearted banter that comes with making a new friend, relaxing in each other's company. The door knocks.

IMANI: Come in!

KATE walks into the office, followed by her father, RAYMOND ARMITAGE, head of Chamberlayne Council. IMANI gets to her feet.

Can I help –

BEN is up and on his feet behind her.

BEN: It's okay Imani... (*To KATE and RAYMOND.*) Hello darling...
Afternoon Raymond.

*He kisses KATE and shakes RAYMOND boldly by the hand while
IMANI watches with a horrified expression on her face, halfway
between shock and pain.*

How are you both?

KATE: Fine darling... You have a jot of lipstick...

*KATE busies herself scraping the lipstick from his mouth.
RAYMOND looks uncomfortable, as does IMANI.*

RAYMOND: Yes we're fine Benjamin, all the better for seeing you
my dear boy... Now, how are you settling in?

BEN: Perfectly Raymond, with the help of my new colleague...
(*He turns to face IMANI.*) Kate, Raymond, meet the very
lovely Imani Shaw; Imani, meet Kate Nelson and Raymond
Armitage: my wife and father-in-law.

IMANI steps forward to shake RAYMOND's hand.

RAYMOND: Good afternoon my dear... By God Benjamin,
you're right! She's stunning!

IMANI: Thank you... Actually, we have met before Mr
Armitage. The 'Arts In Our Borough' Conference, must be
two years ago now. I gave a paper, 'Breaking the Mainstream
Myth'.

RAYMOND: Ah! Please, please, no formalities... You must call
me Raymond. Do you know, that paper must have slipped
my mind... I do know that I was there...

IMANI: Well, never mind, there were a lot of papers that day...

BEN: And... Uh Imani, this is my wife... Kate Nelson...

*Reluctantly, IMANI turns to KATE. There is a simmering unease
between the two women.*

IMANI: Pleased to meet you!

KATE: Yes, pleased to meet you too! Father, you never
mentioned how pretty Imani was when you told us about

the job. It must be difficult for the men to keep their minds on work!

They all laugh, though BEN's seems a little forced.

IMANI: Well, Ben's actually the only person I share an office with, though he seems to be coping just fine. If I was you I'd put my picture in one of those little photo frames you get in the pound shops, stick it on his desk. That way you'll always have an eye on him won't you?

BEN laughs out loud while IMANI chuckles beside him, but RAYMOND doesn't get the joke and KATE, embarrassed, clears her throat. One-nil to IMANI. BEN looks around, takes note of the tense atmosphere, then does some damage limitation.

BEN: We should leave shouldn't we? You booked the table at Razzles didn't you darling?

KATE: Yes I did, and they won't keep it for more than ten minutes so we ought to get along.

BEN: Let me just log out of my computer and we're off.

RAYMOND: *(To IMANI.)* Lovely to meet you my dear. We must all go out to dinner one evening and you must remind me of that paper you read. It sounds fascinating.

IMANI: That would be lovely.

RAYMOND kisses the back of her hand. IMANI turns to KATE and nods.

Nice to meet you. Look after him, he's a good man.

KATE: *(Smiles.)* He certainly is.

BEN comes back.

BEN: Thank you for a perfect first day Imani.

He plants a kiss on her cheek. IMANI tries to hold her smile but it falters a little as BEN backs off and wraps an arm around KATE's shoulder. KATE grins. One all.

IMANI: No worries. See you tomorrow Ben.

BEN: Good night Imani.

RAYMOND: Ta-ta my dear…

KATE nods once and they all leave IMANI alone in the office. She turns to face the audience with a stern look on her face, then sits at the computer and continues to type. Lights dim.

SCENE 5

JONES and SPENCER come from backstage. JONES is carrying three wine glasses and a tablecloth, while SPENCER has a bottle of wine and a candle. Behind them, LAMMING has a small table. JONES and SPENCER are leaning on each other and laughing, while LAMMING puts down the table and faces IMANI, watching her with a grin.

SPENCER: (*Laughing.*) You see the look on her face!

LAMMING: Leave her alone! Look at her, she's shaken! She didn't expect that!

LAMMING walks offstage. JONES and SPENCER lay the table, pour the wine and light the candles.

SPENCER: Well I dunno what she expected really. Oxford educated, played in a rock band, talks like a lawyer… Stands to reason he'd marry outside his race.

JONES: You think so?

SPENCER: That's what the statistics say…

She walks offstage, and comes back with a chair. LAMMING returns with two more. They place the chairs around the table.

JONES: Oi Lamming, you heard what Spencer says? She reckons Imani was stupid for expecting any different from our Ben…

SPENCER: I didn't say stupid! I just thought she was asking a bit much that's all…

JONES: … Seeing as he's a bit educated and he played in a rock band and stuff. What d'you reckon?

LAMMING: (*Thinks a moment.*) Well, I tend to think he's a man caught between two worlds and his desire to exist in both without being torn apart. His fight is one of identity, a struggle to find himself…

SPENCER: (*Walks away.*) See what happens when you take too many acting classes?

JONES: I thought he was quite eloquent...

LAMMING: Will you lot please do your link before they get here? It's like GCSE Drama working with you lot!

JONES: All right, all right, you're not exactly Denzel either!

LAMMING gives him a dirty look, then he and SPENCER exit stage right and left respectively. JONES turns to audience while a half light appears on IMANI. She is sitting and staring into space, looking thoughtful.

As you can see, Imani wasn't exactly pleased to discover that her new boss had married... Well, you know...

SPENCER: (*From the back.*) A white woman!

JONES: (*Clears his throat.*) I was going to say the daughter of a Council Chairman...

SPENCER gives a cheeky grin. IMANI gets up and exits stage right. KATE, BEN and RAYMOND appear, walking towards the table and chairs. They sit and begin to mime drinking and talking.

JONES: ... Raymond Armitage was a former stationer who ran a small shop for ten years before he bought out a supplier and began selling wholesale. He had been the Chairman of Chamberlayne Council for two years when Ben took Kate as his wife. His working colleagues knew how unhappy Raymond was and urged him to see the political advantages of such an in-law. The following year, Raymond offered Ben the job as West Chamberlayne's Senior Arts Officer.

JONES gives a half-bow, then exits stage left. Front lights dim.

SCENE 6

BEN, KATE and RAYMOND begin to speak as though midway through their conversation. KATE and BEN are animated and full of beans, while RAYMOND is quiet.

BEN: ... Raymond, you must see it, it's the most exciting thing to hit the big screen in a very long time... It's got everything... Youth, colour, music... The element of exotica if you like that sort of thing... It was wonderful, really wonderful... In fact, we should see it together...

KATE: Not again! Ben went back and saw it three times, didn't you darling? Dragged me along twice... (*They kiss.*) Now father, you will stay for one more won't you?

RAYMOND: Yes of course darling, then I'll be off. I have to be in Birmingham tomorrow morning. I'll be catching the early train so I must get my sleep.

KATE: I'll get this round...

KATE leaves the living room. BEN slumps on the sofa while RAYMOND takes a seat on the opposite side. There is a long, long silence. BEN begins to speak all at once, surprising his father-in-law.

BEN: I'm really grateful for this opportunity you've given me Raymond. I was a little unsure about it when you asked me, as you might well recall; but when I talked about it with Kate I really felt that there was a chance I could make a difference. And today in the office was like magic! I think Imani and I are going to make a great team, what with her community connections and my wider access... You made the right decision Raymond, asking me to be Senior Arts Officer... I'll make sure I prove it...

RAYMOND: Yes; well you're very kind Benjamin, almost too kind for me to speak home truths – but that would not do at all. Now don't take me the wrong; I value your enthusiasm and passion for the job. I only advise that you wait until you've got your hands dirty before there's any excitement on your part.

BEN: A lot of people have had this job before me haven't they?

RAYMOND: A fair few, that's right.

BEN: Imani said that there were no black Senior Officers before me, is that correct?

RAYMOND: No, that's quite untrue. There was a man... Jerry Baker, something like that. He was black... With us before Imani's time I think... Back when I was Councillor for Arts and Leisure...

BEN: Oh I see... Actually, I think she said there were never two blacks in the office at the same time, not that there was never a black SAO. I had to laugh when she said that. I couldn't quite believe it. Never two blacks eh? How quaint!

RAYMOND: Yes, yes... (*Thinks hard before his next sentence.*) Now Benjamin, you must be quite careful of what Imani says in that office. You're quite right, she's a lovely young woman: charming, vivacious, full of that bubbly Caribbean spirit -you know what I mean by that, being African and all? I'm not being patronising, I just meant it as a compliment to the race.

BEN: Well, actually I'm only half African. My mother's from Barbados and my father's Nigerian. I thought you knew that Raymond.

RAYMOND: Yes well, as I was saying, I love the passion of the West Indian psyche – it's brought so much joy to the world. The only disadvantage is that it sometimes carries a perspective that is hard for others to share. That feeling of being hard done by, not getting their lot – perhaps it's a legacy of slavery isn't it Benjamin, a reminder of how they felt under the whip and chain? And you – you were brought up in your father's tradition were you not? Thank me for giving you this post if you must Benjamin – it was won by virtue of being you. There was no one else who could be SAO for Chamberlayne. Just be you and everything will turn out fine.

BEN: (*Confused.*) Right; thank you Raymond...

RAYMOND gets to his feet, just before KATE comes back clutching lager bottles. BEN is still lost in thought. KATE stops dead.

KATE: Father! You wouldn't dare leave when it's taken me so long to get these!

RAYMOND: Darling I must dash, I should really get some sleep before tomorrow or I'll be insufferable in Birmingham, I'm sure I will. Next time I promise I'll stay longer…

KATE: (*Sad.*) Okay daddy… I'm very upset, but do what you must…

KATE puts bottles down and gives her father a kiss and a hug. BEN gets up and enthusiastically shakes RAYMOND's hand.

BEN: Good to see you Raymond. Thanks again whatever your reasons.

That takes RAYMOND by surprise. He's not sure what BEN means, but is loath to speak out in front of KATE, a die-hard liberal.

RAYMOND: That's okay Ben; you just do the best you can.

KATE: I'll walk you to your car.

They both leave. BEN sits back down on the sofa slowly. He runs his hands through his hair. He puts his head in his hands and stares out into the crowd. He sits back, restless, thoughts clearly flying through his head at lightening speed. He rubs the palms of his hands up and down his thighs. KATE returns.

Never mind eh? More time to ourselves, isn't that right darling?

BEN: Yes; yes, I suppose it is.

She sits on his lap, then wraps her arms around him and plants an big kiss on his cheek. BEN looks around, a little embarrassed but has to smile despite himself.

What's that for?

KATE: Because I'm proud of you. Everything you said at dinner today was spot on. Because you're my husband. Because you're you.

BEN: That's what your dad said; but he didn't make me feel the same way. I wasn't sure what he meant.

KATE: Does anyone? Dad's been a politician so many years I think he's got a built-in PC check for his brain. Ask him a question and he'll give you the answer six different ways and it's up to you to pick the one that suits. That's how he is, has always been and always will be. Once you get to understand him it'll make perfect sense.

BEN: I'm trying babe. You know I'm trying.

KATE: I know.

She looks up and gives him another kiss, then lays her head on his shoulder. BEN still looks worried.

KATE: So... I see you got on well with Imani then?

BEN: Yes...

His mind seems locked on the conversation with KATE's father.

Why?

KATE: Well... I just didn't think she'd be your type you know? I was surprised that you two seemed so pally.

BEN: Not my type? (*He turns and looks at KATE.*) Why wouldn't Imani be my type?

KATE: (*Grins.*) You know...

BEN: (*Grinning too.*) No, actually I don't know.

KATE: You know... You just seem to have... very different personalities if you see what I mean...

BEN: (*Thinking.*) Yes... Yes, you're quite right I suppose... I happen to think that we might be quite complementary, quite complementary indeed.

KATE says nothing. She's sipping her lager and looking into space. BEN peers at her.

You're jealous.

KATE: (*Shocked.*) No I'm not!

BEN: You are! I thought you might have been earlier in the office but I wasn't sure until now. Don't forget I know what you get like. We have been here before.

KATE: Yes, well we needn't bring all that up again Ben Nelson. And I may have been jealous then, but I am not now, I can assure you of that. I was merely making an observation.

KATE sits back on her own chair with her arms crossed, looking put-out. BEN is smiling. He knows how to handle this sort of thing. He moves his chair closer and puts an arm around her, slowly at first, as if to gauge her annoyance level. When KATE relaxes against his embrace, he moves in.

BEN: I love it when you're like this. It shows how much you care.

KATE: I told you –

BEN: I know, I know… You're not jealous.

He strokes her hair. They look deep into each other's eyes. BEN gets to his feet while holding KATE's hand.

Shall we?

KATE smiles, nods and also stands. They leave the bar. Lights dim.

SCENE 7

BEN enters the living room looking pleased with himself. He is fixing his tie around his neck and getting ready for work while MICHAEL wanders in behind him, looking around the room as though it's the first time he has entered. BEN seems jovial and full of good spirits.

BEN: Can I offer you anything to drink? Coffee perhaps, or Tea?

MICHAEL: Oh no, I'm fine really I am. I had a coffee on the way over.

BEN: Well, if you change your mind… Sorry, I'm in a bit of a muddle, first few days on a new job and all… What I'm trying to say is, I didn't catch your name.

MICHAEL: Michael. Michael Cerwin. Kate might have mentioned me.

BEN is appraising MICHAEL with a curious eye.

BEN: Ah! Yes... she did. Pleased to meet you, I've heard a great deal about you Michael.

MICHAEL: Likewise. All very good I have to tell you! I'm impressed Ben! Katie's not an easy woman to please.

BEN: Tell me about it! I'll just go and call her down.

MICHAEL: Thank you, you're very kind.

BEN leaves the room. MICHAEL wanders around picking up pictures and ornaments, studying them with great interest. He sits on the sofa, looking as though he's attempting to mentally prepare himself for whatever may happen next. He seems a little nervous. KATE enters the room, followed by BEN. She's flustered and won't look at MICHAEL.

KATE: Michael... What a surprise... And so early...

MICHAEL: Well, I promised I'd help you paint so I thought the earlier a start we make, the sooner we can get it all done. It'll take ages you doing it alone.

KATE shoots him an angry look, but BEN doesn't notice.

BEN: I think that's a splendid idea darling. I was worried about you doing the decorating by yourself now that I'm working. You should have told me you'd sorted something out with Michael, it's been playing on my mind for weeks.

KATE: (*Quick.*) Michael came around for the first time yesterday. You were so pleased about the job I clean forgot to mention it last night.

MICHAEL: I can always leave it for another time if there's a problem. I don't want to be the cause of any hassle...

BEN: No, no, no, don't you dare even think about it, you're the answer to our prayers – well mine at least! And I'm pretty sure you'll do a better job than I could, being an expert and all.

MICHAEL: (*Baffled.*) Sorry?

BEN: You paint for a living don't you?

MICHAEL: (*Laughs.*) Oh – different thing I'm afraid. Like the difference between running a marathon and performing a hundred yard dash.

BEN: Yes, but which is which?

MICHAEL: Do you know, I ask myself the same question!

Both men laugh. BEN reaches out and shakes MICHAEL's hand. KATE looks like she wants to be sick.

BEN: Nice to meet you at last. You must join us for dinner one night, so we can show our appreciation.

MICHAEL: I'd love to.

BEN: (*Turns to KATE.*) Darling I'm off. See you this evening.

They kiss.

KATE: Goodbye darling. Have a wonderful day at work. I love you.

BEN: Love you too. See you around Michael.

MICHAEL: Bye…

BEN leaves. MICHAEL sits on the sofa looking wistful.

What a nice man…

KATE: (*Livid.*) Listen to me. I do not have to put up with your cockeyed view of the world according to Michael Cerwin, so I suggest that you nip any plans you might have to control my life again in the bud! Do you understand me? If you haven't worked it out by now, the reason I left in the first place was because you were a liar and a control freak Michael. If you want me back in your life in even the remotest possible way, you'll have to work on giving me some indication that's changed, because if it hasn't this is going to be a very short reunion. Am I making myself clear?

MICHAEL: As a bell Katie… (*KATE glares at him.*) Kate… Sorry, don't get annoyed with me, old habits die hard that's all. What I want to know is, when are you going to accept that things are very different now Kate? That I'm older, wiser, that losing you taught me a few things. Don't look so cynical – old Mr Stubborn Cerwin has made some adjustments and I'm fully prepared to be the man you want.

KATE: That's what I'm saying. I already have the man I want.

MICHAEL: Well I'm prepared to be the man that accepts that too. He won, I lost through my own stupidity. All I wanted was for us to be happy Kate, but I never was and suppose I took that out on you. Now we're here years later, mentally in the same place at the same time, even though we're not together. That's a good thing Kate. It really is. We should make the most of it, not tear each other down over things that happened in the past. Help each other like the friends we were before all this. That's all.

KATE looks down at the floor, then, after a long while, back up at MICHAEL.

KATE: Seriously?

MICHAEL: I've never been more serious about anything Kate. Life is good to me now. I want to keep it that way.

She thinks about it.

KATE: Okay… All right then… Would you like a cup of coffee?

MICHAEL: I'd love one thank you.

KATE nods and disappears backstage. MICHAEL sits smiling to himself.

SCENE 8

BEN strolls into the office still looking pleased with himself, a briefcase swinging from his arm. IMANI is already there, wearing reading glasses and typing mechanically into her computer. She takes no notice of him.

BEN: Good morning!

IMANI stops typing. Looks over her glasses at BEN. Turns back to the computer.

IMANI: Morning Ben.

BEN frowns a little but doesn't seem worried by IMANI's actions. Humming to himself, he goes to his desk and looks through some envelopes.

BEN: Hey, letters already eh? Thought it would have been more like a week before I got any – but then I suppose this job's been vacant so long there must be a backlog, wouldn't you say? I'll get them all now I reckon, all the backdated appointments, funding applications, promised grants... And the files are in a total mess, I wish I'd known that before! I mean, I looked through some of the pending projects the last SAO was handling and most were never completed. Can you believe that? Some people had projects the SAO knew about, but never followed up. Some of those people wrote year upon year begging for help, only for WCA to turn a blind eye. Others – only a few of the organisations that had somehow managed to win favour, but enough to matter – were repeatedly given funding despite the fact that they never produced the actual projects they'd received funding for! Can you seriously believe that's still going on in this day and age?

IMANI: Yes, I can believe it Ben. I was here, remember?

BEN: Well yes, of course you were... You realise I'm not saying anything about your working methods Imani. It's clear from the records you were totally dedicated towards giving these artists the chances they deserved. But you see... And correct me if you think I'm speaking out of turn here... I know I've only been doing the job for less than 48 hours while here you are, slaving... Struggling away trying to make things right when everything that surrounds you is wrong, but I really think I've got a handle on this Arts Funding thing – if I am permitted to air my opinions? (*IMANI nods.*) It seems pretty clear to me why we're not seeing more Black and Asian theatre in a mainstream arena, or any working class theatre anywhere that matters. I know it's very early in the game for me to be coming to any conclusions at all, but I'm sure I know what the problem is.

IMANI turns around in her seat, deadpan, looking at BEN as though he was shit on her heel.

IMANI: Enlighten me.

BEN: *(Pause.)* Well… I suppose it wouldn't be news to you in a sense, seeing as you've been here so long. For me it's very important I understand what's going on in Chamberlayne, so I can take that understanding further afield. Basically, going by everything I read… This is a really hard thing for me to say… Well…it seems as though the whole arts funding system is completely corrupt. What you know isn't nearly as important as who you know.

IMANI: Yes. I would say you're one hundred per cent correct in your assessment. Well done.

IMANI turns back to her computer and begins to write in a large notebook. BEN watches her. He's unsure what's going on but is beginning to get the feeling it's something to do with him.

BEN: … Now, I would have said a while back that this so-called 'corruption' was a fallacy, a by-product of the 'chip on the shoulder' mentality –

IMANI slams down her pen, then turns around once more.

IMANI: I'm sorry, I've a mountain of work to do today and I've already wasted a lot of time chewing the fat, so to speak. Would you mind if I just got on with this LAF application? I've got to get it finished by the end of the day.

Without another word, IMANI turns back to her notebook, leaving BEN stunned. Hesitantly, he sits behind his desk, still shooting looks her way. Lights fade to black on office.

Lights up on office. BEN is on the phone while IMANI sits by a desk staring intently at the funding application form before her, though she sometimes reacts to what's being said. BEN's former animation hasn't gone away.

BEN: Yes… Yes Mr Tompkins, everything is going exceptionally well… I'm enjoying the post, I have an excellent assistant… I'm very happy… *(IMANI looks up. BEN isn't looking. She shakes her head and goes back to her work.)* Yes, she's

wonderful actually... Painting the house as we speak...
Of course... Oh you must, it's a marvellous old place...
North Chamberlayne, just off Parliament Hill... She was
saying the very same thing, how much she enjoys Nancy's
company... Well, they're like old chums when they get
together, they don't stop do they? Yes, it's been forever...
Well, you know, there's nothing to stop you coming over for
dinner one Sunday once we get the place ship-shape. I can
filch us a bottle of that Rioja everyone likes so much –

*IMANI stands abruptly, gathers her papers and pens and walks
from the office. BEN watches her departure looking sad and
seems to lose the thread of his conversation.*

... Mmmm... Yes, you're absolutely right, a simple
Chardonnay would be easier on the head... No, no it's not
a problem at all, I just got distracted by something Imani
placed in front of me... It'll be fine... So, how are you fixed
for... this Sunday? About two pm?

Lights dim.

*Lights up on office. BEN is sitting at his desk, alone. He is eating
from a small Chinese takeaway box and looking a little morose.
IMANI comes in holding a MacDonald's bag, but stops when
she sees him. BEN almost jumps to attention.*

Gave up then?

IMANI: I beg your pardon?

BEN: You gave up. Your diet. Can't be too worried about your
thighs if you're eating that kind of stuff. Stones usually
jump from those bags right onto me.

IMANI: Yeah, well I've got a lot more than my weight to think
about this afternoon, so I didn't take much notice actually.

BEN: I see...

IMANI: I think I'll eat in the reccy room today Ben. No
one's there and it'll give me a chance to get on with this
application. I hope you don't mind.

BEN: No, not at all, do what you must. Have a good lunch.

IMANI: You too.

She leaves. BEN watches her go, then sighs in frustration, ignoring his food. He taps an impatient finger on the desk. Lights dim.

A sound of typing can be heard. Lights up on office. BEN is hard at work in a world of his own, absorbed by what he can see on his computer screen. A mug sits on his desk. His fingers are moving fluidly. IMANI comes in on this, walking slow as if she doesn't want to disturb him. She looks at her watch, makes a face, then approaches her desk. BEN finally notices her and stops typing.

BEN: Hey, you're back!

IMANI: Yeah, sorry I was so long. I wasn't skivving, just thought I'd stay in the reccy and finish the app, seeing as nobody was there –

BEN: It's fine, it's fine. How did it go?

IMANI: I think we'll get the money. It's for a multi-media centre in a local youth club, Five Feathers over in West Chamberlayne? A couple of years ago some Black kid was killed in a racist attack not far from there. Since then the managers have been doing all they can to prove how multi-cultural the club and area really is. I think they're planning a short film and a couple of music videos shot on DVD, that kind of thing.

BEN: Sounds perfect. Can I get you a cup of tea?

IMANI: Uh… No thanks…

BEN: Go on, it won't kill you.

IMANI: I'm okay, really.

BEN: You sure? I've just boiled the kettle.

IMANI: Oh…go on then, if you're having one.

BEN disappears offstage. IMANI sits on her desk. BEN comes back with her tea.

BEN: There you go. No sugar.

IMANI: Thank you.

BEN: Actually, the tea's a kind of substitute to be truthful.

IMANI: Huh?

BEN: A substitute. I wanted to make a peace offering but I haven't got anything to give besides a cup of tea.

IMANI: A peace offering? What for, you haven't done anything.

BEN: (*Laughing.*) Oh come on Imani, I'm not a complete dimwit you know. I may not be the most sensitive man in the world but I can tell when I've upset someone, and I've definitely upset you. Yesterday we were best buddies, now you can hardly look me in the eye. It's obvious I've done something or the other. I just don't know what.

IMANI: (*Distraught.*) Ben –

BEN: So you admit that I've upset you at least?

IMANI: Ben, I really don't want to do this right now…

IMANI gets up from the desk and sits in her office chair, clearly uncomfortable. BEN doesn't know what to say.

BEN: Look, I know that talking like this is difficult. I used to have a problem with it too. When I was a kid my father used to hate me arguing with my brothers. There was three of us and I was the middle child, so I always felt as though I was having to keep the peace without taking sides. Whenever there was an argument, my father would gather us together in one room – usually the sitting room come to think of it – and give us each a turn to say what was on our minds. He'd take the role of judge I suppose, telling us when we'd spoken long enough, or stopping us butting in and re-starting the argument. Sometimes it would go on for hours, but eventually we'd always feel better and sort out some kind of compromise. My father helped me come to the conclusion that although it hurts, it's good for a disagreement to run its course instead of letting it fester. The longer you do, the more likely it is that it'll come out anyway, tenfold. That's what my dad used to think.

IMANI: Your father's a very smart man.

BEN: Was. Thank you. I think so.

IMANI: (*Gentle.*) Listen… I hear what you're saying and a large part of me thinks… You know, yeah you're right. At the same time another part of me knows that if I tell you what's been bothering me, that's it. I'll have soured our working relationship and things will change for the worse, which is not the direction we should be heading in. I appreciate your peace offering but I really think it might be best to let this one pass and start over. None of us wants to say something we might regret.

BEN: But I'm worried Imani. I'm worried that if I've offended you already I could go out there and do the same to the very people I'm trying to help. It's really important to me that I can interact with the community at large as an integral component that understands them fully, not some hired black man in a suit that treats them just like everyone else. I mean, come on Imani I'm not an idiot. I know who I am, where I come from. I understand the concept of tokenism. Don't get me wrong, I'm proud of what I've achieved in life but if you can't tell me right here and now what I've done to hurt you, and I can't re-evaluate my actions, and in turn do something about them, then I might as well turn off that computer, get my coat, leave this office right this minute and never come back. Do you understand me Imani? Because I would have failed. I would have failed every black, white, Asian, Indian, Jewish, Muslim –

IMANI: Okay, okay, okay! I'm convinced, just stop talking for a minute will you! I need to work out how I'm gonna say this.

IMANI paces up and down the office for a long while, deep in thought. She stops, and turns back to BEN, reaches out a hand for him.

Come here a minute.

He does, very slowly.

Give me a hug.

He does this too, facing the audience, a strained and pensive expression on his face. IMANI lets him go quickly, leads him to his chair by the hand, placing him on it, then goes back and gets her own. She rolls over to him and takes his hand once more. They're both seated, both on their opposite sides of the office, yet their hands are joined at the centre.

Okay… Promise you'll hear me out until the very end before you try to argue or correct any facts. Remember, your dad's not here to mediate now.

They laugh.

Okay… The first thing I'd like to say is positive. I like you very much Ben Nelson. I know we've barely met in the general scheme of things, but I'm a great believer in spiritual energy and from the moment you walked through that door I knew you were a special person Ben. No word of a lie. Even when I got upset and thought differently, you still proved how special you are, showed me I was right about you. And I like that. I like that you've proven me right and made me feel good about myself. That's a very positive thing.

BEN is nodding, seemingly afraid to say a word.

What I'm upset about is a little more complicated. And you're right, tokenism has a lot to do with it. In case you haven't guessed, I come from the same place as those black, white, Jewish, Muslim, and whatever else you mentioned working-class people. We're well used to tokens being placed in our community, being told they're here for our benefit, to look after our concerns, all the rest. Because we're so experienced in this field it becomes fairly easy to spot the makings of a token. The tell-tale signs, so to speak. We get very worried when we do spot any of these signs, because usually – meaning nine times out of every ten – they're a clear indication of what type of help we're getting.

BEN: Imani –

IMANI: Wait. You promised. (*BEN waves a hand, letting her continue.*) So, what are the tell-tale signs you may ask yourself? How do we know we have a sell-out in our midst? It's quite simple really. There are three main things I've found very telling in all my years in the arts. Still want to hear them?

BEN nods once again.

Number one: the token always comes from a highly educated background. Oxford, Cambridge, some affiliate or another. That way, not only does the token have the highest education, they will also find it difficult to relate in a working class environment. Number two: they get the job because they have friends in high places and are recommended, rather than interviewed as such. Jobs like these are handed out on a need-to-know basis. Any advertising in the *Media Guardian* and the like are purely perfunctory. Number three: *(She fixes BEN with a deadly stare.)* Number three: *(She looks at her feet.)*

BEN: Say it... Say it...

IMANI: Number three: the token always has a white partner. *(She pauses to let this sink in.)* Degrees of tokenism can be assessed by the race of the partner in question. White is very bad, Eastern Asian is less so, Western Asian even less. Mixed-race can be tricky yet passable. Black is good, though number two and one have to be called into assessment before a decision is made. And that, is basically that.

BEN is silent for a very long time before;

BEN: People actually think like that?

IMANI: Every day.

BEN gently extracts his hand and walks to front of stage, a hand to his head, looking distressed. Behind him, IMANI is watching blankly.

BEN: What can I do?

IMANI looks at her watch again.

IMANI: It's way past our home time. Come for a drink with me and I'll explain on the way. I think you should meet some friends.

BEN: Well, if it's late I really should get on and see how my wife is doing with the painting –

IMANI: Ben. You said you wanted to know.

Pause.

BEN: Okay. Okay, let's go.

They grab their coats and exit. Lights dim.

SCENE 9

LAMMING, JONES and SPENCER come back onto the stage with tables, chairs and what-have-you. While JONES and SPENCER busy themselves setting up the bar scene, LAMMING comes to the very front of stage.

LAMMING: So, as you can see –

JONES: Oi! We haven't got time for that! They'll be here any minute and we aren't nearly ready yet.

LAMMING: But I got –

SPENCER: Lamming, Jones is right. We ain' got time for you to be giving us your analytical rubbish, we have to get on.

JONES is wandering around near the back of stage, looking for IMANI and BEN.

LAMMING: (*Livid.*) What about my link?

SPENCER: It's been cut. All that back story stuff's been cut. It gives away too much plot. Now you just say the first line.

LAMMING: What?! Riggs never said anything about that…

JONES: They're coming!

SPENCER: Hurry up will you!

LAMMING: (*Grudgingly jovial.*) And this was the point we came into the story… (*To SPENCER and JONES.*) Bollocks. That was complete bollocks… It won't make sense to the audience without the rest…

JONES: Never mind that, here they come…

LAMMING, JONES and SPENCER take up positions in the bar area of the stage. IMANI and BEN walk on taking no notice of the actors. IMANI carries two bottles of beer.

SCENE 10

IMANI: God, I wish I never said anything to you now Ben. I wasn't trying to upset you in return. Remember you did ask.

BEN: I'm not upset.

They sit at the table.

IMANI: You're a bad actor and an even worse liar. Course you're upset, I did everything but call you a traitor to your race. I shouldn't have said a word.

BEN: Well I'm glad you did. I'm really not upset Imani; stunned is a better description. Can you remember what it feels like to be walking down the road and have a stranger tell you your fly is undone? Or to be out for dinner and have your date tell you that you have a stain on your shirt? Close your eyes and imagine yourself in a situation like that Imani. Could you do that for me please?

IMANI: Of course.

She does as she's told.

BEN: How does it feel?

IMANI: *(Thinks for a long time.)* Embarrassing.

BEN: Exactly.

Behind IMANI and BEN, a black man comes into the bar and greets JONES, SPENCER and LAMMING. This is DON. He soon gets into deep conversation with the actors and doesn't look IMANI's way.

IMANI: But there's no reason for you to feel like that –

BEN: Oh yeah?

IMANI: Yes! Look, the main reason I told you all that was cos you're not like most of those people I normally see operating in the arts. And it's not just what you say; if I had a penny for every time I've heard a token talk about what we need, more inclusion, and all the other key words that keep them in a career while doing bugger all for the arts, I'd be phat enough to buy my own multi-media building! What's different about you is your passion Ben, your sincerity when you're speaking about what needs to be done. That's what appeals to me. Trust me, if I thought you were one of those types through and through I would have hid my feelings and paid you no mind and nothing would have changed. I've done it before. At least now we have things out in the open. We can do something about them.

BEN: True. What?

IMANI: What? What?! You already know what Ben.

BEN: Do I?

IMANI: Of course you do. (*Sighs.*) You outlined the plan yesterday. 'What's missing from funding bodies is patience and a desire to build a working relationship with the artists around them.' If we're gonna be a team you better remember what you say cos I'm gonna hold you to it. Still believe it?

BEN: Yes, without question.

IMANI: Then that's your mission: start hooking up with the people that need your help. They're all around you Ben, there's no reason not to start right away.

BEN: Right away? What do you mean?

IMANI: Ben, I have to tell you something. As well as working for WCA, I also volunteer for an organisation called the COT Project.

BEN: COT? As in, what you keep a child in, C-O-T?

IMANI: That's the one! COT stands for Children Of Tamana, a place in Ancient Kamit where many people believe the Black Civilisation grew to maturity. The project I'm involved in has vowed to continue that task, bringing positive teachings, spirituality and healing to sons and daughters of Kamit.

BEN: You said that word before. What's Kamit?

IMANI: The original name for Egypt. Egypt's actually what the Greeks called Kamit, while Kam was the word for Black in those lands. Kamit meant Land of the Blacks, which is why even today we're the only race that calls ourselves by our colour. We did it to ourselves as a celebration of our skin tone.

BEN: I see…

IMANI: Anyway, the COT Project is made up of all aspects of the Black community, though we generally find most of our members come from the artists end of the spectrum. It would be the perfect place for you to meet Black practitioners of all kinds. We actually have a meeting tonight.

BEN: Tonight?

IMANI looks over at the bar, where DON has been waiting.

IMANI: *(Waving him over.)* Oh look, there's someone you have to meet! That's Don, my boyfriend.

BEN: Ah!

DON comes over and grabs a seat.

DON: Hi babe – *(Kisses IMANI, then turns to BEN.)* Saw you when I came in, but your conversation looked well serious so I thought I best leave you alone.

IMANI: Thanks babe. This is Ben, my new SAO, Ben this is Don, my other half.

DON: Pleased to meet you mate!

BEN: You too! So how long have you been a couple?

IMANI: Nearly three years, innit babe?

DON: Best three years of my life!

They kiss again. BEN looks pleased by their interactions.

IMANI: You can see why he's lasted, can't you Ben?

BEN: I certainly can! Would you like a drink Don?

DON: I'm fine thanks mate, sorted for the minute. So how are finding it working with such a moody cow? Ain' you 'ad enough already?

They laugh, while IMANI makes to strike her boyfriend. He dodges out of the way.

BEN: Well… (*They wait, looking at him.*) It's been two days of extreme contrast, but very informative nonetheless. I think I've learnt lots already.

DON: (*Appraising him differently, speaking in his best 'cowboy' voice.*) You're not from these parts are yuh now?

They all laugh again, BEN the hardest.

BEN: No, you're right, I'm not. I was brought up in Barnes for most of my life actually.

DON: Oh; nice was it?

BEN: Yeah, I had a great childhood despite what you might have heard about places like that. It was good for me. Now I think I should live where there are more of us, if you know what I mean.

DON: Glad to hear it mate!

IMANI: Don works with young actors. He set up a drama group that meets at St Luke's Church twice a week and puts on shows every three months. They're brilliant.

BEN: Really? How long have you been doing that?

DON: Close to eight, nine years now. The kids come and go mostly, but we have a core of trained actors, (*He points at LAMMING, JONES and SPENCER.*) that assist me in looking for others, holding workshops and all that lark so I'm never doing it alone. We've had some great reviews and we always sell out.

BEN: Who's funding you?

DON: Funding! Don't make me laugh! We've been refused so many times I'm starting to think we must smell…

BEN: (*Looking at IMANI.*) But, I would have thought –

IMANI: Don't look at me. Don can't come and see me cos it would be unethical. He's been to see every SAO we've had even before I worked for West Chamber Arts and nothing ever came of it. Between me and you, I even filled some of those damn application forms myself and that's the only time I've been refused. I don't know what it is about what you do that they don't like babe, but they don't like it one little bit.

DON: (*Smiling.*) She gets so worked up about it, but I always say we'll survive. We've survived this long...

BEN: That's the trouble with Black art. It's so busy trying to survive, trying to keep its head above water, that it never gets to operate at full capacity.

DON and IMANI exchange glances.

You should come down and see me in the office Don. Imani might not be allowed to help, but there's absolutely no reason why I shouldn't be able to give you advice at the very least. How are you fixed tomorrow?

DON: Tomorrow? That's great –

BEN: Pass by about twelve. We can go for lunch and firm things up.

DON: Thanks Ben, I'll really appreciate whatever you can do –

IMANI: Ben was just saying he'll join our meeting tonight, weren't you Ben?

BEN: Well... Kate will be worrying awfully...

DON: Who's Kate, your missus? It's part of the job, she'll understand you working late won't she?

IMANI and DON get to their feet.

IMANI: Course she will, Kate's a very nice lady. She seems very understanding.

BEN: Yes, she's lovely –

DON: Come on then, chop, chop, it's only five minutes away. We'll have you home by nine at the latest Ben, we promise!

BEN: (*Getting to his feet.*) All right, all right, I'll come along for a bit! But I may leave early, I warn you!

IMANI: It's up to you Ben! Leave when you like, but you must stay for half an hour minimum, okay?

BEN: Sure I will.

IMANI: You won't regret this…

They exit the stage. JONES, SPENCER, and LAMMING also get up and leave. LAMMING stops for a minute, turns to the audience as though he's going to say something, but JONES grabs him and pulls him offstage. Lights dim.

End of Act One.

Act Two

SCENE 1

Lights up. LAMMING, JONES and SPENCER march on stage looking like they're in the middle of a heated argument. They speak in low hushed tones, LAMMING the most animated of the trio. They pause near the wings for a moment, still arguing and shooting quick glances at the audience in between. Suddenly, LAMMING breaks off and walks to front of stage.

LAMMING: Yeah, well they're gonna hear what I have to say one way or another…

SPENCER: Just do the bloody link will you?

LAMMING: You sure you don't mind? I feel a bit guilty – it's yours and it's a good one! 'Let me bring you up to speed…' I'm feelin' that bit!

SPENCER: *(Sighs.)* Nah I don't mind. You go for it.

JONES: Break a leg!

LAMMING gives JONES a sarcastic smile and walks to front of stage. He pauses, looking into the audience, searching for sympathy.

LAMMING: Good evening ladies, gentlemen and mini-you's. Welcome back to our premier production of *B is for Black*, we hope you had a most comfortable interlude. Now. Earlier this evening you may have heard some sections of this piece that you found a mite unsettling. Let me take a moment to clarify what was meant…

JONES: Lamming…

LAMMING turns around. JONES gives a winding up signal with his hand. LAMMING sighs and turns back to the audience.

LAMMING: Time is short, so we will have to reconvene at a later point, when I will break down the essence of Imani's rules. It should be enough for me to say that in life there is such a thing as action and re-action, a pushing and pulling of the elements that –

SPENCER noisily clears her throat.

Okay… Gotta take care of business. We'll talk, yeah?

(*Goes back into presenter mode.*) Good evening, ladies, gentlemen and mini-you's. Welcome back to our premier production of *B is for Black*, we hope you had a most comfortable interlude. Let us bring you up to speed with what you've missed…

LAMMING steps back into the bar scene with JONES and SPENCER while IMANI, DON and BEN enter stage. BEN is clearly high from his experience. They sit at the table.

DON: … So, when the Spanish reached the Americas, they were in for a shock all right – everywhere they looked there were paintings and carvings and huge statues with flat noses and full lips – and that weren't all! My History teacher used to say that there were even pictures of white people drawn on the walls in chalk and mud…

BEN: I've heard that too, but not for a long time… When I went to Iceland the Icelandic people were claiming they discovered America…

IMANI: Like you can discover a place where people already live…

DON: I know what they meant babe, the Icelandics were closer to America than the Europeans.

BEN: All they'd have to do is follow the land from Alaska down south. It's simple migration.

IMANI: When did you go to Iceland then?

BEN: Years ago, for my honeymoon. Kate was livid at first! She wanted to go to Benidorm, Mexico or the Caribbean – in other words, anywhere hot! As soon as we got to Reykjavik she changed her mind. It was easily the best holiday I've ever had, and I've travelled a fair bit.

IMANI: Iceland? No thanks love. What's in Iceland besides a distinct lack of Black people?

BEN: Glaciers, dolphins, whales, hot water geysers, natural mineral pools, extinct volcanos, mountains, twenty-four hour daylight in summer and, amazingly enough, Black people! Not many but enough to make you think 'no wonder we've got problems. Whites must be thinking these damn Blacks get everywhere!'

Laughter.

DON: (*Standing.*) I'll get 'em in shall I? Ben, wha' you 'avin blud?

BEN: No thanks Don, I really should be going. Kate must be out of her wits by now.

DON: Fair enough. Back in a jiffy.

He leaves. IMANI watches him go, then reaches over and takes BEN's hand.

IMANI: Thank you.

BEN: What for?

IMANI: You're the first SAO that's ever come to one of our COT meetings. Even Jerry Baker was too busy for us; probably contributed to him getting sacked too. It does make a difference Ben, trust me it does. So thanks for taking that step.

BEN: That's okay. I really enjoyed myself tonight Imani. It was an insight into how much I need to learn.

IMANI: In what way?

BEN: I don't know yet... The one thing that kept running through my mind is that these people are human beings. Most of what they're talking about and asking for isn't some irrational want, like a spoilt child crying for sweets, but real and necessary tools of survival. I must admit Imani, I rather feared I'd be hearing the old 'Down with Whitey stuff' you expect from these type of things. I think there could have better means of articulating some of the arguments I heard, but overall I was very impressed...

IMANI was listening avidly to the first part of BEN's speech, but by the end her eyes are glazed and she is clearly somewhere else.

IMANI: Hmmm… Great, that's great Ben.

BEN: You're tired. I need to see my wife. Thank you Imani –

BEN gets to his feet.

IMANI: No, not tired at all Ben, just daydreaming… (*She gets to her feet too.*) See you partner.

They hug. DON comes back with the drinks.

BEN: See you Imani.

DON: Off then are we?

BEN: Yes, to finally attend to my duties as a husband! Nice meeting you Don! (*They shake hands firmly.*) Don't forget, tomorrow, 12pm, the WCA office.

DON: For sure!

BEN leaves. DON and IMANI stay standing still, looking at each other for a long while. After a moment they both smile and hug. Lights dim.

SCENE 2

Lights up on RAYMOND, MICHAEL and KATE all drinking wine and catching up on old times. They are laughing hard. KATE and MICHAEL still wear clothes splattered with paint. MICHAEL sits on the sofa with RAYMOND while KATE is sitting on stage left, where she can get a good view of MICHAEL. Her frosty attitude towards him seems to have thawed.

RAYMOND: (*Still laughing.*) Good God Michael, you seem to have had the most wonderful life since we last saw you… Such experiences!

MICHAEL: That sounds like the ideal inspiration for a toast actually Raymond! Lady and gentleman: I bid you raise your glasses and join me in celebrating one of life's most invigorating gifts – experience!

RAYMOND: To experience!

KATE: Experience!

They clink glasses.

RAYMOND: It's good to know you're still alive and painting.
I was always annoying Katherine by asking what had
happened to you, what you were doing now.

KATE: He isn't fibbing!

MICHAEL: Well thank you very much Raymond. It's nice to
know I was missed by someone! (*KATE looks hurt. MICHAEL
snatches a look, pretends not to notice but changes tack
anyway.*) But seriously, I think I needed that time. Back
then I was the type of guy that was always in a relationship.
I couldn't function without knowing I had a woman beside
me, even if she didn't like being there very much. After Kate
and I split I was in such a state there was no way I could
manage another relationship. All I had left was myself,
which was pretty fortunate at the time, as I didn't really
know who I was. So that was it. I spent days at a time with
no company and tried to find the things I'd lost; the things
that made the real Michael Cerwin tick.

KATE: And what did you find?

MICHAEL: Well, obviously I found I had a genuine love for
painting that went far beyond a hobby. I don't know if this
makes me sound crazy or something, but I realised that
if I go for long periods without painting I fall into a state
similar to depression. I'm argumentative, moody, restless
and uncharitable...

KATE: So you didn't paint for most of our relationship then?

*KATE and RAYMOND laugh, but MICHAEL seriously contemplates
her question.*

MICHAEL: Can you remember anything I did?

KATE: (*Realising it wasn't a joke.*) No – as a matter of fact, I
can't... Oh, there was that piece you just sold, the bad trip –

MICHAEL: I did that one before we started going out. I wanted to give it to you on our first date. You came to my house, remember?

KATE: (*Vague.*) No… All I remember is that… Lovely piece of artwork.

MICHAEL: (*To RAYMOND.*) This is the painting your daughter said reminded her of psychedelic vomit…

They all have a chuckle at that.

But as well as the painting I found that I needed time away from people. I've got a personality a bit like a sponge I'm afraid – I soak up whatever's going on around me. Hanging around student bars long after I'd left Uni and going to all those parties just turned me into one of those people that needs to be loved by everyone that doesn't matter. In short, I was an arsehole. Now I largely keep away from the party scene and concentrate on living life, collecting more of those experiences we were talking about. It's a much better way to live.

RAYMOND: Indeed. Indeed it is.

As RAYMOND speaks there's a knock on the door. BEN's head pokes in.

BEN: Evening all. I'm not interrupting anything am I?

KATE: Of course not darling, come in. We've been wondering where you got to.

BEN steps into the room.

BEN: How are you Michael, Raymond?

RAYMOND: Splendid…

MICHAEL: Very well, thanks. Great wine you've got.

BEN: Thank you. (*Kisses KATE.*) Darling, I had the most wonderful day. Well, it wasn't the best to start with but eventually it turned out fine.

RAYMOND is listening with deep intent.

KATE: Really? What happened?

BEN: Well, Imani and myself had a bit of an argument –

KATE: An argument? About what?

BEN: Politics I suppose. I'm afraid you were right last night about us being polar opposites. But to cut a long story short, we avoided the issue all day then eventually managed to iron out our differences. She invited me to a Black networking club she regularly attends called Children of Tamana –

MICHAEL: Cot?

BEN: Exactly. A number of Black arts practitioners go to those meetings, so she thought it would be a good idea for me to attend, get the lay of the land. (*Sighs, clearly pumped up.*) Darling, it was amazing. Some of the speakers have a lot to learn about delivery and their speeches could have done with some minor editing, but the points they made… And the passion… I even learnt some things! Did you know that when the Spanish went to the Americas there were already pictures of Africans and Europeans on their walls?

MICHAEL: Yes, that's quite right. And carved statues in the jungles.

KATE: I've never heard that before. That's amazing darling.

BEN: Isn't it?

BEN looks over at RAYMOND, who has been watching silently.

Did you know that Raymond?

RAYMOND: Yes, yes I did. Though I hardly think it makes any difference to the run of world history –

BEN: Oh, I have to disagree with you there Raymond. Ancient Mayan and Aztec civilisations were considered among the most advanced in the world. Their architecture, astrology, their calendar of world events making predictions from then until way past now – these things are scientifically respected everywhere. If Africans were in the Americas long enough to have been painted on walls that are thousands of years old, world history as we know it is missing a vital chunk of truth about where that knowledge came from.

RAYMOND: Yes; yes, I suppose I can see what you're getting at.

KATE: It all sounds very interesting darling. Would you like some wine?

BEN: Actually, no. I will have a cup of tea though. (*KATE gets up.*) Don't worry I'll make it.

BEN heads stage left.

KATE: I'll come anyway.

KATE and BEN exit stage left, leaving RAYMOND and MICHAEL alone. There's a long, awkward silence.

MICHAEL: Well… It's nice to see Katie's with a good, intelligent man isn't it Raymond? I met Ben this morning and he seems to be a top chap. Well-mannered, educated –

RAYMOND: As are you. As are you.

MICHAEL: Yes… Yes, well… Not meaning to overstate my earlier point, but I think I had other…issues to deal with besides my manners and education when I was with Kate.

RAYMOND: But you're a different man now, are you not? Older, wiser… Experienced…

MICHAEL is looking at RAYMOND warily, wondering what he's getting at.

Let me explain myself. When I look at you Michael, I see a man who desires something he can't possibly speak of. A man who perhaps has a hope that the current situation might…dissolve sometime in the near future. I recognise the look in your eye Michael. I was your age once – many moons ago of course, but I haven't forgotten what is was like to love unconditionally. Be prepared to forgive any past solecism.

MICHAEL: I don't know what you mean.

RAYMOND: Michael, I need you to do something for me. A small favour that won't take much time.

MICHAEL: Go on…

RAYMOND: I'm worried about the influence Benjamin's work colleague might have on him. It's only been two days and she's already got him going to meetings where they discuss the type of things we've just heard –

MICHAEL: And? It's an interesting topic, I think.

RAYMOND: Well, I myself am not adverse to the ideal of Black Consciousness, though there are many in my council that would disagree. Unfortunately for Benjamin, he was hired to enforce the Status Quo, not make waves that could drown this community. Chamberlayne has been bogged by racial tensions since the first Caribbeans stepped from Windrush onto these streets. Like it or not, if Benjamin keeps talking as he was tonight he's bound to offend someone, somewhere. What I'm asking you to do isn't far from what you're doing already Michael – be his friend. Keep an eye on him, tell me his state of mind, what he may be planning. If things look like they're going out of hand I'll be able to step in and stop him before he ruins a perfect situation for himself and my daughter.

MICHAEL: So you want me to be a squealer? A tattle-teller?

RAYMOND says nothing, shrugs.

What do I get out of it?

RAYMOND: I'll endeavour to do all that I can to influence and smooth things along so that what you need – favourable conditions in which to air your unspeakable desire – can be achieved with little or no effort on your part.

Silence. Both men are thinking quite hard. BEN and KATE come back bearing steaming mugs of tea.

BEN: … Oh, so if I jumped off a bridge would you do that too?

KATE: Don't be silly Ben, I saw you boiling the kettle and all of a sudden I wanted a cup of tea, end of story! Leave me alone, you're such a tease!

BEN: Only because you're so easy to tease…

MICHAEL: (*Standing.*) Uh… I'm going to be off now.

KATE: Okay Michael, thanks ever so much for your help –

BEN: Yes, I can't tell you how happy I am to have you assisting poor Kate. Let me give you something –

BEN starts fishing for his wallet. MICHAEL looks horrified. BEN stops.

MICHAEL: No, no really you mustn't. It's the least I can do seeing as I was such a terrible boyfriend.

KATE: Ah… You weren't the worst you know; not by a long shot.

MICHAEL: The fact that I made the list at all doesn't sit well with me I'm afraid Kate. (*Kisses her cheek.*) See you tomorrow. I may leave early though, get on with some of my own work.

KATE: Whatever you can manage is perfect.

BEN: Are you sure you don't want any money for your troubles?

MICHAEL: No honestly, there's no need. Bye Raymond. I'm sure we'll see each other soon, now I'm back.

RAYMOND: Yes; I'm sure we will.

MICHAEL: 'Bye everyone!

BEN: You take care Michael.

MICHAEL leaves.

(*Yawns.*) Well, I think I'm about ready for bed darling! Coming?

KATE: Yes, I feel quite sleepy now; must be all that painting I've been doing. It wears you out!

BEN: See, there you go again! You're a follow-fashion girl darling! My mother would have told you so!

KATE: (*Slapping his shoulder.*) Good night father. The spare bed's all made up and I left the radiator on it case it gets cold all right? Try not to get us up too early.

RAYMOND: Yes, good night you two. See you both in the morning.

BEN: Night Raymond. (*To KATE as they leave.*) Hear that, 'follow-fashion'? I haven't completely lost my roots if I can remember that, have I?

KATE: No of course not darling, that would never happen...

They're gone. RAYMOND sits on the sofa looking as though the weight of the world is on his shoulders. Lights dim.

SCENE 3

Lights half up. IMANI is alone in the office once again. She is holding a sheet of A4 paper in front of her and behaving very oddly. Every now and then she performs a random sentence to an invisible audience.

IMANI: '... Since time immemorial Black Culture has been irrevocably linked with art...' Shit! That's not right. (*Bends over paper and writes.*) 'Since...the...dawn...of the... African...Civilisation... Black Culture has been tied like a rope, to art.' (*Looks at what she's written.*) Oh...you can do this! Okay Imani, think, think, think... 'Since...'

She bends over her desk and begins writing once more. BEN enters the office and immediately begins squinting.

BEN: Morning! Wow, it's dark in here!

He flicks a switch. Lights up full.

IMANI: Hiya...

She hardly takes her eyes from the paper. BEN looks at her warily.

BEN: You're early. (*Pause.*) I haven't upset you again have I?

IMANI: No! No, not at all, how are you Ben? (*Gets to her feet and gives him a big kiss.*) It's just that we've got this COT thing next week and I promised I'd prepare a speech, but it's all going wrong! The woman meant to deliver the speech has thyroid problems. They're gonna operate over the weekend and she reckons she won't be able to speak for ages! I'm trying my best to write something for the person that'll take over, but I still haven't finished those LAF applications and there's three more to go. It's just too much for me at this point in my life! (*Relaxes.*) Anyway, that's my concern; how are you, Kate wasn't too upset about you being late was she?

BEN: No, she was fine, just a little worried. I think I might need a mobile from now on.

IMANI: Why not? You're probably gonna have a lot more late nights if you're hanging out with the artists all the time. A mobile will be the best thing for both of you. Don't get Pay-As-You-Go though, it's way too expensive.

BEN: I haven't got a clue what you're talking about. Actually, I might need your help with all of that stuff; I probably couldn't tell the difference between a phone and a CB radio.

IMANI: Fine, you know where to find me!

They smile at each other. IMANI goes back to her speech while BEN checks his in-tray and switches on the computer. He walks offstage. IMANI looks up to see where he's gone, then tries writing again. BEN comes back and watches her.

'Since the world began to turn, Black people have been known to practise art in many forms...' Shit!

BEN: I'll do it.

IMANI: Huh?

BEN: I'll do your speech. Write it and read it if you like. I used to be a member of my school's debating society and there was precious few people who could top me. It's quite easy to slip back into that mindset – even last night when I was talking to those speakers I had to bite my tongue so I wouldn't correct some of the things they said. I can't help it. I don't know why.

IMANI: Probably because you talk the way we're meant to write.

BEN: (*Smiles.*) Probably.

IMANI: Well give it go then. It can't go any worse than it's already going...

She hands him the paper.

77

BEN: Thanks… *(Looks it over.)* Well, right off the bat your first sentence could be simplified… That's the trouble when most people write, they think too much about long words and complicated ideas when the best thing you can do is be as concise and basic as possible. Think of the best way to get your message across with minimum effort. Your speech has all the relevant information, it's just the sentence structure that's all over the place… I mean, look at your opening line. Instead of all that complicated stuff, all you have to say is: 'Since the dawn of time, the African civilisation has used art as an expression of their culture.' And that's it. You're off. You can say what you like after that.

BEN looks down to see IMANI staring at him in awe.

IMANI: Wow Ben. I couldn't do that like you. I've been here all morning trying to write this and you think up a perfect first sentence in five minutes. Not even that!

BEN: You could do it, you just haven't had the practice. Like most people. It's just talking without sounding like you're thinking about it. Anyway, you get on with your LAF apps and I'll have a tinker with what you've got and we'll see what we can do. It's not as if I've got lots on anyway. In fact, I'm pretty free until lunch.

IMANI: Great! Thanks Ben, you're a babe!

BEN: Don't worry about it.

BEN sits at his desk and gets to work right away. IMANI goes over to a filing cabinet and sifts through some of the files. When she has what she wants, she turns and looks at BEN. She's smiling triumphantly. IMANI sits back at her desk, still beaming. Lights dim.

Lights up. IMANI is still at her desk working on her LAF application. BEN has his head down working on his speech. There's a knock on the office door.

IMANI: Come in!

DON pokes his head around the door.

DON: All right darling? Not you Ben, I was talking to the missus!

All laugh. DON comes inside and kisses IMANI, who gets up and gives him a hug.

IMANI: How are you babe?

DON: Lovely! Not too early am I Ben, thought I'd make an effort and that!

BEN: No, not too early at all. Let me just finish this last sentence and I'll be ready to go.

DON: Sure thing blud.

Ben begins to write furiously. DON pulls a face IMANI's way. IMANI beams.

IMANI: B's writing that speech I was supposed to do for Paulette Wilson next week. He's doing a good job too –

DON: Paulette 'oo? Never 'eard of her.

IMANI: Wilson. Remember – the woman with the thyroid problem?

IMANI gives DON a pointed look and pokes him in the ribs. DON is looking at her blankly as if unsure of what's going on. BEN, concentrating on the A4 paper in front of him, is taking no notice.

DON: Oh yeah – Paulette. Poor cow, she's ever so ill at the minute.

IMANI: Yeah, such a shame. Mind you, it's a good thing we've got B to take over the Fort, innit Ben?

BEN: Sorry? Oh, you're waiting for me aren't you? (*Writes one last sentence.*) Okay, I think that's it! I'll type this up later Imani, but you can read it if you like and make changes wherever you see fit – you know, factual evidence to back up your claims, spelling errors, stuff like that. I shouldn't be more than an hour, hour and a half for lunch, max. Is that all right?

IMANI: Do what you like, you're my senior here, not the other way around.

BEN: Fine then. See you in a bit.

DON: (*Pointedly.*) We'll talk later Imani, all right?

IMANI: Yeah.

They leave the office. IMANI watches the door for a minute, far away, then in a dream-like state turns and goes for BEN's desk where the speech is sitting almost as if waiting for her to read. IMANI thinks so anyway. She picks it up, unable to keep the smile from her face, and begins. As her eyes travel the page, her smile gets wider. At some point she draws in her breath, or chuckles and shakes her head. The office door knocks. IMANI puts down the speech and looks up.

Hello!

MICHAEL comes in.

Can I help?

MICHAEL: Yes, I was looking for Ben Nelson, Senior Arts Officer; he does work here doesn't he?

IMANI: He does, but you've just missed him – he left for lunch five minutes ago. I'm Imani Shaw, Assistant Arts Officer – can I help you at all, take a message or anything?

MICHAEL: Pleased to meet you. (*He offers a hand to shake, which she takes.*) Yes, if you could just tell him I passed by to say hello and have a chat. I'll pass by again soon enough.

IMANI: Okay then.

MICHAEL: Okay.

IMANI grabs the speech and continues reading. MICHAEL watches her a moment longer, then walks from the office.

(*On his way out.*) See you...

IMANI: (*Without looking up.*) Bye...

The office door closes. Lights dim.

SCENE 4

JONES, LAMMING and SPENCER all walk to the front of stage. They stand in a single file line and speak as one.

ALL: Meanwhile…

They turn on their heels and walk offstage.

SCENE 5

BEN and DON walk to the table both with drinks in hand. BEN clutches a large folder. They sit.

DON: … That year the community centre gave us five days to do the show, and we were packed every night – people came back two and three times – yet all we could get them to agree to was a box office split, so none of us made any real money… Pocket change, that's all we did, couple 'undred but nothing really worth our while. I tell you, if it wasn't for the kids I woulda given up this lark long ago, become a benefits advisor or something with a regular wage. It's bloody ridiculous waiting to get paid this way…

BEN: (*Looking through files.*) Your sales report isn't as good as it could be. Not bad, but you had two slow nights to begin with…

DON: Yeah, well that's only to be expected innit? Change ah venue, limited fliers, no money for radio or newspaper ads. No one willing to review a five-day run for obvious reasons…

BEN: … By the time the review comes out the run is over, I know, that's what all the papers say.

DON: But getting a two-week run with no money is murder for us mate, let alone three weeks. Imagine if we'd been in the community centre that long. The way our audience figures were going we'd have made loads of money for them and us, but they just wouldn't let it happen, even when the initial five days went well.

BEN: What about Jean Withers at Pulse? Have you dealt with her before?

DON: (*Morose.*) Yeah…

BEN: What happened?

81

DON: That was our last show, *Sex and Violence* –

BEN: Great title!

DON: Yeah, it gets people's attention I tell yuh that much! Anyway, it was a kind of exploration of the modern attitude towards the sex and violence that surrounds kid's lives from birth until adulthood. We did it as a series of short set pieces all worked up from improvs into a script written by one ah the kids.

BEN: Which you directed?

DON: That's right. Jean read the script, loved it, give us two weeks at the Pulse and a vague promise that if we were successful we could at least do more shows, then we went ahead.

BEN: And?

DON: The sales figures and reviews speak for themselves.

BEN looks through the sheets of paper. DON waits.

BEN: You had a bad two days at the beginning of the second week.

DON: Tube strike both days. But look on the bright side blud, we still got –

BEN: Forty the first night, sixty the next. Yeah. Not bad at all, considering.

DON: We're supported by the local community, that's why.

BEN: So what happened after that?

DON: Well, when we went back to Jean about our next show she told us they were all booked up. That if we got funding come and see her, but otherwise the season was already set.

BEN: That's doesn't sound like Jean.

DON: What can I say? That's what she told me...

BEN reads some more. DON watches.

BEN: You've got fantastic reviews from some very important people.

DON: I know. I don't understand what we're doing wrong.

BEN reads further, turns the page, sees that he's finished and looks up at DON.

BEN: Okay; I think I can honestly help. With all of this information it should be easy to put together a funding package that makes sure the kids get paid and you don't have to work for JSA! I mean, what you do is what they say they're looking for Don. It's ridiculous that you've been left to struggle all these years.

DON: Well, I hope you're right. It would really be something to be able to treat the kids like professionals for a change. You should come to a rehearsal too – if you got time.

BEN: I'll make time – it would be very interesting to see what you guys do.

DON: It's a deal.

They shake.

You're a good guy B –

BEN: B? Is that my street moniker or something now?

DON: (*Laughs.*) Yeah, you could look at it like that. I just said it cos that's what Imani called you in the office. Don't you like it?

BEN: No – no, it's fine. Just a little strange is all…

DON: Listen blud, don't you worry about strange. I dunno what you've done to my missus, but she really believes in you B – her re-christening you is probably just the tip of the iceberg. You keep reading speeches for her and you'll see.

BEN: Oh, don't you worry, that's okay by me. You're a lucky man, you know that Don? Imani's smart, beautiful, full of integrity… Writing that speech is the least I can do.

DON is acting as though he's very nervous all of a sudden.

DON: Well: I know that this might sound weird coming from me Ben, but don't let Imani push you too far. You know what women are like eh? Give 'em what they want and they'll walk all over you until they're tired of lifting their feet, then they'll still wanna use your corpse as a footrest. I love Imani with all my heart but sometimes she can get carried away. Watch out for that blud.

BEN: Okay...

DON: (*After watching BEN for a long time.*) Look: never mind what I just said, okay? I'm so used to being knocked back I can't help casting my cynical eye over everything, even me own missus. You and Imani will make a great team, I can see that already. (*He raises his drink.*) To Ben and Imani.

After a second, so does BEN.

BEN: Ben and Imani...

They knock their drinks together. Lights dim.

SCENE 6

LAMMING, JONES and SPENCER storm onstage in that order. LAMMING is obviously full of high spirits and in a much better mood than we've previously seen. JONES and SPENCER seem to be trying to shut him up.

LAMMING: Wait, wait, wait, hold up a second! (*To lighting man.*) Hey, you up there, Mr Lighting Man! Hold up a sec mate, hold on...

JONES: What the hell are you doing now?

SPENCER: Messing things up. Like he always does.

LAMMING: No, you lot don't understand, this is great!

SPENCER: What's great?

LAMMING: This! What happened then!

JONES: Lamming: do you mind telling the both of us what in God's name you're going on about?

LAMMING: Okay; I'll take it slow, I know you guys aren't used to thinking on your feet. (*JONES and SPENCER shoot each other looks.*) I was backstage thinking about Imani's three rules, watching everything, when it suddenly hit me – the scale of what we're doing, what we're involved in...

JONES: Lamming! You're not making any sense.

LAMMING: See what I mean? You guys can't possibly comprehend the enormity of what's happening on that stage cos you don't have the vested interest I have. A man like me buys into this shit a lot easier than you guys.

JONES: I know you need me to ask the million dollar question, so I'll do you a favour just this once. Why?

SPENCER: Wait, don't tell me: cos you studied at RADA, right? You just didn't wanna tell us before cos you were worried we might be intimidated by your skill –

LAMMING: Very funny, but wrong. It's cos I'm a Black man Spencer! A Black man!

Silence.

SPENCER: Yeah, Ali G has the same problem…

JONES and SPENCER collapse into fits of laughter.

LAMMING: Can't you talk in a civilised manner without being sarky for one minute? You're not funny and you're not clever, it's just sad okay? (*JONES and SPENCER are still laughing.*) I knew you guys wouldn't get it. What we're seeing here is classic stuff you know; that last scene between Don and Ben, Don trying to warn him about Imani, not being exactly sure what he's warning him about – that's classic tragedy there mate I'm telling you, can't get better than that.

JONES: Well, I'd hardly call this classic material, especially not when our writer's clearly ripped off Shakespeare –

LAMMING: Sssh! (*Looking into audience.*) Who doesn't these days?

JONES: – And then goes on to try and lure the audience into his story with poorly advised shock tactics like those terrible 'rules' you seem so fond of. Honestly! I've kept my mouth shut long enough, but seeing as you constantly feel the need to express your feelings, I think I should too.

LAMMING: This'll be good!

SPENCER: Excuse me; don't you lot realise we have a show to perform here or what?

LAMMING: Wait a minute Spencer, let him have his say and then you can have yours, all fair –

SPENCER: I don't want my say! I wanna get this job done, then I wanna go home! Simple!

LAMMING: Go on Jones, don't mind her.

SPENCER gets mad and storms offstage.

JONES: On closer inspection of the script, I happen to think that this play is racist –

LAMMING: Oh! Racist! That's a good one!

JONES: – on the grounds that it vilifies white people. Look at all the white characters in this script. What do they have in common? They're all evil bastards who want to put down your race. That's not reality!

LAMMING: Not yours. Anyway, they're not all bad. What about Michael?

JONES: From page 103 onwards his character development takes an awful turn.

LAMMING: Yeah, but he's not racist is he?

JONES: Well, yes… Institutionally.

LAMMING: What about Kate then? And you! Are you saying you're racist too!

JONES: Not yet! But look here – (*Pulls out A4 sheet, walks over to LAMMING and starts pointing at it.*) Even this argument is pre-written to make it seem as if I agree with their views. It's unfair and I protest that from this moment, I refuse to be a caricature…

SPENCER comes onstage followed by BEN. They stand stage left with their arms folded looking very unhappy.

LAMMING: But you're not! Listen Jones, Imani's rules had nothing to do with white people and everything to do with Blacks in a majority white environment and how they handle themselves. You might find it hard to deal with, but for me it's a refreshing change to hear this stuff. Every play I've been in I've done the standard actor's thing – read my part, sod the rest. I even did it with this play too! But sitting in the wings, watching what was going on I realised this is probably the most important play I'm never gonna see – if I let that happen.

JONES: Why is it so hard following your train of thought?

LAMMING: Cos I'm a deep brudda, you get me? Anyway, what I'm saying to you is, I want to see this play. An' I will you know.

LAMMING walks into the audience, climbs up to sensible spot, removes a reserved sign and sits. JONES is incredulous, looking from left to right unsure what to do next.

JONES: But – what are you doing – you can't sit there, it's against the rules – (*Spots SPENCER and BEN.*) Oh hey, how's it going? Good show?

BEN: Do you mind? We're waiting to come on…

JONES: Of course. I'll get on it right away.

BEN: Thank you.

BEN and SPENCER walk offstage.

JONES: (*To LAMMING.*) Bastard! (*Straight to audience as LAMMING laughs.*) Life seems to be progressing quite nicely for Ben Nelson. After a great meeting with Don he gets back to the office to find that Imani has read his speech and loves it – in fact, she can't wait to hear it out loud. The following week is full of nerves and anticipation for Ben, and he decides to keep news of his public appearance very secret, just in case things don't go as well as planned. This is very unusual, as he normally shares every waking moment with his wife at the very least. Ben's discomfort does not go unnoticed by Kate. Just when it all seems like too much to hold back, his big night finally arrives…

JONES makes to walk offstage, then changes his mind at the last moment and climbs into the audience beside LAMMING as the following scene continues below.

LAMMING: All right mate! Where's the popcorn?

JONES: Shut up! You've caused enough trouble already!

JONES sits. LAMMING laughs again.

SCENE 7

A group of people are gathered in the bar hanging out when BEN walks into the room with IMANI beside him, DON in tow. Lots of nods and raised glasses in his direction. BEN smiles at all, looking at ease as IMANI guides him to their usual table. DON, who takes his seat last, isn't as jovial as we're used to.

BEN: Well! I don't know quite what I expected but it wasn't a reaction like that!

IMANI: They loved you B, they really did. I knew the speech was good and it was one thing reading it, but to hear the feeling you put into those words... You're a natural at this, you really are!

BEN: Like I told you, it's only a case of practice –

IMANI: Will you shut up and take a compliment?! You're too modest by far B, you should accept the fact that you're no ordinary mortal, shouldn't he darling?

DON: You were amazing B. No word of a lie blud, that speech was on the money, like you'd been at it years. Well done.

BEN: You're not having me on are you, trying to make me feel good? I mean – you seem a little quiet tonight Don, if you don't mind me saying...

DON: Nah man, I wouldn't kid you like that for a minute B, it's not my style. Just been a long day rehearsing with the kids and all, don't mind me.

BEN: Yes, and then to come here straight afterwards must be pretty gruelling.

IMANI: Ah! My little workhorse!

IMANI gives DON *a kiss, which he doesn't react to. She backs off, a little confused but says nothing.*

BEN: When I think about it though, it was a great feeling being up there, making people think, laugh, getting into the rhythm of the words, ad-libbing, all of that…

SPENCER approaches the table.

SPENCER: Hi there – Ben?

BEN: Yes, that's right, hello.

SPENCER: Hi. My name's Melody Spencer; I'm not anyone important or anything, just a COT member who loved the speech you made. I was wondering, has it been published?

BEN: No – no. I'm not really in this line of work… It's just something I tried as a favour –

SPENCER: Oh, that's a shame. If it was published I would have given a copy to my son, he really needs that type of inspiration in his life… Anyhow, I just wanted to say it's about time we heard more speeches like the one you read and keep up the good work.

BEN: Thank you Melody…

SPENCER: See you next week I hope?

BEN: Yes, I think you will.

SPENCER leaves. BEN *gets to his feet.*

IMANI: Leaving already? Or you going to chase up more adulation from willing female admirers?

BEN: Leaving. One admirer in my life is good enough for me.

IMANI: (*Gets up and gives him a hug and kiss.*) Okay… Well done again B. Look at you! Done in under two weeks what most SAOs couldn't do in a whole career. I'm proud of you!

BEN: Be proud when we start getting money in for the artists; anything else is premature.

IMANI: Of course.

Another kiss on the cheek. DON watches closely. BEN offers a hand to shake, which DON manages to the best of his ability.

DON: Nice one blud. I'll give you a call this week.

BEN: No worries. Take care you two.

He leaves. IMANI sits down and turns to DON. Her cheery nature is gone.

IMANI: All right. Do you mind telling me what the hell's the matter with you?

DON: I'm fine.

IMANI: Don, don't play the arse, you're not fine and everyone can see it, even B. Now I want you to tell me –

DON: Cor, can't you go five seconds without putting that man's name in your mouth. B this, Ben that, it's all I've been getting all week! Jesus!

IMANI stares at him for a long time.

IMANI: Ah: now I see.

DON: No you don't. You don't see shit Imani and that's what's bothering me. You don't see cos you don't want to look.

IMANI: It's jealousy, that's what it is. Not even of me and Ben – of the type of man he is, that's all. It's quite natural.

DON: It's not that at all Imani, and you know it. Don't make me out to be someone I'm not.

IMANI: You can admit it babe; it's okay. I felt intimidated by the accent and the height and the complex words too, but he's such a nice man you can't hold any of that against him –

DON: That's not what I'm talking about –

IMANI: It's just the way he was brought up, that's all. I mean, Barnes for God's sake! Can you imagine that Don, to be surrounded by nothing but white people, no rap, no Dasheen, no African Pride hair grease, no cocoa butter, no Buju, no rice and peas, guineps, ackee and saltfish…

DON: (*Harsh whisper.*) Stop! Will you just stop! I'm not jealous and even if I was who would be to blame for that? I'll tell you who. You! Since the day he stepped into that office you haven't stopped going on about him and I wouldn't mind if I really thought you fancied him, that would be normal, that would make some kind of sense, but what you're doing is nothing but manipulation and you better stop it Imani. You better stop or me and you are gonna have a major bust up, I'm telling you now!

IMANI watches him a minute, stunned.

IMANI: Manipulation… Is that what you think I'm doing?

DON: (*Kisses his teeth.*) Why did you lie about that woman being ill? Not being able to make your imaginary speech? (*IMANI looks him in the eye but doesn't say a word.*) Everyone I asked at today's meeting told me you said Ben was making this speech last week. Why did you tell them that?

IMANI: You saw how fired up he was at the last meeting. If you think I'd miss an opportunity to get someone like him on board, you're sadly mistaken. He's an asset!

DON: He's a Senior Arts Officer Imani! Getting Ben involved means a conflict of interests and you know it. The council's never gonna allow him to stay in office and speak out at COT meetings like some Marcus Garvey revolutionary! He's gonna get in all sorts of trouble.

IMANI: They let *me*.

DON: That's cos you're small fry love – he's the one that matters, the one with access to the purse strings, and they ain't gonna have it, you watch. Look at me as a prime example if you don't believe it.

IMANI: So that's what you think I am Don? Small fry?

DON: Nah love, don't even try those ones. That's what they think and you know it.

IMANI: (*Relenting a little.*) It was only one speech. One speech to prove he means what he says and isn't just mouthing off like the rest of them. Come on Don, you know how it is. He's got a white wife, was practically given the job as a wedding present and all the rest... I've got to make sure Don. I can't be let down again. One speech for God's sake!

DON: And if he decides he wants to make another? Are you gonna be the one to tell him what I just said?

IMANI: Well; if he wants to, how the hell can I stop him –

DON: Thought as much... (*He gets to his feet.*) I'll be staying at mine tonight Imani. It's not right what you're doing to that poor guy and I ain't gonna condone it no matter how much you try to convince me. Talk to you soon.

He leaves.

IMANI: (*Loud.*) Don, don't be stupid, come back – (*She stops, looks around, thinks about it. Next line to herself.*) Fine. Fine.

Lights dim.

SCENE 8

KATE is enjoying a late night drink alone, in front of the TV. BEN enters the room.

BEN: Hello Mrs Nelson

KATE: Why, good evening Mr Nelson. A pleasant one for you I trust?

BEN: Most pleasant indeed darling – most pleasant indeed. Yours?

KATE: Marvellous darling. You just missed Michael. Said to give you his best.

BEN: (*Looking at his watch.*) Did he?

KATE: Yes; we watched DVDs and polished off another one of your bottles. I hope you don't mind.

BEN: That's what they're here for.

He bends over to give her a kiss. KATE reaches over, grabs him by the back of the neck and pulls him down. They hold that position for a while before BEN backs off.

You're drunk.

KATE: Am not!

BEN: Tipsy then.

KATE: Well: all right I'll give you that, but I have had half a bottle to myself. And I'm quietly drunk that's all, far from raving.

BEN: Of course…

He pours, lifting the bottle to the light when he only gets half a glass. He shrugs and sits on the sofa next to KATE.

KATE: So how was your night?

BEN: Good, really good darling. Tonight, for once in my life, I think I can safely say that I did something really amazing.

KATE: Whatever did you do?

BEN: I – well, you know Imani invited me to her Children Of Tamana meeting last week –

KATE: Yes…

BEN: Well, I went again this week –

KATE: That's what I assumed –

BEN: But Imani was in trouble because she had this speech she was supposed to write for the meeting and no one to read it – well, she had someone to read it but the woman was sick, so Imani had to find someone else –

KATE: Why didn't she read it herself?

BEN: Why – I'm not sure. I don't think she's confident that way –

KATE: She struck me as pretty confident in all ways…

BEN: Yes; anyway, she had no one to read her speech so I stepped in and said I'd write and perform it. (*KATE is nodded zealously, over-doing her listening wife bit but not really*

93

paying attention.) Which is what I did tonight! I wanted to tell you last week but I was so nervous I thought it best I do it and not tell anyone.

KATE: How did it go? Well I suppose?

BEN: Better than I could have imagined. Darling, I really got into the whole idea of performing again – it was just like being in the band, only this time I really knew what I was doing and it showed. I got a standing ovation – well, stumbling actually: the Calabash Afro-Caribbean Pensioners Group seemed most impressed.

They both laugh.

But the main point is that I reached people on that stage tonight darling. I spoke from the soul and they heard me and connected, just as I hoped they would. My heart hasn't stopped pounding since I stepped up to the lectern, I tell you that much! That speech has definitely done something for me tonight Kate, over and above the political. I feel alive again, I really do. I feel strong...

KATE: Of course you do darling...

BEN: ... And I have Imani to thank.

KATE thinks about that for a moment.

KATE: So, what was the speech about?

BEN looks at her, smiles.

What?

BEN: Nothing.

KATE: So?

BEN: So what?

KATE: Your speech. What was the topic?

BEN: (*Sighs.*) I started by talking about Black Art and its cultural links across the Diaspora; then I went on to our present situation, with most indigenous Blacks finding it next to impossible to practise their arts. I tied the whole thing up by highlighting the wealth of social ills Black people face living here, particularly the young, and made the point that had unhindered artistic expression been allowed from the get go, many of those social ills could have been cured.

KATE: (*After small silence.*) Yes; yes, that makes incredible sense…

BEN: (*Laughs.*) It's far too late for this kind of conversation…

KATE: It is not!

BEN: Well you're far too drunk –

KATE: Ben Nelson, for the last time I am not drunk or dim! And while I admit I'm not an expert when it comes to the African Diaspora, it would be foolish not to admit that I must have some knowledge.

BEN: Because you're married to me, right?

KATE: I beg your pardon?

BEN: You think you know what goes on in the African Diaspora because you're married to me, don't you? That's obvious. And very wrong.

KATE: I did know Black people before I married you Ben!

BEN: (*Smiling.*) Is that so? Tell me this darling – how often do these many Black people you've come across in your life actually visit you and pass on their knowledge of the African Diaspora?

KATE: (*Quiet.*) Are you trying to embarrass me?

BEN: In front of? Come on darling, don't be upset, I was just teasing you again –

KATE: (*Snaps.*) Well you shouldn't because I don't like it, I've told you before! (*Gets up.*) Oh, now look what you've done!

KATE slams down her glass and leaves the living room. BEN, frowning, watches her leave, then downs his glass and follows, flicking the light switch. Lights dim.

BEN: Darling! Darling, don't be upset it was a joke…

SCENE 9

Lights up on LAMMING and JONES. For a moment they don't notice, then LAMMING looks up at the ceiling.

LAMMING: Ay! Ay, wha' you doing? Put that light out, don't you know there's a play on?

LAMMING cracks up to himself while JONES elbows his side and tries to slide down in his seat trying not to be noticed.

JONES: Stop it! We've obviously missed a cue –

SPENCER strides out onto the stage looking livid.

SPENCER: Are you guys quite finished playing school kids, or do we have to bring Riggs to throw you out on the cold streets of South London? And it ain't nice out there I'm telling ya!

JONES: What do you mean?

SPENCER: I mean if you lot don't get your arses off those seats and backstage you're both sacked by order of the management and I get your wages. Okay?

SPENCER storms offstage without waiting for a reply. LAMMING looks at JONES.

LAMMING: We better go. I didn't even think we got wages, but I don't wanna risk it.

JONES: Yeah. I quite liked it up here too.

They leave their seats and walk offstage still talking amongst themselves.

LAMMING: That's a bit harsh innit? The sack. After all the years we put into this company.

JONES: There's no loyalty in the business any more…

LAMMING: You'd think they'd take it as a sign of appreciation, us watching their play, but no…

JONES: It's a major compliment!

LAMMING: If I wrote a play I wouldn't mind if the actors wanted to watch it, I tell you that much…

LAMMING and JONES exit. Lights dim. SPENCER creeps back out and stands front of stage. Lights immediately up.

SPENCER: Sorry… A bit of a mess backstage at the minute… It was my cue… Sorry… Don't tell them lot will you? (*Clears her throat, smiles, all professional now.*) Six weeks later…

She turns and walks offstage, stops before she gets there, looks up at the lighting man and waves his way.

Sorry!

She walks offstage.

SCENE 10

BEN sitting at his desk with a sheet of A4 paper in front of him, the phone to his ear. He doesn't look as calm as we have previously seen.

BEN: Hello? Yes hello, could I speak to Bryony Furniss please? Ben Nelson, West Chamberlayne Arts. Thank you. (*Pause.*) Hello? Could I speak to Bryony please? It's Ben Nelson, West Chamberlayne Arts. Oh, an arts application I submitted about a month ago, from… Yes, all right. Okay. (*Longer pause.*) Oh Bryony, it's Ben Nelson here, West Chamberlayne Arts… It's about the application from Kids Company I'm afraid… Must be sick of hearing that name I imagine… I was actually wondering if you could spare some time to explain more about why we aren't eligible for your fund. I know I left a message yesterday, but I'd really like to be able to tell Don why he didn't get the money. I'm sure you understand. Give me a call back, you know the number. Thanks Bryony.

BEN puts the phone down. Consults his piece of A4 paper. Picks up the phone.

Okay then… (*He dials.*) Hello? Hello, is that Steve Wellington? Yes, it's Ben Nelson West Chamberlayne Arts, how are you? Oh yes, settling in quite well I think…. No, not at all, I've just got a project I'm really quite keen on and when I'm keen I don't mind working the odd late evening…

Yes... That's right, and without passion what do we have?
Exactly... (*Pause.*) Yes, I was actually... Have you? Oh,
that's a shame because it would be great if we could talk
about... Yes, I realise it's late. I've been trying you all day
I'm afraid, just got the answerphone. Well, we hadn't heard
back and it's getting difficult to explain to Don... Yes, of
course... What time tomorrow? Okay, I'll call back then...
No I understand, if they've gone home... Okay, bye then...
Bye.

*BEN puts the phone down and gently rests his head against the
desk. He lays like that for a while before he gets up and starts
pacing the office. He walks up and down three times before
he turns and picks up the phone. He stops with it halfway to
his ear and waits. He puts it down, closes his eyes, takes a
deep breath. He picks up and dials quickly, putting the phone
to his ear again.*

Hello? Raymond, is that you? It's Ben... How are you? Yes,
I didn't think I'd catch you but I thought I'd try... Great,
great... Yes, well actually I wanted a favour if you could... I
need some advice and I thought you might be able to help...
The office... Yes, that's fine... I'll see you there in about 20
minutes? Perfect. See you Raymond.

*BEN puts down the phone and thinks a minute. Then he picks
up his papers and folders, turns off everything in the office,
flicks the light switch and leaves. Lights dim.*

SCENE 11

*RAYMOND walks into the bar, looks around, then unbuttons
his jacket and sits at the table. For a moment he waits a little
impatiently, tapping his fingers on the table, getting out his
newspaper and scanning the news before laying it down and
tapping again. IMANI walks past without a coat. She's carrying
some files and almost shits herself when she sees RAYMOND sitting
there. He doesn't see her. Behind him, IMANI gets her act together
and works out her story before she approaches.*

IMANI: Raymond?

He turns.

RAYMOND: Diana?

IMANI: Imani. Imani Shaw. I work with your son-in-law Ben, at WCA?

RAYMOND: Of course, of course, I remember the face never the name, much apologies…

IMANI: Not to worry I know how it is. Having a late lunch?

RAYMOND: No actually, just an afternoon drink.

IMANI: Ooh, that sounds nice.

RAYMOND: Yes; and what are your plans for the evening?

IMANI: Oh, I'm just going over next year's COT events with a few of the team; I'd say come over and join us but we'll probably be off within the next ten minutes.

RAYMOND: Well I hope it all goes smoothly.

IMANI: Thanks Raymond, have a good meeting.

RAYMOND: Thank you.

IMANI leaves. RAYMOND sits waiting. JONES comes out wearing an apron and carrying a mint julep cocktail on a silver tray. He gives the drink to RAYMOND, who looks pleased but not surprised.

JONES: Compliments of the management Mr Armitage.

RAYMOND: *(Getting out his wallet.)* Why thank you, thank you very much. And could I get a bottled lager, whatever you have will do.

JONES: Certainly sir. Don't trouble yourself, management will get that one too. Won't be a moment.

JONES leaves just as BEN gets through the door. RAYMOND spies him, puts away his wallet and waves. BEN approaches the table.

BEN: Good evening Raymond, how are you keeping?

RAYMOND: Splendid Benjamin, splendid! I took the liberty of ordering you a bottle of lager, I hope you don't mind.

BEN: Not at all Raymond, not at all. In fact, I think I could use it.

RAYMOND: Oh?

JONES comes back with a bottle of lager, which he places in front of BEN.

BEN: I'll tell all in a minute, once I've settled in. How's council life treating you?

RAYMOND: Same as ever my dear boy, same as ever. Endless stuffy meetings in endless stuffy rooms with endless stuffy people. But it's work, and we must all work my boy, must we not?

BEN: We must.

RAYMOND: Cheers.

BEN: Cheers Raymond.

They clink glass. RAYMOND sips his cocktail and smacks his lips together.

RAYMOND: A perfect Mojito. Reminds me of Habana, '77; my wife and myself couldn't get enough of these. Morning, noon and night we'd be drinking and do you know, I'd never, ever wake up with a hangover? 'Ernest Hemingways' they call them in Cuba – apparently they were his favourite drink too. It only takes a mouthful and I can see it all you know Benjamin, the children, the bands, the colours; Julie –

RAYMOND breaks off and stares into space. This is the closest to a human being we've seen in him.

BEN: You must miss her a great deal.

RAYMOND: Every day my dear boy; every day. (*Collects himself.*) So, what is it you had to see me about in such a hurry?

BEN: I was hoping I could bend your ear actually Raymond, glean some advice from you.

RAYMOND: If I can help I'd be glad to.

BEN: It's about one of my clients, Don Kenworthy. He runs a project called Kids Company over in West Chamberlayne…

RAYMOND: Yes…

BEN: Well it's a very perplexing thing. I was approached by Don because he told me that despite the fact he's been running a successful theatre group for close to eight years, he's never received any funding from any local arts bodies –

RAYMOND: Never?

BEN: Much less any regional departments. Not one bean from anybody…

RAYMOND: I find that very hard to believe.

BEN: Well, it's the God's honest truth Raymond –

RAYMOND: I didn't mean to imply that you were lying –

BEN: What I mean is, I've got all the forms that he sent and I looked them over, so we have proof of his rejections. Now, it wouldn't be so bad if it was Don was running an adult company of Cambridge graduates, because they very obviously don't meet this borough's funding criteria. What gets me is the fact that Kids Company is a fully multi-cultural group with an age range of 16-30 years old, operating in the middle of Queensbury Housing Estate, peopled mainly by youths who previously robbed, took crack, stole cars… And now they perform theatre. In other words, they're doing exactly what funders say they want, but are rejected regardless.

RAYMOND: Yes. I see what you mean.

BEN: (*Getting fired up.*) And that's not the end of it. After I looked over Don's papers I decided to come on board and fill out his forms, look over his budgets, send his apps out with a WCA recommendation on headed paper. And do you know what Raymond? We've been rejected by every single funding body I've applied to. Can you believe that? Every single one. Oh, well that's not strictly true of course – the ones that haven't rejected us just didn't call back. Ever. I was chasing them up today and a lot of the time they're people I know, but that only tends to make it worse. I end

up getting fobbed off and charmed, but not getting any
money.

RAYMOND: What were his accounts like?

BEN: Spot on. No real money coming in or out, so not much to
account for really.

RAYMOND: So how have they been maintaining themselves for
eight years?

BEN: Don's pocket according to him. And a much reduced work
method: limited sets, volunteer actors, box office splits
worked out with willing venues…

RAYMOND: Hmmm. I can't help thinking that because your
man is set up and running already, his chances of receiving
funding are seriously hindered. Theatre funds mostly exist
to aid new and emerging companies, not those operating
successfully for eight years or more. His decision –

BEN: But that's bullshit Raymond; please excuse my language,
but your reasoning makes no sense! We've got funding apps
dating right from the beginning, before Kids Company put
on a single production and the story was still the same.
Sorry, you're not eligible for funding. They rejected him
until he put almost a decade of work into the project, then
tell him one of the reasons that he might not be getting any
money is because the company performed professionally for
several years. Might! They weren't even sure about that!

RAYMOND: Now Benjamin, calm down –

BEN: (*Quieter, but still forceful.*) That's the worst thing about it!
From what their records tell me Don has appealed, written
letters and had numerous meetings, but no one seems to
be able to give conclusive reasons as to why they're not
funded. Nothing! (*Flicks through the files.*) All these sales
reports, reviews, audience questionnaires to prove that all
they need is help, and the system simply refuses to look at
the information. It's thoroughly frustrating!

RAYMOND: So I see…

BEN: Sorry Raymond… It's just that these six weeks were a chance for me to prove what I could do, the changes I could make; all I've done is the complete opposite… I shudder to think what Don makes of me… We used to talk or meet twice a week, but I hardly see him now and I know it's down to my complete lack of success. I haven't had one successful application for any of my clients Raymond; meanwhile Imani not only manages to raise money for the Five Feathers Film Project, but The 3rd Avenue Multi-Media Poetry Slam too! What's Don supposed to do? He's got a show to put on in a month's time and if he can't rely on me then I'm useless, aren't I?

RAYMOND: Indeed.

BEN: So what next Raymond? Do you know anyone who could help, someone connected to a tax-break deal perhaps, or some small funding body I might not have uncovered –

RAYMOND: Now Ben –

BEN: Nothing big at this stage; I mean, I know we can't get the set we wanted, but maybe we could pay the actors' travel expenses and give them a small subsidy –

RAYMOND: Well –

BEN: Cause it's important Raymond, it's really important that I don't lose their trust at this stage, not when I've built so many bridges. If I can't get funding for a project of this nature then I'm just the same as any other SAO and that's not the image I want to project –

RAYMOND: Benjamin Nelson! (*BEN looks up, startled.*) You cannot ask my advice and then forbid me from getting a word in edgeways my dear boy. It's simply not done! (*Takes a deep breath.*) Now, in answer to your query I'm afraid the answer is no. I cannot help you. I'm sorry Benjamin, but this one is out of my hands.

BEN looks at him in complete shock. He never expected that.

BEN: No?

RAYMOND: Let me explain something to you my dear boy; something I believe I should have taken the time to say a long while ago and overlooked because my assumption was that you understood. Now I know different; but never mind. Ignorance can be rectified, if the spirit is willing of course. You see Benjamin, in the world of arts funding there are two types of applications that reach our desks: the type of applications we fund, and the type we do not. The type of applications we fund are... To cut a long story short, the types that appeal to the current marketplace; financially, aesthetically, morally. Take theatre for instance: in theatre the audience that spends the money – the real money Benjamin – don't want their world to change or boundaries to shift. And why would they? Would you spend money to sit and listen to some white man telling you how wicked and evil your race is?

BEN: But that's not what –

RAYMOND: Do let me finish. As I was trying to say, the type of application that largely doesn't receive any real funding, is the kind of socially inclusive blame-it-on-the-system art that seems so predominant within the working class community, especially – now hear me out Benjamin – especially the Blacks. Now, I believe I know Don Kenworthy's work. The play I saw was exactly the kind of thing I'm talking about – reverse racism, poverty-stricken setting, lots of politically incorrect speeches... Funders don't go for words, much to my dismay. They want dancing, rap, musical entertainment –

BEN: Like a professional talent show?

RAYMOND: Yes, that's right! And if you can weave a storyline out of it, more's the better, but if you don't they don't even mind! That's what gets the funding.

BEN: What if that's not what the talent wants to do?

RAYMOND: (*Laughs.*) Benjamin! Oh, Benjamin! The talent he says! The talent! Good God dear boy, you're talking like a Hollywood agent, not the Senior Arts Officer of West

Chamberlayne Arts! Now Benjamin, listen to me – you must stop this nonsense. You have a good, well-paid job, a beautiful wife, a fine house and a career ahead of you. Don't blow it all with grandeur notions of changing the world because it won't happen, not in your lifetime anyway. I've seen this type of thing before you know. You've got too much to do my dear boy, too much to lose: don't risk being a martyr to people you don't even know! You are not them! Think about it! Now it's high time we saw the old Benjamin again, the man we all know and love! Stop this nonsense and give us the old Benjamin back, eh?

BEN: *(Takes his time.)* I think… I think that the old Ben was a product of your imagination… *(He gets to his feet.)* I think the old Ben was a person you dreamt about while you slept, then woke up wishing for him so hard you convinced yourself that he really existed.

RAYMOND: Now Benjamin, don't be ridiculous. Sit down –

BEN: No. I won't sit down because I'm not being ridiculous. Because unless you can look at me Raymond, really look at me and see me for who I am, there's not point sitting at a table with you. Is there now?

RAYMOND: Well, come now Benjamin –

BEN: That's not who I am Raymond. I'm Ben.

BEN turns and exits the stage. RAYMOND sits there for a minute, thinking hard. He pulls out a mobile, dials, puts it to his ear and changes his mind, ending the call. IMANI comes out followed by SPENCER and at least three women with their coats on, all at the back of stage. RAYMOND gets his jacket and makes a speedy exit while they talk.

IMANI: Okay, so I'll speak to you guys over the weekend but basically we're all set, right?

SPENCER: Sure. This is gonna be so fantastic Imani! It's the best idea you've ever had!

IMANI: Thanks babe, but don't get too excited yet! We've still gotta announce it at this week's COT meeting and then it'll have to be put to a vote and then we'll have to tell him at least!

The women laugh.

SPENCER: Nearly forgot about that!

IMANI: What does his opinion matter anyway, he's only a man!

SPENCER: Yeah, we're the real brains behind the organisation anyway! Children Of Tamana Focus Group rules!

IMANI: Hear, hear! (*Looks around to see if anyone's listening, notices RAYMOND is gone. Smiles.*) So, all being well, Ben Nelson is set to be the new managing director of the Children Of Tamana! Isn't that wonderful!

They group-hug.

SPENCER: Oh, I love you guys you know! Does anyone want a lift, I can fit you all in…

IMANI: Yes definitely, seeing as I'm still in Don's bad books… Let's get outta here…

SPENCER: (*As they leave.*) Huh, when are we ever out of their bad books? It's too much trouble watching your Ps and Qs hoping you won't piss them off. I give up trying a long time ago love… The thing with Grant, yeah, is that he loves to hold a grudge suttin' bad Imani, I'm telling you… If I've told the man once I tell him a million times that don't work with me, but does he sort it out? Does he hell! I tell you…

The women leave the stage. Lights dim.

End of Act Two.

Act Three

SCENE 1

Lights up. KATE sits on the sofa with her head down, looking very much alone. Right now she's about as active as a life-sized ornamental statue made of china. MICHAEL's jacket hangs on the sofa's right arm. KATE's smoking a cigarette and drinking a cup of tea while staring into space. The radio plays Britpop.

MICHAEL: (*Off.*) Kate? Kate?

KATE is lost in her own world, far from her West London home.

(*Off.*) Katie! There's somebody here for you!

KATE doesn't say a word. MICHAEL enters the room.

Kate, didn't you hear me? There's somebody at the door for you, didn't you hear the bell?

KATE: I don't want to see anyone.

MICHAEL: Oh – okay. (*Turns to leave, stops and turns back to her.*) Don't you even want to know who it is?

The statue stirs. KATE shrugs. MICHAEL looks worried.

KATE: It won't make any difference.

MICHAEL: It's Imani Shaw, the woman who works at Ben's office? She's –

KATE: Let her in.

Pause.

MICHAEL: But you just… Okay, you're playing with me, right?

KATE: No, I just don't want to see anybody except her. Let her in.

MICHAEL studies KATE.

MICHAEL: Kate, are you all right?

KATE: For God's sake Michael, please let's not do this now, especially not when we have a guest waiting. I'm fine, I just have things on my mind. Now could you see Imani inside? Please?

MICHAEL: Sure.

MICHAEL leaves. We hear a mutter of conversation from the passageway before MICHAEL comes back followed by IMANI, who seems cheery and full of life.

IMANI: Katie, how are you darling? I hope I'm not intruding or anything; (*Walks over and plants a kiss on KATE's cheek.*) but I was passing through the area and I remembered that you guys lived around here and so I thought oh! Let me stop and say hello to Mrs Nelson, I don't see you nearly enough! How you doing girl?

KATE: Fine, fine. Just taking a little time out from my day…

IMANI: Well yeah, it's well exhausting moving and doing up your own place, and it doesn't happen overnight either! My mother was working on her place for 15 years before she scraped up the money to make it as she really wanted. Imagine that! 15 years of sanding, polyfilling, painting, screwing –

MICHAEL: Now that last one… That last one sounds like heaven!

IMANI: Ooh, listen to naughty!

IMANI and MICHAEL crack up, while KATE strains at giving even a polite smile. She still doesn't like IMANI very much. MICHAEL notices her discomfort.

MICHAEL: Listen Kate, I should go –

KATE: No! I mean, you've only just got here and you've off to the loo, then I've got you answering my door like a servant –

IMANI: And don't leave on my account, I wasn't stopping or anything. I just called for a quick talk with Kate, that's all. I won't be long.

KATE: With me? I thought you came looking for Ben.

IMANI: You don't mind do you love, I'll only be five minutes of your time? I know what it's like when you're trying to relax.

KATE: Uh... Yes, of course. Sit down. Would you like some tea?

IMANI: No thanks babe, that's all right.

MICHAEL: I'll be in the kitchen.

KATE: Thank you Michael.

MICHAEL exits stage right.

IMANI: Your brother?

KATE: Whatever gave you that idea?

IMANI: You seem to have a trusting relationship.

KATE: Michael's a very old friend.

IMANI: You can always tell. I don't know what it is, but you can. I can anyway.

KATE: Not working?

IMANI: No, I had some leave coming so I decided to take it, let B deal with all that madness! It's been so long since I took a real break, what with all that time we spent waiting for a new SAO! Whether it was my wisest decision or not is another thing.

KATE: What do you mean?

IMANI: Under the circumstances.

KATE: (*Snaps.*) What circumstances? (*Pause.*) I'm sorry, that was ever so rude of me –

IMANI: Don't worry about it. You're anxious about your husband and I'm talking to you as if you work in the office with us. I should apologise. I will – I'm very sorry for talking to you as if you know what's going on Kate.

KATE: Well... Well, apology accepted...

IMANI: So, we'll start again. Let me be clearer. I wasn't sure whether it was a wise decision to leave Ben alone in the office because I think your husband has some issues that he's not dealing with very well Kate; I'm sorry, but that's the honest truth. Over the last few weeks I think I've got to know Ben very well and I'm not sure if I sound melodramatic; but I think I've watched him change a little. Now, before you say anything I know how I sound coming over here and saying all of this stuff to you, but you have to believe me when I say that I'm worried about where this could all be leading –

KATE: You don't have explain yourself. I've seen it. He's changed towards me too.

IMANI sighs, bows her head and then reaches for KATE's hand.

IMANI: Katie, don't worry. You're not the cause of his change. You're too kind and loving a woman to have ever made him begin thinking like he is. To be truthful – to be truthful, if you have to blame anyone it should be me.

KATE: For?

IMANI: Introducing him to the Children Of Tamana. The bookstores and books he's been reading; don't tell me you haven't noticed. Making B… Making Ben read that speech I couldn't manage not so long ago.

KATE sits back on the sofa, an ornamental statue made from china once more.

KATE: Tell me about it.

IMANI: Now Katie, I'm gonna say something you might not agree with but you must hear me out, okay? Some of it might not make sense because of our…because of our cultural differences you know, but if you hear me out I'll try and explain.

KATE: You mean I might not understand because it's a Black thing don't you?

IMANI: (*A little shocked.*) You go girl! But yeah – yeah, I suppose it is.

KATE: Go on. It's not the first time I've been told as much.

IMANI: (*Uncomfortable.*) Okay… The reason I felt I had to give Ben those books is cos he seemed so out of touch with his culture. He's the kindest, most good-natured man I've met bar none, and he really has a great awareness of who is – but when it comes to what that means in a wider context – who the rest of us are – I'm afraid that your husband was sadly lacking. So I gave him the books, introduced him to the Children Of Tamana, talked about Africa and its wonderful history… And as Ben started to know more I began to notice a strange air about him. He wasn't cheerful in the mornings any more. We wouldn't talk in the office, he'd just sit with his head in a book and read whenever he had free time. Then I went and let him make that speech and it all speeded up like one of those old-time films. He wouldn't talk at all. He fell out with clients. Forgive me if I'm prying, but Ben told me something about a disagreement he had with your father? Katie, no word of a lie, when I heard him shouting at an arts officer last week, calling him a racist and what-not I got scared, I really did cos apps get turned down all the time, you win some you lose some and I got my app approved so it can't be racism can it? I'm Black and the kids getting the money are mostly Black, so how can that be? I mean you know me girl, I ain't no liberal or nothing but Jesus, there are limits you know? I warned Ben about the bad elements of the group but instead of listening to me he went straight for them, damn what I might have to say.

KATE is so stunned she hardly knows what to do.

KATE: So… These bad elements… Who are they?

IMANI lowers her head.

I'm sorry you can't say, how stupid of me I know you can't say.

IMANI: If only I could, but…

KATE: I understand completely Imani. And I appreciate the risk you're taking even coming here. But tell me something else if you can. This has been going on a long time, yes?

IMANI: Since that speech really. Months now. I think what's really happening is Ben feels bad about not being able to get any of his clients funded, including my boyfriend –

KATE: Your boyfriend is one of my husband's clients?

IMANI: Yes, you didn't know that? (*KATE makes a face.*) I'm sorry, obvious question. Yeah, he can't get his clients funded so he's blaming it on racism – one of those Black things I was talking about Katie. Most of us deal with that Malcolm X stuff in our teens; it's almost our way of rebelling, you know? By my age, we've long come to terms with our place in the world – or not. Ben was obviously taught something else growing up but his response to all that knowledge was the same; it's just his age that's off-wack. All you can do for him is represent the real world, the world of sanity, the modern world.

KATE: (*Tearful.*) I know what you mean. I've been wondering what's wrong with Ben for weeks, I just couldn't work it out. I never would have guessed if you hadn't told me.

IMANI: Like I said, I was there in the office with him seven and a half hours every day. I was bound to notice something. The apps were the last straw though. I took a look over them when Ben went to lunch one day. Put it this way – if I'd have filled 'em in, I could practically guarantee they would have got that money.

KATE: You think so? They were that bad?

IMANI: What can I say? It takes practice, I've had a lot more, that's all it comes down to. (*Looks at her watch.*) Oops, have to go; I've got lots on and I only put pocket change in the meter.

KATE: Yes, they're awful aren't they? If I never had a permit I think I'd die.

IMANI: I have one, but it doesn't work in this part of Chamberlayne.

KATE: Doesn't it? That's a shame. Let me see you out.

IMANI: Thank you…

IMANI and KATE exit stage left. A moment later MICHAEL enters stage right looking like a man on the run. He straightens up when he sees the room is empty and sits on the edge of the sofa, putting his head in his hands, covering his face. When he takes them away he's beaming. He begins to laugh to himself, silently but with force until he can hardly control himself. A door slams. He sits up straight and wipes the grin from his face. KATE returns, shuts the door and stands with her back against it.

KATE: Did you hear that?

MICHAEL: No. All right, a little.

KATE comes over and sits down very near to MICHAEL.

KATE: Did you get the gist?

MICHAEL: Yes. Yes, I think so.

KATE: What am I going to do Michael? I told Imani I'd been wondering what was wrong with Ben, but that was a lie. I knew, deep down I knew this would happen, ever since that night –

MICHAEL: What night?

KATE: The night of Ben's speech. Remember I told you what he said to me?

MICHAEL: Something about… Not knowing enough about Black people?

KATE: Exactly! How am I going to deal with this Michael? Imani made me swear secrecy on my own doorstep! How am I going to convince Ben I know what he's been going through if I can't say who told me? I can hardly pretend I'm an expert on Black psychology all of a sudden! According to him I don't know anything!

MICHAEL: Well I don't –

KATE: This is insane, absolutely insane!

KATE leans over and puts her head on MICHAEL's thigh, who recoils, but before he can move her arms are around his waist. He's very uncomfortable.

MICHAEL: Katie –

KATE: Hold me Michael.

MICHAEL: This isn't right Katie –

KATE: *(Lifts head.)* Michael, I can assure you I am not entertaining thoughts of us getting back together: I'm merely asking for a sympathetic hug between friends. If you can't do that, what was the point of staying anyway?

MICHAEL: Katie – *(Thinks.)* Oh all right, seeing as you put it so nicely.

KATE: Thank you.

They only hug a second before a key sounds in a door and they leap apart as though electrically charged.

MICHAEL: See what happens…

KATE: Shush!

BEN walks in, all smiles. He carries a number of books beneath his arm.

BEN: Evening all, how's everyone tonight? Michael?

MICHAEL: Oh! I'm great Ben, I really am, greater than I've been for a long very time, really I am…

KATE: *(Cool.)* We're fine Benjamin. How are you?

BEN stops and takes another look around. Something smells fishy.

BEN: Is everything all right?

Silence.

MICHAEL: I better go.

He gets his jacket, still hanging on the right arm of sofa.

BEN: Kate, why is he going?

KATE: Just let him…

BEN: Why are you going Michael?

MICHAEL: This has nothing to do with me. Catch you later Ben.

He's gone before BEN *can turn around.* BEN *continues his turn until he faces his wife again. She looks afraid.*

BEN: Kate? What's going on?

KATE: Nothing Ben. I was just talking with Michael about certain things and he felt it best that I talk to you instead. That's why he left.

BEN: I see… He seemed very anxious…

KATE: (*Smiling.*) That's Michael's nature. He's always anxious.

BEN: (*Serious.*) I wouldn't have thought so.

KATE's smile withers.

So… You wanted to talk?

BEN *sits on the sofa and places his books on his knees.* KATE *finally notices them, and as she sits beside him and takes his hand we can see her scanning the covers.*

KATE: That's a lot of books to read.

BEN: I'll be skimming them mainly. For research. I've been asked to make another speech at the next Children Of Tamana meeting. I've already lots I want to say, but I wanted some historic quotes too, so…

KATE's head has fallen in despair, mainly due to the tales IMANI *told of her husband and what she can now see for herself.* BEN *trails off, as he can see that what he's saying is making* KATE *uncomfortable. He looks at her with concern.*

Kate? You did want to talk didn't you?

KATE: Yes Ben, I think we must. I'm… I'm worried about you darling –

BEN: Worried?

KATE: Yes; you seem so distracted these days. We don't seem to talk any more, we hardly go out –

BEN: But I'm working darling; you can see how much work I have to do –

KATE: And when we do talk it's always about the same old political issues that you say I'm not qualified to talk about –

BEN: I never said any such thing!

KATE: Yes you did. The first time you actually suggested it was months ago, but since then you've found other ways to let me know. Sometimes you don't answer my questions. Other times you give me that silly little laugh, almost like you want to shut me up but don't know how. Mostly you give me that look Ben: the look you're giving me now, the sympathetic look that says I don't know what I'm talking about? Do you know what I mean by that?

BEN: No, no I don't know what you mean Kate, because I'm not thinking along those lines at all –

KATE: Ben! Will you face up to the truth! You're pulling away from me! Aren't you?

BEN: Now Kate, please don't be silly, I love you with all my heart –

KATE: You're pulling away because you think I don't understand your culture and that was okay before when neither of us had any Black friends, but now you do and frankly you find it a embarrassing don't you?

BEN: Kate Nelson, would you stop this at once –

KATE: That's why you don't show me the books you're reading. You think I wouldn't be able to make sense of them. That's why you don't answer my questions, and most of all, why you don't take me along to those COT meetings either. What would they say Ben? What would they say if we walked into that hall together, arm-in-arm? What would they think of your speeches then?

BEN bows his head and gives himself time to gather his thoughts.

BEN: Now Kate, I'm going to say this once and only once. You've got it all wrong –

KATE: Oh, I've got it wrong?

BEN: Kate – let me have my say. I walked through that door happy as Larry and God alone knows what I walked in on, but since that point I've been...attacked by a barrage of accusations with no factual grounds whatsoever and I resent it Kate. I resent that you could ever think that way about me. Now, let's start with the books. (*He passes them over one by one.*) This is the *Metu Neter*; a book of Egyptian Cosmology. It explains the meaning behind their spiritual beliefs and meditation techniques – no bogeymen, no kill whitey statements, no Black power fists… Just peace and equality for all…

KATE: (*Thumbing through the book.*) *The Black Founders of Civilisation*… Not much equality there…

BEN: Kate, it's an established fact that Africans were the first race on earth…

KATE: You're making that face again. What are the others?

BEN: (*Sighs.*) *The Black Celts*, a study of the ancient African tribes that formerly lived in England, and *Ancient Future*, another book of Egyptian Cosmology. Look through them, read them yourself if you think I'm hiding anything. None of them have changed my former beliefs or the way I feel about you. Now; let's deal with the subject of your questions. The reason I don't answer them is because most of the time I don't have the answers Kate! Because I don't know! You can't expect me to be a Professor of African Studies in the little time I've had to learn and read. In fact, I probably know only a smidgen more than you! As for the COT meetings, there's a simple explanation for that – I just didn't think you'd be interested. If you are, then we'll go, no problem. Okay?

KATE: Well… Yes, of course that's okay. I'll read a book… I think I'll take this one, is that all right?

KATE holds up the Metu Neter.

BEN: Well, I was going to start that tonight –

KATE: But darling look, you've got two more you could start and you're not going to read all three at once. I could try a few chapters and see what I think –

BEN: Okay darling; you go ahead.

KATE: Thank you. (*Gives* BEN *a kiss on cheek.*) I'm sorry if I was short with you but I was honestly worried darling. Maybe all we needed was to clear the air. I'll go upstairs and try these chapters right away, we'll talk and I'll come along to that COT meeting, then everything will be fine. Won't it darling?

BEN: Of course it will darling. Of course it will.

KATE gives BEN another kiss on the cheek.

KATE: Love you darling.

BEN: Love you.

She leaves. Finally, BEN can't help thinking. He sits looking at his books, turning them over in hands, then opens a page. Lights slow dim.

SCENE 2

Lights up. IMANI is sitting in the bar reading The New Nation. *LAMMING walks up wearing an apron and carrying a cocktail on a tray. He places it beside her. IMANI says a quiet 'thank you' and goes back to her paper. LAMMING leaves and MICHAEL walks into the bar. He looks around, spies IMANI and begins to smile. He waves over LAMMING, talks in a voice too low for the audience to hear, then begins a slow saunter towards the table. IMANI looks up.*

IMANI: Hiya.

MICHAEL: Afternoon.

IMANI gets to her feet. They kiss European style while holding hands – a quick peck on each cheek. They sit.

Managed to get out of the office okay then?

IMANI: Yeah. I told B I had food shopping to do and no time to do it. He seemed a bit preoccupied with his new speech to be honest, he didn't seem to mind lunching on his own.

MICHAEL: A new speech? That's good.

IMANI: Yeah, he'll be making it tomorrow night and Children Of Tamana are pulling out all the stops to guarantee he's heard; hopefully, it's gonna be our biggest meeting for years! (*Looks around for* LAMMING.) Have you ordered a drink? I can get you one if you like.

MICHAEL: That's okay, I asked for a bottle of lager. I'll get yours too, it's my treat. Don't forget I invited you to lunch Imani.

IMANI: Thank you; I know what I want, I come here all the time so when you're ready to eat just let me know.

MICHAEL: Sure.

They sit in silence, staring at each other.

IMANI: So... Michael... I was very intrigued by your call this morning. You do know I haven't a clue why I'm here, right?

MICHAEL: (*Laughs.*) Right.

LAMMING *comes back with* MICHAEL's *lager. He places it on the table, nods and leaves.*

Did you want to order?

IMANI: Yes, after I've heard what you've got to say. Is that all right?

MICHAEL: Fine with me. Okay Imani, I won't keep you waiting any longer. I called you because I think we have vested interests. That different as we may seem, our circumstances actually make us very similar. I called because I see an ally in you Imani.

IMANI: (*Smiles.*) An ally? You make it sound as though someone's at war.

MICHAEL: I heard what you told Kate. For someone like her, someone that hasn't had much experience of the world outside her world, what you said would make perfect sense. It's kind of like telling a sheltered child a ghost story – it's easy to scare them with untruths and imagination because they haven't been exposed to the real world. Funnily enough, when I listened to you talking to her I tried to picture myself telling an Iraqi kid a ghost story. Think it'd be easy to scare an Iraqi kid?

IMANI: I imagine not.

MICHAEL: Because they've seen the real world, right? Real nightmares, real death, real life…

IMANI: I…suppose. But what's that got to do with what I said to Kate?

MICHAEL: Kate's a sheltered child Imani. I'm an Iraqi.

IMANI: Interesting analogy, but… Where is it taking me?

MICHAEL: What I'm saying is I've mixed with Black people before. I've read a lot of those books, even travelled to a few of the places they talked about and encountered a lot of suspicion and mistrust – at first – but never racism, never militancy. And Ben – I mean, come on Imani, look at Ben. Only a sheltered child would believe he could be a militant, because a sheltered child has no concept of what militancy entails.

IMANI: This is all very clever stuff… Only I still don't see what you're getting at.

MICHAEL: You lied Imani. (*IMANI opens her mouth to protest.*) Okay, maybe lie's too strong a word – you exaggerated. I wondered why for a while but then I realised what was going on underneath it all – well, I thought I realised, but I could be wrong, I can admit that –

IMANI: What do you think's going on then Michael?

MICHAEL: I think that you need a division between Ben and Kate. I think you went to that house to drive a wedge between them for your own good, not to help Katie. If she wasn't so unstable she would have noticed herself.

IMANI: Unstable? In what way?

MICHAEL: Let's just say that she has a difficulty… With depression…

IMANI is nodding with a poker face. She leans forward so that MICHAEL and herself are very close. MICHAEL does the same.

IMANI: So, supposing you were right. Supposing I wanted to drive a wedge between Kate and B. What would I want to do that for? And – this is the part I find really intriguing – how would that make us allies?

MICHAEL: Why else would a woman want to come between a man and wife Imani?

They stare at each other.

IMANI: (*Hopeful.*) Because I fancy him?

MICHAEL shrugs.

And that would make us allies because…

MICHAEL: It would make us allies because I feel the same way about Kate. In fact, there's more to it than simple fancy. I love her Imani, I always have. That means we have a common goal. Doesn't it?

IMANI looks deep into MICHAEL's eyes as if to assess how serious he is. LAMMING appears, hovering by the wings. When she's satisfied she breaks out into a wide grin.

IMANI: You know what Michael? I think it does. (*She looks up at LAMMING, waves him over.*) And I think I'm ready to order.

MICHAEL: Great stuff!

IMANI looks over her menu. MICHAEL watches her. Lights dim.

SCENE 3

Lights up. BEN sits with his speech on his lap, an opened book by his side, lips moving as he concentrates. KATE walks in. She's clutching the Metu Neter *by her side, her finger keeping a page while she stares at her husband. BEN doesn't notice her and keeps reading and muttering beneath his breath, referring to his book every now and then.*

KATE: Ben?

No reply.

Ben?

He looks up.

BEN: What is it darling? I've less than an hour to tighten the end of this speech and I really haven't time for chit-chat. Are you well?

KATE: I'm not sure… I'm not sure…

KATE walks further into the room. She seems in a daze.

BEN: Kate? Whatever are you talking about?

KATE: Do you think you could bring yourself to let me read your speech darling? If I promise I won't come to your meeting tonight, would you at least let me read your speech?

BEN: But you're perfectly welcome to come tonight darling.

KATE: Well, I'm not entirely sure that I should. But I'd like to read your speech very much, if you don't mind.

BEN: Now?

KATE: If you don't mind.

BEN hands the speech over.

BEN: It's still quite rough in places…

KATE takes the speech and puts down the Metu Neter, *makes herself comfortable on the sofa and begins to read. BEN watches her with baited breath. KATE's breathing starts to get deeper and more rapid as she moves further down the page. Soon she can't handle any more and she throws the speech down beside her, jumping to her feet and moving towards the door.*

Darling – darling, what's the matter?

KATE: I can't Ben… I can't, I can't…

BEN: What are you talking about?

KATE: I can't do this!

BEN: What? What can't you do?

KATE: This! This charade of understanding liberal wife! This attempt to be the English woman who condemns her country and people for what they did in a past too far back for most of us to remember! I can't do it because I don't feel that way darling! I can only speak for me Ben, what I feel and what I know and I'm a good person, not a racist!

I simply refuse to study books that generalise and openly degrade my own race in order to understand the man I married!

BEN: No one said you had to read books to understand me –

KATE: Yes you did!

BEN: I wanted you to read them to understand my culture –

KATE: Well I didn't marry a culture Ben, I married a man! A good, kind, strong man who didn't see sex or colour, only the goodness, kindness and strength in other's hearts! A man I can't find no matter how hard I seek him out, a man that's disappeared –

BEN: (*Snaps.*) Kate, you're being preposterous and you know it! Maybe you never thought you'd married a culture as well as myself, but I did! I've never been allowed to forget it. Eat these foods, talk about these books and plays, discuss only your politics. And if I'm seen to stray across any perceived cultural boundaries then I'm liable to be warned – by Arts Funding bodies, or Paul Tompkins; even by your own father. Yes Kate, you married a culture as well as a man. What bothers me at this point is my realisation that you expected something else.

KATE: What... What do you mean?

BEN: Don't feel bad darling, it's not just you. It seems like everybody thought that because I was kind, good-natured and honest, that somehow translated into me being different from the rest of my race. Almost as though those traits were abnormal for us. That I'd be able to pretend the things that happened thousands of years ago and continue right to this day weren't happening at all because they didn't happen to me. That I could carry my schooling and white wife like a free pass into the world of turn a blind eye, I'm all right Jack, we don't give a fuck. Didn't they? (*Shouts when she doesn't answer.*) Didn't they?

KATE: Ben, stop you're scaring me –

BEN: (*Still shouting.*) Good! Maybe it's about time you knew what it felt like to be scared, to have your heart pump and feel the blood running in your veins! Maybe you should learn to feel as alive as the real world does, outside your ivory towers of wine bars, opera and members-only restaurants –

KATE: Ben, will you stop! You're talking like one of those awful books and I don't like it! I don't like it one bit!

BEN: (*Still shouting.*) Maybe you'll get it then; what it feels like to have someone chastise who you are and what you do! Maybe you'll start to look around and see all the Black people cast as gun criminals in the news, sex objects or idiots in soaps, mad-men or drug addicts in documentaries while our singers and songwriters are reduced to puppets who only get limelight as long as they pretend it's not happening! Maybe when you see that you'll understand that the way you feel when you read that book is the way most of us feel every day of our lives. That disposing of the feeling by fighting against its root cause is the only way the rest of us can live.

KATE: (*Tearful.*) You really... You really hate us don't you...

BEN: (*Sighs and smiles.*) I don't hate any of you. In fact, I love you all a great deal. It's the reason I could live as I did for so long and the reason why I can't take it any more. I'm not prepared to settle for less from any of you Kate. Especially not you.

KATE is sniffling but not really crying. BEN picks up his speech and book then walks to the door and stops.

You say that you're not racist Kate, but you are. Wait, don't say a word – you are. We see your father every week without fail, but months could pass without us seeing anyone from my family and you don't even notice. You said it yourself, we've never had any Black friends in all the time we've known each other and up until recently, you didn't notice that either. Worst of all though Kate, was the way you reacted to Imani when you finally got close to a real Black woman. Like the wife of a plantation owner, scared her husband might seek favour from his slave. I was the whitest Black man you'd ever met, wasn't I Kate? Your father wouldn't have it any other way.

BEN walks over to KATE and kisses her on the forehead. She's still and silent, savouring his accusations with her eyes closed, as if immersing herself in his anger.

I love you. I'll never stop loving you.

He leaves. A minute later a door slams. KATE wipes her eyes, then calmly walks out of the room and returns carrying a suitcase which she heaves as though quite full. She gets to the telephone, and dials, occasionally wiping a tear from her eye. As she speaks, she continues packing her suitcase.

KATE: Daddy? Daddy, I have something to tell you… Yes daddy… Tonight… Right this minute… Yes, if you could… Oh, must you? I'm really not in the mood to see anyone… I see… I can be ready in half an hour… Yes Daddy… See you soon… I love you…

Lights dim.

SCENE 4

The bar is full. A gathering of COT members are hanging around. DON is in a corner alone looking around angrily at everybody. IMANI is pacing up and down looking very nervous until BEN walks through the door.

IMANI: B… B, you're here…

BEN: I wouldn't let you down Imani…

They hug. Over her shoulder BEN sees DON. He stiffens as he lets IMANI go, but she doesn't notice.

IMANI: Now we've got reporters from the *Nation, Voice, Caribbean Times, Chamberlayne Chronicle* and some guy from the *Standard* that said he knew you from University. London Tonight said they might come and film for a small local news piece – apparently they like the fact you're an Arts Officer turned political hurricane…

BEN: That's Don isn't it?

Now it's IMANI's turn to stiffen.

IMANI: Yes. Yes it is.

BEN: I haven't heard from him in weeks. Did you give him my messages?

IMANI: Of course I did, he was just busy with the play. I told you that.

BEN: Yes you did…

BEN walks over to DON while IMANI watches helplessly.

Don?

DON: All right B?

BEN: I'm surprised you're here. I thought I'd be the last person you'd want to see.

DON: Not at all B. Just hard at work you know…

There's a very awkward silence.

BEN: Well… Well, I just wanted to say… Don't give up on me Don.

DON: I never did mate. Never did.

They shake hands firmly, rueful smiles on both faces.

You know, B –

IMANI appears as if by magic.

IMANI: Sorry to interrupt, but we should make our way upstairs to the hall now, we're already ten minutes late. Don't want to keep everyone waiting do we?

BEN: Of course not. I'll see you upstairs Don.

DON: See you later mate.

BEN walks offstage. DON gives IMANI the dirtiest look he can muster, which she returns in kind before following BEN offstage. DON shakes his head in wonder, then turns just in time to see KATE, RAYMOND and MICHAEL walk into the bar. MICHAEL has his arm firmly around KATE. DON's jaw drops, then he slips away. Lights dim.

SCENE 5

SPENCER brings on a lectern and puts it down onstage. Lights up. COT members begin to crowd around the lectern, including LAMMING, JONES, SPENCER, KATE, RAYMOND and MICHAEL. A buzz of energy is in the air. IMANI approaches the lectern and addresses the audience as if they're part of the crowd. Lights dim on crowd, while IMANI is spotlit. The crowd begin to applaud. DON, keeping well hidden, watches from the sidelines.

IMANI: Thank you; thank you. Children Of Tamana, once again we gather together for spiritual replenishment and sustenance. To remind ourselves of who we once were. To bring the old ways into this new millennium and carry the sons and daughters of Africa back where we belong – back to the cradle of civilisation. (*Pause for clapping.*) Tonight is a special night for all of our members. For those of you who don't know why, I have only two words for you. And those words are – Benjamin Nelson. (*More clapping, and some cheering too, IMANI speaks over the noise.*) Now Ben – now Ben is a recent addition to the fold, but a most vital addition nonetheless. In his short time with us he has made himself an invaluable asset to our cause, and shown himself among our keenest of researchers. Judging by his last speech, which had members requesting another as if this were Choice and my name was Jenny Francis (*Laughter.*), I'm more than confident in his ability to amplify our message to the masses in his own unique way. So Children Of Tamana; Children Of Tamana, without further ado we bring to you: Mr Benjamin Nelson…

Whooping cheers as BEN takes the lectern wearing glasses and looking quite stern. The crowd fall silent, waiting for him to speak. For a while he says nothing, perhaps realising the gravity of the moment, relishing the minuscule line drawn between before and after. He catches sight of RAYMOND, MICHAEL and KATE and visibly stiffens. RAYMOND shakes his head and draws his finger across his neck. BEN stares at him, and begins to smile. Then he speaks.

BEN: Children Of Tamana, I bid you good evening and welcome. (*He waits as they murmur a greeting in reply.*) Today I come to you a changed man in many ways: a variation of the person you saw standing at this very lectern, in this very hall, all of those weeks ago. Today you see someone who held a belief so strongly he was prepared to reason, prepared to debate, argue, fight; even die for what he believed was good and proper – for his rights as a whole human being. We talked of that belief at length the last time I was up here, didn't we Children? (*Smiles.*) Some of you seem confused. Some of you are saying to yourselves, 'What's he talking about, his last speech wasn't about beliefs! It was about Black Art and its relation to Black Culture! He's right about one thing though, he has changed innit! He's stark raving mad now, that's what he is! Raving mad!' But I must ask you to bear with me. I must ask you to take time and hear what I have to say. For I am not mad; in fact, if you take time and listen I think you'll find that the complete opposite is true. That, like a sinner who lived his whole life in darkness only to finally find Jesus, I have seen the light. But hear me out another minute Children. For this light is not religious in nature. It doesn't emanate from the Holy Ghost or Son of Man. You can't find this particular truth in scriptures or churches, can you? No. You find it out there, on the streets, in the shops and restaurants, banks and schools: the whole world over. You find it on your television and cinema screens Children. The truth, according to us – the Black race. Someone should write the definitive book on that. Perhaps one day, someone will... (*Pause.*) What is this truth I'm talking about you may ask? What is this thing that Black people know but won't talk about for fear of reprisal? What is the sham perpetrated in offices and board rooms nationwide in the name of assistance? Easy. The English language being that great and all-expansive tool for communication that it is, it can be explained in only one word Children – and that word is – multiculturalism. (*Big cheer from crowd,* BEN *shouts over them.*) This new.... This new, oh-so-cool and trendy term has become our by-word for racial equality, for all that's good and right in our fair land; for the England that wipes away its past and steps bravely into the new millennium fully aware of who it was and who it should now be. Even the Collins Dictionary I found classifies the word in a positive light; it says, and I quote: 'Multiculturalism – 1. The state or condition of being multi-cultural, or 2. The policy of maintaining a diversity of ethnic cultures within a community.' If you look up the word Multicultural you'll find, and I quote: 'Multicultural: consisting of, relating to, or designed for the cultures of different races.' (*BEN looks into the audience as if in deep thought.*) Now, when I read that I had to think carefully. It was a time where I was analysing the concept of multiculturalism very seriously, and to be presented with such a precise definition of terms was heartening in one light; disappointing in another. See – when I thought about it – really thought about it – although the term is bandied about like street slang, we very rarely see any evidence of the specified points in action: 1, the state or condition of being multicultural; 2, the policy of maintaining a diversity of ethnic cultures within a community; or even 3, consisting of, relating to, or designed for the cultures of different races. Speaking for the arts sector, which in the past was a sector specifically targeted for its lack of success in this area, I can safely say that we are being failed. Nothing has changed. As some of you may know, I hold the post of Senior Arts Officer at West Chamberlayne Arts. For close to four months I have been attempting to gain funding for ethnically diverse theatre groups to perform shows at venues known for their...lack of melanin, so to speak. I have faced four months of being fobbed off, lied to, ignored and being turned down, often for no good reason. Then I began to think – I'm a Senior Arts Officer and I can't get these shows funded. How is anyone else going to manage, anyone who doesn't have my skills in filling out applications, handling themselves in meetings, budgeting and the like. Then it really hit me. They won't manage, will they? And that's the whole point!

The crowd roars. BEN soaks it all up, looking a little shocked as though he has never had a reaction like this before. KATE and MICHAEL clutch each other looking scared, while RAYMOND storms up to IMANI, very red in the face.

RAYMOND: Stop this! You must stop this tomfoolery at once!

IMANI, looking shocked herself, nods and makes a move towards BEN, who quickly turns back to the crowd and raises a hand to quiet them. They fall silent in an instant. He continues. RAYMOND looks livid as IMANI shrugs back at him.

BEN: So after that, of course, I had to test my theory out as best I could. I looked up the seasons for mainstream theatre venues – not the few known for putting on Black and Asian plays, but the big ones, the ones that have claimed funding on the understanding they'll open their doors to diversity. Do you know what I found Children? Not one venue has one play by an ethically diverse company, anywhere in the country – yes, they have Black plays imported from South Africa, or by African Americans, or even Black British actors playing West Indian, African American or South African characters – but not one single play that tackles the diversity of modern Britain out of more than twenty mainstream theatre venues nationwide. Not one that accepts us as an intransigent component of this vibrant society, instead of being other, Johnny foreigner, former immigrants who came here begging for acceptance. So what other conclusion am I to draw but the surety that when it comes to multiculturalism as defined by my Collins English Dictionary, they don't want it! Which means they don't want us. Which means we have to fight, Children, if only for our cultural survival! We have to fight!

The crowd goes wild once more. BEN, clearly in the zone now, turns over his papers, but it seems as though he's lost something. RAYMOND is busy arguing with IMANI. He's trying to get past her in order to stop BEN's speech, but she won't let him past, even though she doesn't seem pleased either. She placates him, then approaches BEN herself, who shoots her a quick glance but continues on.

How do we fight I hear you ask? What means must we take in order to grasp what's ours? I'll tell you Children… I'll tell you… (*Looks up from his papers.*) We must take our fight to highest channels. We should petition, march, lobby our local councils to give us our fair due as the laws and the reports see fit. We should demand to be recognised for who and what we are as our ancestors in Kamit once did: not ethnic, not urban, not multicultural – but Black people Children. Black people – sons and daughters of Africa long gone but never forgotten. Black people! Visualise the word and all it conjures, all the colours and sounds and life and spirit that makes up you, me, us – our people. Visualise it right now, Black with a capital B and remember my Children, from this day forward… From this day forward the capital B is for Black!

Uproar from a crowd at fever pitch: KATE and MICHAEL are looking more than alarmed now, while IMANI walks up to BEN and visibly tells him that the speech is over. He shakes his head, pushes her aside and looks through more papers. RAYMOND storms past IMANI while she's wrong-footed, grabbing BEN's arm and attempting to hoist him from the lectern. Bad idea. After resisting as best he can, BEN pushes him away with one arm and RAYMOND falls backward on his arse, unhurt but very embarrassed. The crowd cheer, but BEN raises his arms again. Silence falls.

Children! Children hear me! (*Points at RAYMOND.*) Here is the face behind our lack of progress in the arts; here is the man that has made sure we never reach the heights that history shows we're capable of, one of those scared to death by the idea of Black progress! Look at his actions! I stand up here and speak the truth and what does he do? First he sends a lackey, a Black woman that we all know, a member of our own project to do his dirty work for him; (*BEN looks daggers at IMANI.*) then, when that doesn't work, he resorts to brute force to try and hurl me from where I stand – but Children, I will not be moved until we get what we came for! We will not be moved until we get what we came for! Look at him: look at them both and remember

this day forever, as history shows this is the strategy used
to defeat us time and time again – Black and White side
by side, monkey and organ grinder, house slave and slave
master standing together in hope of banishing the wolf from
their shared door. And it's the same in every facet of our
existence! We are being failed in every department, every
direction and everyone knows it! I've done the research. (*He
flicks through papers.*) According to broadsheet newspaper
headlines earlier this year, the 2001 census revealed that,
and I quote: 'While Britain becomes more multicultural,
second and even third generation immigrants are still the
most deprived in society'. Figures revealed by the census
prove that, as Black people we are twice as more likely to be
unemployed, half as likely to own our home and run double
the risk of poor health. But we knew that already didn't we
Children? We knew that from living it day in, day out for
the last 50 years we've lived in this country as immigrants,
never mind those that came here before Windrush, the
one or two in a neighbourhood that managed to live in
isolation from the rest of us. But we cannot let then do this
any more Children. We cannot allow them to give us the
worst housing, the worst jobs, the worst education unless
we conform to heart-wrenching prospect being a house
nigger – yes I said it, a house nigger – because what else is
a Black person who allows themselves to be used like that,
other than an evil creation of the white mind just like that
awful word? We cannot allow them to bleed our motherland
and kill our kids at bus stops, then go to every length they
can to deny us justice! Children, I will say this once and
once only; they must, give us what we want! (*Lower.*) And
if they won't; if they won't yield to reason and morality, if
they won't abide by their own laws, if they won't provide
the justice we've been screaming for so long... All that's
left for us to do is take it from them Children. Take it from
them at any cost! Fight for our right to live –

The crowd roar and yell drowning him out; only there are
shouts of 'Take it now!' And 'Give us our rights!' Along with
all the cheering. Before BEN *can say more someone yells 'Come*

on!' And they rush from the stage leaving him looking on in bewilderment.

Wait! Hey, come back! I haven't finished!

They pay him no mind. DON *rushes up to* IMANI, *who is standing in a shocked daze.*

DON: I hope you're satisfied Imani. I hope you're satisfied you wrecked a man's life for nothing. I'm just glad he finally got to see you for who you really are.

He turns and walks offstage. IMANI *doesn't move, just closes her eyes as the shouting and smashing of windows begin.* BEN *watches* DON'*s exit, then turns to see* KATE *and* MICHAEL *staring straight at him. They lock eyes. Lights dim on lectern, then stage.*

SCENE 6

JONES *removes lectern. Lights up. More sounds of heavy rioting come from outside. A hangdog looking* BEN *walks into the bar to see* IMANI, RAYMOND, KATE *and* MICHAEL *huddled in a tight group, talking. They stop when they catch sight of him and* BEN *stops walking. He looks haunted, deeply shaken by what has happened.* KATE *turns away, while* MICHAEL *looks from her to* BEN, *unsure.* RAYMOND *is back to his solid self.* IMANI *breaks away from the group.*

IMANI: B, what were you thinking –

RAYMOND: (*Loud.*) I'll deal with this Imani.

She looks back, then steps aside and lets RAYMOND *step forward.* MICHAEL *stands beside him protectively.* BEN *looks at them with pure disdain.*

BEN: You'll deal with this Raymond? You? I think this is a little out of your remit, wouldn't you say old boy? There's a riot going on out there, not one of your council meetings –

RAYMOND: (*Angry.*) You act as though I don't know that! You act as though I wasn't there to see the whole thing, you stoking them up then letting them go out there on the street and behave like...like monsters! Well, just in case

133

you've taken complete leave of your senses I'll gladly inform you that a room full of civilised people saw the whole thing too! You're going to be punished for what you did tonight, every sentence and every word, every shove – you'll be punished, mark my words.

BEN: (*Calm.*) That's good Raymond. That's good, let it all out, let me hear it all once and for all so I put it right up here; (*Taps his head.*) for safekeeping. Bring it on.

RAYMOND: Say what you like Benjamin, we all know the real truth. You've lost you're grip on reality haven't you? Verbally abusing my daughter, attacking me, causing decent, well-meaning people to riot – when will all end Ben, when will it end? I can tell you something for nothing – I'm not waiting around to find out. You can forget about working for West Chamberlayne Arts, and forget any former association we might have had. If you want to salvage any pride out of this matter you'll give yourself up to the police at once –

BEN: Wait a minute. I don't want your job anyway Raymond, but the police!? There's no need for any police –

RAYMOND: You are mad aren't you? Benjamin, you've just made a speech that's driven people to the streets in violence. In legal terms, that's known as incitement to riot. As I'm a councillor and not a barrister I don't know how many years that carries, but it's very likely most cases end with a sustained prison term...

BEN: What... You're lying...

MICHAEL: He's not Ben.

BEN wanders over to a distant corner of the stage as if sleepwalking. IMANI steps forward and follows him.

IMANI: B; the best thing that you could do right now is give yourself up to the police. No pain, no fuss. Everybody goes home safely. What d'you think, eh?

BEN: I think you show a distinct lack of loyalty Imani, now more than ever. What about your wanting me to be

Children Of Tamana's leader? You'd give up your leader that easily?

IMANI: (*Cold.*) How did you know about that?

BEN: Jean Withers at the Pulse let it slip. You did say she talked a lot.

IMANI: Yes. Well, although I did hope that you had leadership qualities that would befit the Children Of Tamana, I'm afraid that's changed now B, what with your speech and… all. In fact, I think it would be safe to say everything has changed…

BEN looks daggers at IMANI again until SPENCER suddenly appears looking bedraggled. The noise of the riot gets louder behind her.

SPENCER: Leave, you lot, now! I'm serious, you better get out of here! The police are coming, people are moving back up this end of the street, and it won't be long before they're here. Oi, get moving will you!

KATE: Michael –

MICHAEL: I think we should take her advice –

IMANI: There's an exit around the back we can use. Follow me.

They move stage right looking at BEN. Ignoring them, BEN moves stage left.

KATE: Ben?

RAYMOND: I hope you're going to give yourself up Benjamin – it's the safest option you have!

BEN: If any of you must know, I'm going to see if I can advise those rioters to cease. I started it and now I'm going to finish it.

KATE: Ben, that's madness! You can't be serious!

MICHAEL: They're likely to have you for breakfast just as soon as look at you Ben, you really should reconsider…

IMANI: B, listen to them; give yourself up! You'll only get hurt!

BEN: As if you care Imani. As if any of you really care.

BEN exits. SPENCER watches him go, then looks around.

SPENCER: Go!

She takes her own advice. IMANI, RAYMOND, MICHAEL and KATE form a single file line and leave. KATE is holding MICHAEL's hand. Noise of riots increase until almost deafening. Lights dim.

SCENE 7

A bang against the office door. A jangle of keys in the darkness. The keys are dropped. The door moves. Whispers and curses before they're picked up. The office door is pushed open and a shadow walks in, flicks a light switch. Lights up. It's BEN, his tie gone and his shirt open, carrying a gym bag. He looks around the office. The filing cabinet is open and files are scattered everywhere. Chairs are overturned. BEN walks inside, puts his bag down and collects all the files, rights the chairs and puts the phones on the hook. He then sits down and puts his feet up on his desk and closes his eyes. After a moment he opens them again. Looks at a pile of paper he placed on top of the files. Picks up a single sheet, looks at it and laughs a rueful laugh.

BEN: *B is for Black*, by Benjamin Nelson… *B is for Black*… Benjamin… Nelson… (*Clears his throat.*) Children Of Tamana, I bid you good evening and welcome…

He can't do it. Before he realises what's happened he's laughing out loud, then he starts to cry in big silent gulps. IMANI appears by the office door. At first BEN doesn't notice her, but when she takes a further step into the room he senses her presence and looks up, wiping his eyes. IMANI stops in her tracks.

IMANI: You knew I was here. Sensed me didn't you B? Told you I felt a spiritual connection between us, didn't I? It's still there, still working despite everything.

BEN: Don't give me your crap Imani. I know how you do things now, your little smokescreen to hide who you really are. Raymond's words aren't the only thing that I stored in my head today Imani. What you said to me; what you said will stay with me forever…

IMANI: What? What I said about turning yourself in? You said worse if I remember rightly. Anyway, one doesn't necessarily contradict the other does it? I mean, I can ascertain we have a spiritual connection while also thinking what you did up there tonight was wrong, can't I? Surely the two aren't mutually exclusive?

BEN: Why don't you go away Imani? I used to like hearing you talk but now it just gets on my nerves. You're a traitor and I don't have to listen to you.

IMANI: Oh but B; I can't go away. I just can't. I was the one that called the papers and told them about you. I was the one that booked the bar. I called the caterers, bought the plastic cups, all the drinks that went in them and guess what? everybody knows it B. That means everybody knows I'm associated with you. The only way I can disassociate myself is if I have a hand in your coming in. Which is why I can't go away.

IMANI steps forward.

BEN: Stay away from me you bitch! (*IMANI stops, unfazed.*) I think there's a little more to it than that! You were the one that took me to Children of Tamana, got me into this Black Power stuff in the first place. You encouraged me to write that speech, read my proofs and told me it was fine, and now you expect me to help you run out on me! I can't believe your nerve!

IMANI: You're confusing yourself. I didn't tell you to write, nor did I read prior to you getting up at that lectern, any of the last portion of your speech. In fact, I had to stand there horrified, with my heart in my mouth while you went on about capital Bs and Black people taking what they want and all that shit you were spouting B, while everybody's looking at me to do something about it. Me, Ben! And that's all it was you know – shit – at the end of the day! You can't possibly shit-stir with people that are desperate, people that are hungry because of the very corruption you talked about in the earlier part of your speech – the part that I liked, the part I fully supported. But I and the Children Of

Tamana will not condone what you made happen tonight, there's no way we could. Even if we wanted to –

BEN: So that's it? After everything you said about the three rules and proving myself, I go out and put my neck on the line only to have it chopped off at the first opportunity while you help lift the axe?! Have you the faintest idea what I risked up there on that lectern; what I gambled away for a cause you're willing to drop at the first sign of trouble! I've lost my job, my wife, probably my life and liberty too' and all you care about is protecting your own skin –

IMANI: Will you stop saying that? It's as if you believe that if you repeat it enough times you'll make it come true. I haven't dropped the cause and I'm not doing any of this to protect my skin: I'm doing it to protect the Children Of Tamana. For the last time Ben, you're a liability. Can't you see that? If we condone what you said it means we condone the results and that's not good politics B; that's BNP, Le Pen politics, the kind of politics that cause us to end up like the Black Panthers, and I'm not going to let that happen. Not when I've worked so hard for this organisation for so many years. Now, if you let me take you in I'll hand you over quietly and calmly, then the organisation can look after you within a legal framework. A few months later, when everything's died down the organisation will formally announce Children Of Tamana's new leader to the media and press and the pressure on you will die. You'll make it up with Kate, get a new job and live the rest of your life in relative peace and comfort B. Come on; don't let's make things worse. You can't stay in the office anyway – the police will be forced to search here at some point.

BEN: Nice try Imani; looks like they've already been. And I told you, I'm not going anywhere with you. That's the last of it. Now go away.

IMANI steps forward again.

IMANI: Come on will you! You're not thinking straight and it shows. Everyone can see it! You're making bad judgement calls left right and centre! I'm just trying to re-adjust your focus. Did you know our people were going to riot tonight? No. Did they listen when you told them to stop? No. Don't make another bad decision tonight and pile it sky high on top of all the others. Listen to me B. I'm trying to be your friend. Come with me to Chamberlayne Station.

BEN's head falls. He seems sad.

BEN: (*Laughs.*) You know Imani... You know, when I first met you I used to think that in other time...you know, in another life, if things were different and we were different people, maybe we'd –

IMANI: Yeah. Yeah, me too B.

BEN: But that could never happen here and now, in our time could it?

IMANI: No.

BEN: I almost wish it could. If it could, then none of this would have happened. Would it?

IMANI: No B. I don't suppose it would.

BEN: I really thought you were somebody different Imani.

IMANI looks up in shock.

IMANI: What do you mean by that?

BEN: You said that in a few months the Children Of Tamana would announce their new leader to the press. Mind telling me who that new leader would be?

IMANI: Oh! Well, there weren't actually many candidates to pick from...

BEN: Yes –

IMANI: And seeing as things had been fine the way they were before when it wasn't as official, no hiccups, no stress or anything, I thought it best that I come out as Children Of Tamana's official leader, maybe even with a pre-written press release condemning your earlier speech. Now, before your start calling me a traitor all over again I realise that it might sound harsh B, but that's the way in politics and you could even help me draft that latter speech if you felt in the mood for it – it's months away, so you've got plenty of time to decide. But basically, yes; I'll run the show. Most sensible option really.

BEN: Yes... I thought you might say that... Most sensible option. The safest option. Like Raymond says...

IMANI: Yes. So B; (*Big smile.*) have you decided or what? I don't intend to stay in this stuffy little office all night waiting for you. Are you coming out with me? Or am I leaving you behind?

BEN thinks for a moment.

BEN: All right. All right, I'll come out with you.

IMANI: Thanks B. You're doing the right thing.

BEN: I know.

IMANI reaches out a hand for him. He takes it and she pulls him to her in what she probably imagines is one last hug. It quickly begins to get a little more intimate than that. They neck and nuzzle. IMANI puts her hands to his face, caressing his cheek. At her touch BEN comes to his senses and puts his hands around her throat, starting to squeeze. IMANI tries to fight but he's far too strong for that. He pushes her to her knees and locks his hands even tighter. IMANI struggles, but can't free herself. Abruptly, BEN lets go. Panting and sweating, he walks away from her. IMANI is looking at him, shocked, holding her throat and coughing. BEN stumbles against a desk, pushes himself upright and steps forwards until he reaches front of stage then stops and closes his eyes. His breathing calms. He comes back to himself. He falls to his knees with tears on his face. He begins to sob. Lights slow dim.

The End.

MOJ OF THE ANTARCTIC

Mojisola Adebayo
in conversation with Lynette Goddard

Edited by Lynette Goddard
(Royal Holloway, University of London)

Moj of the Antarctic was written and performed by Mojisola Adebayo, and produced by The Antarctic Collective at the Lyric Hammersmith, 2006 and the Oval House Theatre, 2007. The play is inspired by the real-life story of light-skinned African American slave Ellen Craft who in 1848 cross-dressed as a white man to escape slavery, with her darker-skinned husband, William Craft, accompanying her as her servant. Their daring escape is documented in William Craft's *Running a Thousand Miles for Freedom* (Baton Rouge: Louisiana State University Press, 1999 [1860]). In this interview, Mojisola Adebayo speaks with Lynette Goddard about writing and performing the show.

What was your impulse for creating Moj of the Antarctic?

I am very interested in the way black people use performance and performance skills in their everyday lives. I was researching African American history, African American figures, slavery and slave narratives, and I discovered the story of Ellen Craft, and I wanted to find a way of telling the story. At around the same time, I got really interested in Antarctica and I saw this advert for writers and artists to go to Antarctica and then I wondered about whether there was a way to bring together Ellen Craft's story with Antarctica. I was interested in her crossing boundaries in terms of race and gender, but also the geographical boundaries – she went from the Deep South in Georgia way up to the North to Boston, from Boston over to Britain where she lived in Surrey for a while, before eventually going back to the United States. The crossings of all of these boundaries fascinated me and I started thinking about how to extend her incredible real-life odyssey into a theatrical odyssey by taking her to Antarctica.

Coincidentally, around the same time, I went to the Gambia on holiday. As a tourist, I took a boat trip through the Gambia River, which was really moving as thousands of African people would have crossed that river to be held [in the holding port] on James Island, before being transferred to the slave ships to be taken to the Americas. At the bottom of the River Gambia there would be souls of Africans that threw themselves into the river to try to avoid being held as slaves. Going to James Island was incredibly moving, not just because this was a historical place that could have been an Auschwitz of Africa, but also that this island is disappearing into the sea because the sea levels in the Gambia are rising. The coast is eroding, and the islands are disappearing, which is the effect that climate change is having on Africa, and our history is disappearing into the sea in the same way that those Africans disappeared into the sea. I wanted to make something that would record a part of history, but would also bring it up to the present day to look at the erosion of history in the really physical way, the erosion of that island, but also to look at the erosion and forgetting of our stories and our heroes like Ellen Craft who are really not known about.

Yes, it's really important to tell these untold stories from black history as there is so much missing knowledge of the past to be recovered still. The show connects the past with the present and links a range of different themes such as race, gender, and sexuality with big global issues such as climate change. These might actually be seen to be quite disparate themes, so what sort of challenges did they pose for you, to bring them together in one play?

Huge challenges! I wanted to do the subject of climate change real justice, but at the same time not create a polemical or agit-prop piece. The form of an odyssey, an epic life journey, provides a useful structure, where through one life you can take a massive journey and take in loads of different characters and issues. Homer's *Odyssey* and novels like *Moby Dick* are epic and enormous in scope, so the challenge is doing that in a play. Having a one-woman show makes it easier, because you're looking at the life of one person; so the audience can follow one person and through that go to all of these big issues and big places. If it was a bigger cast it would have been harder to do that.

You remove Ellen Craft's husband, William Craft, from your version of the story and you engage your character Moj in a lesbian relationship with a woman called May. Why was it important to queer the story?

My play is inspired by William and Ellen's love story, but I also wanted it to be true to my experience, and to weave in the queer stories that have always been there in African history and the African Diaspora that are not ever told. It was important to me that the play was inspired by her but wasn't her exclusively, that somehow there would be a projection from her incredible journey, so, in a sense, it's as much about me, about who you can become as it is about who anyone is or was. From a twenty-first century position, I see what Ellen Craft did as a wonderfully queer thing, part of a queer history and legacy. It's nothing to do with her sexuality, but is about her transgressing the boundaries of gender. I chose a female lover for her because I'm acknowledging that there are many stories of female lovers in our history that I will never discover because they have never been written down and have never been acknowledged.

You open with the play with a comment on the way that binary language systems fix us into either/ or categories, such as Africa/Antarctica, black/white, male/female, homosexual/heterosexual, and in a sense your character is crossing those binaries. I agree with you that we can claim that as a 'queer performance'.

It was really important not to confine the story in twenty-first century language, so the words queer, lesbian, gay or homosexual are not in the play. All we know is that she had a lover called May and it's not explained or described particularly. It's a very tiny part of the story, but it's very much part of who she is, before the confinement of language around sexuality.

You incorporate quotations from iconic white writers such as William Shakespeare, Samuel Coleridge, Homer, John Milton, and theorists such as Karl Marx and Charles Darwin. Can you speak about the process for creating a play with these sources?

I wanted to write a period piece, a mid-nineteenth century play, and I immersed myself in reading lots of writing of that period. I read every slave narrative from the mid-nineteenth century that I could get hold of – a lot of mid-nineteenth century classics – such as *Moby Dick,* important writers like Darwin and Marx, poets such as Coleridge, and a lot of poetry about slavery because I wanted the piece to have a really poetic voice. I not only wrote in that kind of idiom, but used huge sections from the period. In the same way that I'm queering black history, in a sense, I'm Africanising the European literary voice. My background is in devising performance, so creating *Moj of the Antarctic* felt like a devising process, except that the writers I was devising with were all dead. I felt like me, Marx, Darwin, Frederick Douglass, Harriet Jacobs and Ellen Craft were all in the rehearsal room together and I was trying to make *The Communist Manifesto* fit with Darwin and rhyme.

So when you bring all of those voices together, what comes up is, the dead white European males in dialogue with important figures from black history.

It was quite a magical experience. There was something supernatural about it – as though it was not fixed in the here and now. It did feel as though I was communing somehow, in the same way that Alice Walker sees herself as a medium and says that *The Color Purple* was written through her.

You've included a familiar African storyteller – a griot – and you create a complex, rich and multi-layered performance that uses spoken word, physical movement, dance, poetry, song, character playing, multimedia slides projection, and audience interaction to mediate themes of black women, slavery, and gender/ racial performativity. How do you see the work within traditions of black performance?

It very much feels like it is within a broad African, Caribbean, and black British aesthetic. There is something so beautiful about the live experience, and I think it's important to use everything that we have, all of the body, all of the light – whatever props and physical materials you can use – singing. Let's use everything and anything in order to tell a story and wrestle with big questions, together. Sometimes I do wonder where I get this from, if there is something in my cultural memory, if it comes from the way black families talk, the way that we watch television, or the way that we worship.

Do you always see this being performed as a solo piece?

The only way I could see this being performed by more than one person is that the storyteller could be another person. My original intention was that there would be two people on the stage, myself and a creative and theatrical sign language interpreter. Jacqui Beckford is a wonderful interpreter performer and to me it just had to be me and Jacqui there on stage. One of the really big aims of the project is the bringing together of black and queer people in a space and one of the successes of the piece was that the Antarctic Collective producing the play and the audience were so diverse, including a mainly Caribbean Pentecostal church group, youth of different races, gay, white, middle-class men, Antarctic photographers, people who were interested in climate change, and deaf people. This was really was important to me as it's a personal passion of mine to make work that is as accessible and encompassing as possible and I don't want deaf people excluded from that.[1]

Did your aim to make it accessible, inform the overall style of the piece then, as you use vibrant visuals in Del La Grace Volcano's multimedia slide projections of your trip to Antarctica and the performance style is very physical?

Absolutely! This was very influenced by seeing a Graeae production of a play called *Peeling* by Kaite O'Reilly, which is not black theatre, but very accessible theatre. Jenny Sealey and Graeae Theatre Company have liberated me to see the other possibilities for language. In future productions I would hope to take those visuals, the physicality, and the BSL interpretation to another level. The director, Sheron Wray's, background was in dance and choreography and her idea was that it would be accessible, because she thinks in pictures. The way she directed me is so gestural that I'm almost signing with my body.

You've previously worked with Black Mime Theatre Company, and I could see some Black Mime influences in terms of the sketch book style of performance, the use of songs, the rapid shifts from one char-

---

1   Jacqui Beckford presented BSL (British Sign Language) interpretations of selected performances of *Moj of the Antarctic.*

acter to another, the use of humour and the very physical nature of the performance. Can you tell me about how your previous performance experience feeds into the style of presentation in this piece?

I'm really glad you asked me that as it's an opportunity for me to acknowledge the incredible legacy of Black Mime Theatre, under the leadership of Denise Wong. Black Mime carved out a distinctive style that really is black British that was never matched by any other theatre company and influenced so many of us, but they are pretty much excluded from the canon of British theatre. Certainly, a lot of the influence of Black Mime is still very much in my work.[2]

I recently saw the rehearsed reading for your new show, Muhammad Ali and Me, *where the central character is called Mojisola, and I know you're also developing work about Matt Henson, Gladys Bentley and Tituba. Is your work a kind of auto-bio-mythography, finding ways of integrating your own biography with the stories of these historical black figures?*

That is such an inspirational idea, the making of new myths. I am passionately interested in recording histories, and I make work for me as much as anyone else. I've been ashamed over the years about how little I know about black history, so writing *Moj of the Antarctic* was an opportunity for me to read some key texts in black history, like Frederick Douglass. All of these plays are an opportunity for me to educate myself about black history, to be inspired and excited and reinvent myself again and again through the influence of these people, and to heal my own life in some way.

And to heal others too, other black women, queers, lesbians, and people who want to learn about black history. The performance resonates with ideas of oral traditions as a powerful way to reclaim and restage black history. The mulatta woman is so often represented in films like Imitation of Life *as a tragic figure who fails in her attempt*

---

2   Black Mime Theatre (BMT) (1984–97) aimed to develop a new movement in mime that made the form accessible for black performers and audiences. Their shows incorporated physical theatre, mime, movement and contemporary dance forms. BMT toured their innovative brand of sketchbook style shows nationally and internationally, including several appearances at the London International Mime Festival.

to pass, but Ellen Craft succeeds in her passing. So it's empowering and uplifting to present this play as an example of a real-life woman's successful passing.

In the play, Moj's father is her white slave master, but she is black, in the same way as I feel that I'm black. My mother is white Danish, but my experience of living in Britain is as a black woman. Moj in the play is treated differently when the crime of letter writing between her and May is discovered. The slave master decides on the level of punishment on the basis that Moj has his blood and she's brown and the slave May is darker-skinned than her. This is an important acknowledgment for me, that as a mixed-heritage person I have been and will be treated differently. I have been privy to racist comments on the basis that my mother is white, and the door has been opened to me more, as though somehow I'm not really black, that my mum has given me a passport out. I know I may be treated differently, but in terms of how I feel, I feel black.

Moj of the Antarctic:
An African Odyssey

by

Mojisola Adebayo

with quotations from Ellen and William Craft,
Samuel Coleridge, Charles Darwin, Frederick Douglass,
Frances Ellen Harper, Homer, Harriet Jacobs, Karl Marx,
Herman Melville, John Milton, Phillis Wheatley,
Harriet Wilson, William Shakespeare, Percy Bysshe Shelley,
Ernest Shackleton, Harriet Beecher Stowe
and other spirits…

**A one woman play performed with
photography, video, poetry, light, dance, movement,
music, storytelling and song**

*Dedicated to Ellen Craft and all our
Afri-Queer Ancestors*

Moj of the Antarctic was created by Mojisola Adebayo and the Antarctic Collective. It was first performed at Lyric Hammersmith 14 November 2006 and later developed at Oval House Theatre London.

The Antarctic Collective are…

Writer/Performer **Mojisola Adebayo**

Visual Artist **Del LaGrace Volcano**

Director **Sheron Wray**

Designer **Rajha Shakiry**

Composer **Juwon Ogungbe**

Lighting Designer **Crin Claxton**

Production/Stage Manager **Samantha Nurse**

Visuals Editor **Sue Giovanni**

Assistant to Composer/Sound **Debo Adebayo** aka DJ Felony D

Administrator/Academic **Dr Carole Jones**

Academic **Dr Lynette Goddard**

Sound Recording **Paul Chivers** with **Will Joyce**

Sign Language Interpreter **Jacqui Beckford**

Production Assistants **Faith Yimini, Sasha, Yvonne Redway, Ornella Cameron**

Voice Coach **Andrea Ainsworth**

Moj of the Antarctic: An African Odyssey was developed as part of Lyric's MIX programme funded by Deutsche Bank.

Mojisola Adebayo and the Antarctic Collective gratefully acknowledge the support of Arts Council England and their in-kind supporters.

1 PROLOGUE

This play text is one element of a physical theatre choreographed performance with visuals, movement and music, after Ntozake Shange's 'choreo-poem' style. Yet it may be performed without the all the elements of the original production. In the original stage design there is a bookcase which transforms into a kitchen, a rostra with a trap door and a nineteenth-century style globe and telescope. The images are projected onto a huge screen made of paper which is crumpled in the top left hand corner.

'THE ANCIENT', a West-African female griot (storyteller, historian, singer, mystic), enacts a ritual: she sings, circles the space in a shuffle, speaks in tongues and sprinkles libation.

THE ANCIENT: (*Singing.*)
'Planets on planets run their destin'd round
And circling wonders fill the vast profound'[1]

After singing she addresses the audience.

Once,
We were
Gondwana,
Africa and Antarctica
Antarctica and Africa
One content
Continent.

Before.
Before
Nakedness
And the snake.

Before Enlightenment.
Before Enwhitenment.
Gondwana.
Where day and night danced a duet
In step,

1 Phillis Wheatley, *Complete Writings* (Harmondsworth: Penguin, 2001), p 38.

Together.
Two million years ago…

Gondwana:
Africa.
Antarctica.
A history of
The future:
Antarctica melts,
Africa sinks,
We all disappear.

One million
Two million
Three million more!
From ice to sea to land to shore!

Melting
Rising
Flooding
Seas.
Salt to soil
Drought
Disease.

Desert.
Desertification.
Creatures
Comforts
Coasts
Erosion
Forest.
Deforestation.
More land
More light
More wind
More flight
Of souls,
Soaked.

Tempest
Justice
Tempest
Just ice
Just us
Washing away
Sand and land and memories
Memories.

One melts,
The other sinks,
We all disappear:
Magic!

Imagine:
Gondwana,
Once
We were
One.

But,
Gondwana
Split
Like a family,
Tectonically,
And no one could remember
How it happened.

Yet in understanding through
Opposites
The ancients believed
In what they could not see,
By the stars
They perceived
Antarctica
Must
Exist
Somewhere…
Arctic

Anti-thesis
Antarctica.

And then
Eventually
You were
Uncovered
And you had grown cold.

THE ANCIENT gestures towards the video. Awe inspiring music grows.

You were discovered,
So now we know
If Antarctica exists
Then the world is a globe,
And if the world is a globe
In a tilting procession
Inclined to be eccentric
Obliquely orbiting
The sun…

Then are we not
In a tilting procession
Inclined to be eccentric,
Living with the inevitability of unpredictability
In the knowledge that we can predict the inevitable
Make the inevitable vetible
Vary the variable
Protect the vulnerable
Apply eco logic
To anthropogenic
Action?
And through adaptability and change
Be sustained
Or let the last one turn the lights out!

Blackout. She moves to another position. Lights up, she pops up through the rostra trap.

She said:

If Antarctica exists
And the world is a wobbling wanderer
Then nothing is straight
And no one is straight
Forward.
If the world is a globe
Then there is no above
No below
No North or South
No heaven or hell
No white or… (*She prompts audience to respond.*) black
No male or… (*She prompts audience to respond.*) female
No God or…(*She prompts audience to respond.*) Devil
Magic!

Just a magnetic pull.
And so
Through this pull we
Puuuuush
Through the cracks in the pack ice
To reach our destination.

She sets the stage for the next part of the story – bookcase, telescope.

Our destiny,
Our nation,
Land ahoy! (*She looks through the telescope.*)
America!
Somewhere in the middle
Of the nineteenth century!!!
Where once
Moj was a slave… (*Quick costume change.*)

2 THE BIG HOUSE

We are in the library of a rich Southern plantation owner's house.
It is day-time and hot outside. In the library there stands a globe,
and a telescope. MOJ *a nineteenth-century house-slave in her late*
teens/early twenties enters sweeping the library. She stops, notices
the books and begins to secretly read various sections.

MOJ: 'We are sleeping on a volcano…

Do you not see that the earth trembles anew?

A wind of revolution blows.

A storm is on the horizon.'[2]

And only the fittest survive![3]

In my own century

Nature faces subjection

To man and machinery

Chemistry and industry,

Railways, electricity

Steam-navigation

Clearing whole continents

For cultivation

Conjured out of the ground

Are whole populations![4]

And only the fittest survive![5]

Mutation

Modification

Transition

---

2 Alexis de Tocqueville, quoted in Eric Hobsbawm, *The Age of Capital* (London: Abacus, 2004).

3 See Charles Darwin, *The Origin of the Species* (Oxford: Oxford University Press, 1998 [1859]).

4 'Subjection of Nature's forces to man, machinery, application of chemistry to industry and agriculture, steam-navigation, railways, electric telegraphs, clearing of whole continents for cultivation, canalisation of rivers, whole populations conjured out of the ground – what earlier century has even a presentiment that such productive forces slumbered in the lap of social labour?' (Karl Marx and Friedrich Engels, *The Communist Manifesto* (London: Orion, 1996 [1848]), p 11.

5 See Charles Darwin, *The Origin of the Species* (Oxford: Oxford University Press, 1998).

Or extinction…

Family relation to money relation women are the means of production
money relation to blood relation we are the means of production[6]

All that is fixed fades away
Everything antiquates
All that is solid melts into air
Ev'rything holy is profaned[7]

'A wind of revolution blows.
A storm is on the horizon!'[8]
And only the fittest survive
Only the fittest survive!
Only the fittest survive!

A cascade of paper leaves from books falls from above, like snow. In the chaos, MOJ finds a photograph which has been hidden in a book. The photograph is of the slave master, who is also her father, as a young man. This makes her laugh. We see a photograph of the master projected – it is actually a photo of MOJ dressed as MASTER.

Maaaaassssa! Oh papa! So you weren't always a paaaastor.
Dandy!
Daaaaaaaddy!
Look at you, looking at me, looking like you!
In your ruffs and cuffs velvet cloak top hat and cane like puss-y in boots,
With the ladies and the liquor, and the tobaccaaah!
Maybe you were a dancer – 'de rum and de bum and de baccy!' – (*Song / dance.*) before you were a defiler!

6   See Marx and Engels, *The Communist Manifesto*.
7   'All fixed, fast-frozen relations, with their train of ancient and venerable prejudices and opinions are swept away, all new-formed ones become antiquated before they can ossify. All that is solid melts into air, all that is holy is profaned, and man is at last compelled to face with sober senses, his real conditions of life, and his relations with his kind' (Ibid., pp 8,9).
8   Alexis de Tocqueville.

Beat.

It's only ONE book you read NOW.

MOJ sermonises, playing the MASTER.

'Out of whose womb came the ice?
And the hoary frost of heaven, who hath gendered it?
The waters are hid as with a stone,
And the face of the deep is frozen.'[9] Job, 38.

Beat.

A – Men.

To audience.

Massa is a collector of books and bodies,
scriptures and slaves...
Gets them both at harbour market,
then lets them dust and decay.
He only tends to the Bible these days.
The others he just keeps so he can 'know thine enemy'.
Well then let them all be for meeeeeeeee!!!

Takes in the whole library of books, then hears MASTER's footsteps.

– Yet be still, the iceman cometh!

MASTER: Maaaaaaaj! What you playing at in there?

MOJ: Cleanin suh, takin good care of your lie-brary.

MASTER goes.

(*To audience:*) From the swish of the slave driver's cape,
round the sound of the horn at dawn,
Until the eclipse of six hundred brown eyes I toil
And boil...
But when his back is turned
It's my turn to learn.

Letting the audience into a secret.

I am taught by an angel from the dark side of the moon.

9 Book of Job, Ch. 38: 29-30.

And her name is May.
She teaches me to read-um,
She says 'Moj, (*MOJ playing MAY.*)
it's how you'll win your freedom.
But don't tell Massa, if he was to know,
He'd be reading me a sentence I don't ever wanna know'.

MOJ plays MAY playing the ATTORNEY, and then the JUDGE.

'Commonwealth of Virginia, Norfolk County. In the circuit court. The Grand Jurors on oath present, that Miss Sarah Anna-Marie Jones,[10] being moved and instigated by the devil on the fourth day of July, in the year of our Lord one thousand eight hundred and fifty-four, did teach a certain black girl named "May, a field slave" to read in the Bible, to the great displeasure of Almighty God…Victor Vagabond, Prosecuting Attorney'…

And Judge Scalawag said 'Miss Jones, stand up. You are guilty of one of the vilest crimes that have ever disgraced society; judge and jury have found you so. You have taught a slave girl, "one May Jackson, a field slave", to read the Bible. No enlightened society can exist where such offences go unpunished. The Court, in your case, do not feel for you one solitary ray of sympathy, and they will inflict on you the utmost penalty of the law. In any other civilised country you would have paid for the forfeit of your crime with your life, and the Court have only to regret that such is not the law in this country. The sentence for your offence is that you be imprisoned one month in the county jail… Sheriff, remove the prisoner.'[11]

One day
When I'm truly free
I'll read books by Negroes!

10   The real name of the woman in this true story was Margaret Douglass.
11   Paraphrased from a quote by William Craft, *Running a Thousand Miles for Freedom* (Louisiana: Louisiana State University Press, 1999 [1860]), p 18.

I'll read: (*She suddenly sees the following writers in the audience, gestures towards them, names them.*)
Ignatius Sancho! Frances Harper,
Harriet Wilson, Harriet Jacobs, Phillis Wheatley!
Perhaps the sons of Equiano will even be readin' meeeeee!
But in the Greenwich meantime
I'll say these books are mine
By rights my 'inheritance'
And with this knowledge I'll make a recompense
A small 'reparation'
For the rape of my mother-nation.

MASTER: (*Calling from upstairs.*) Maaaaaj!

MOJ: Cleanin suh!

MOJ resumes cleaning.

But I guess you all want me to say
what happened to the slave-girl in the story,
May.
Well,
She got stripped, whipped
and taken away
from her family,
just like how my mother got taken from me.
But God sent me a teacher,
But God sent me a teacher.
And that teacher is she:

Transition to MOJ looking through the telescope and calls to MAY whom she sees outside.

(*Hushed.*) May... May...

MOJ decides to gently call MAY by singing a forbidden Yoruba song in order to attract MAY, she mixes this by singing 'Bringing in the Sheaves', a Christian hymn, loudly for the benefit of the 'inside' world, the master world, as a distraction.

Eiye n'sunkun
O n'beru f'ormor re

S'e b'oun lo fo lor

Wa iranlorwor fun ite eiye?

/Bringing in the sheaves, bringing in the sheaves, we will

cooooooome...

I daduro lo wa nsin ninu igin la

Ko le mpada lor le

/Rejoicing! Bringing in the sheaves –[12]

Massa comes into the room. MOJ *stops singing suddenly, fearful.*

Massa! Finished my days duties suh. I'm just off to my cabin now...

She goes to leave. MASTER *stops her in her tracks. Threatening.*

MASTER: Heard you singing Moj...

MOJ: That's right Pastor Reverend Captain Justice Massa Suh, I was singing... I just a good Christian Suh, happy to sing when I serve, just like David singing the Psalms with Jonathan! (*MOJ remembers a verse.*) 'Let everything that has breath (*Sharp intake of breath.*) – praise the Lord'. Psalm...23? (*MOJ pretends not to know the Psalm.*)

MASTER: Psalm 150.

MOJ: That's right Suh. I forgets. (*Beat.*) I'm off to my little cabin now suh.

MASTER: (*Ominous.*) That's my girl. Good girl. Good night.

Transition into MOJ's *cabin. She sits and writes a poem to* MAY. *Underscored with music.*

12 'Bringing the Sheaves' by Knowles Shaw. Yoruba song lyrics by Juwon Ogungbe: 'The bird is crying, fearful for her chicks, wasn't it she who flew away to find support for the nest? Now she is stuck in the big tree, and she can't go home'. The Yoruba spelling is phonetically paraphrased here for pronunciation.

3 MOJ AND MAY

MOJ writes a poem by candlelight in her cabin. The words appear on the screen. Underscored with piano.

In the day
You darken in the sun
Like Solomon's
Beloved
While I
On the inside looking out
Am jealous of the overseeing sunlight
Who has gained the right
To kiss your face and arms.

I steal a look
Through the master's telescope
And survey the blue black night
Of your skin:
A shimmering crystal sphere
Made visible
By my desire.
I gaze in awe
And join the cotton dots to trace
The graceful shape of you
Celestial,
You are what myths are made of.

I find you in the shade
The night is a shadow the sun has made
And in this little corner of inner outer space
I pray to have a little more time.

All that matters in the universe
is you.
All matter in the universe
is attracted to you
And though our poles are as opposite
As night and day
This pull is gravitational

We are magnetic
It's scientific, we are a force
We can never be separate.

Pyramids
Are aligned
By your eyes
Of light and heat;
You radiate
Energy
In sheets;
Your smile is a constellation
Of scintillating stars
In which I read my destiny
And hope one day
To draw a map,
To find a way,
To navigate
this gutted ship
of 'ancestral oak',[13]
To your
Volcanic shore.

MOJ sneaks outside past the slaves quarters to visit MAY.

MOJ: (*Loud whisper.*) May!

MAY comes to the door.

MAY: (*Sexily.*) Moj! What you doin here at this hour?… School's closed.

They flirt.

MOJ: I was hoping I could get some…private tuition.

MAY: Oh yeah, and how you gon pay for that?

MOJ: Brought you a poem.

She offers the poem, MAY takes it.

13   From Percy Bysshe Shelley, 'Similes for Two Political Characters of 1819', in Marcus Wood (ed.), *The Poetry of Slavery* (Oxford: Oxford University Press, 2003), p 301.

MAY: Better be good. Otherwise… I just might have to give you detention.

MOJ goes inside MAY's cabin. Their love-making described in a dance.

4 THE PUNISHMENT

Shocking daylight. MASTER has found the poem.

MASTER: Now what would two Niggers be doing with words?…

MAY: Moj, don't say nothing.

MOJ: Massa I beg Sir, I 'pologise Sir, didn't have nothin to do with May Suh it was me wrote the poem, with my own hand Suh –

MASTER: 'These filthy dreamers defile the flesh, despise dominion, and speak evil of dignities… Woe unto them! For they have gone the way of Cain… Raging waves of the sea foaming out their own shame; wandering stars, to whom is reserved blackness of darkness forever' – Jude 8.[14]

MOJ: Massa I beseech you, forgive me, the fault is mine, I wrote the poem!

MASTER: Writing is forgivable, and almost a natural pastime to select in one as…fair as you, Moj. (*He turns to MAY.*) But May Jackson, field slave. Have you learnt nothing?

You above all should know a reading heathen is a mortal sin.

You shall not disgrace this house as you did the house of Sarah Jones.

And since I cannot teach you to forget how to read,

Any more than I can teach you to forget how to breathe…

Let prevention be the cure.

MASTER gets the whip, which is a transformation of MOJ's waist band.

And let the punishment fit the crime.

Let all God's creatures be made pure.

14   Jude, verses 8-13.

And let the duty to all white men be mine.

Moj, hold out your hand. (*MOJ reaches her hand forward, palm up.*)

May, open your eyes. (*MASTER pulls at MAY's face to open her eyes.*)

MOJ / MAY: (*A terrifying scream.*) NO!!!!!!!!

MASTER: OPEN YOUR EYES till I whip you blind!!!!

Transforms to gently singing the song below, juxtaposed with whip cracking. Stark. Slow. Terrifying. Red light.

MOJ: (*Sings a verse from the song 'It's your blood'.*)[15]

Train tracks cut across her eyes,
A forest spread on her face,
Roots descended into her neck and chest,
Her head split like fallen fruit
was unrecognisable as human.
Blood
and water
flooded
the wretched earth
and her feet
melted
into the mud.
What have I done,
what have I done
with words… (*MOJ breaks down.*)

I could my love offer no protection. All I could do was stand and bear witness to this atrocity. Yet even if there had been a thousand brothers present, none of our voices would match the testimony of a solitary white man. No court room would try the pastor for the murder. There was a saying in those days… 'It was worth a half-cent to kill a negro, and a half-cent to bury one.'[16]

15 Lyrics by Michael Christ, Vineyard Music, 1985.
16 Frederick Douglass, *Narrative of the Life of Frederick Douglass, An American Slave*, ed. by Houston A. Baker Jr. (London: Penguin, 1986 [1845]),

5 THE PLAN

MOJ bandaging her hand.

MOJ: And so, having lost my lover in a bitter blizzard of
blows too cruel to behold, there was no reason for me to
stay. So, I determined to take my leave. Like Frederick
Douglass before, 'freedom now appeared, to disappear
no more forever. It was heard in every sound and seen in
everything… It looked from every star, it smiled in every
calm, breathed in every wind, and moved in every storm.'[17]
Freedom was all around. But how to take it?!

My grandmother was an African. Born on a slave ship, in
the Atlantic Ocean, birthed through the muted screams of a
mother's lips bolted. Her father threw himself into the sea
with chains about his feet, he would rather become a fossil
than see his family treated like cattle.

*Still image of black Antarctic glacial erratic rock transforms
into MOJ's great grandfather dancing on the deck of a ship,
played by MOJ.*

(*Sung.*) 'Full fathom five
[my great-grandfather] lies
of his bones are coral made:
those are pearls that were his eyes,
Nothing of him that doth fade,
But doth suffer a sea-change
Into something rich and strange
Sea-nymphs hourly ring his knell
Ding-dong, ding-dong bell…'[18]

His wife, my great-grandmother, died shortly after she
arrived in America, killed by a disease brought about by
this…strange change in climate. My mother, and baby
brother, were sold away from the plantation, after Massa
had his fill of her. Freedom. How to take it and at what

p 69.
    17   Ibid., p 85.
    18   William Shakespeare, *The Tempest* (London: Penguin, 2001 [c. 1611]),
p 40.

cost? Much as I hated myself, I had no desire to be ravaged by blood hounds in the woods. If I wanted simply to be tortured and die, I should do it myself and not let a dog lick his lips with it. I wanted to live, though I did not know why. Perhaps it was the 'instinct to survive'… And so it was whilst dreamily dusting the words of European scholars that I had my first revelation…

It occurred to me that the only creatures to walk truly free upon on the earth were men. White men. Rich white men. And they did not even know it. Free to take a long drive, free to take a long bath. Free to have and free to waste. My master had destroyed my last 'vestige of earthly joy'[19] in his vicious travesty of justice. And so my plan was simply to divest of the cloth of victimhood and transvest to liberty. Having 'nothing to lose but my chains',[20] I decided to play a white man for a while… Sojourner Truth? I would Sojourn for fiction! But I would have to learn how… Naturally, I looked to their books… (*MOJ takes a book from a shelf and reads the title.*)… 'Moby…Dick'.

6 THE REHEARSAL

The text in bold below from Moby Dick *is heard as voiceover with underscored music – with visuals of Antarctica in all its WHITENESS: Icebergs, snow, light…*

'Though in many natural objects, whiteness refiningly enhances beauty, as if imparting some special virtue of its own, as in marbles, japonicas, pearls; and though various nations have in some way recognised a certain royal pre-eminence in this hue…and though this pre-eminence…applies to the human race itself, giving the white man ideal mastership over every dusky tribe; and though, besides all this, whiteness has been even made significant of gladness…there lurks an elusive something

19 Harriet E. Wilson, *Our Nig*, ed. by R.J. Ellis (Nottingham: Trent Editions, 1988 [1859]), p 32 (emphasis added).
20 Paraphrased from Marx and Engels, *The Communist Manifesto*, p 55.

in the innermost idea of this hue, which strikes more panic to the soul than that redness which affrights in blood... Witness the white bear of the poles, and the white shark of the tropics; what but their smooth, flaky whiteness makes them the transcendent horrors they are? [21]

During the above MOJ *has transformed the bookcase into a 'kitchen', household objects on it including: flour, a cheese grater, a first aid bandage (large one), a huge knife, a rolling pin, an old iron, some water, some dough, a clothes peg... Male clothes are also nearby.* MOJ *reads from* Moby Dick *as if it were a recipe book.*

MOJ: 'How to make a white man?...'

She finds the right recipe and follows the instructions. A clown-like farcical scene ensues.

How to make a white man:

- MOJ *takes her skirt off (trousers on underneath).*
- *Puts flour on her face.*
- *Grates her chin with cheese grater.*
- *Bandages her breasts down (with audience help).*
- *Goes to slice her bottom with a carving knife – changes her mind.*
- *Rolls her bottom with rolling pin instead (audience help).*
- *Irons her hair straight.*
- *Constructs a penis from dough – badly. Gives dough to audience to help her.*
- *Pins her nose with clothes peg.*
- *Chews and swallows her lips.*
- *Retrieves the new improved penis from the audience (applause for them!).*
- *Reduces the size of the penis.*
- *Puts on a waistcoat, coat and white gloves, hat, then a cravat around her neck.*

21 Herman Melville, *Moby Dick* (Oxford: Oxford University Press, 1998 [1851]), pp 168-175.

- *Dances to the music – as a white man.*

7 THE ESCAPE

A short very contained sequence, all in the moment of stepping over a boundary. Image of a scarf melting away into the snow.

MOJ: As quiet as a Quaker I crept out of my cabin. Softly my toes like 'moonlight on water'.[22]

8 THE TRAIN

Upbeat optimistic energy.

MOJ: With my rainy day dollars, and my father's features, I bought a ticket to Boston. The train was packed!

A whistle blows. All the physical bustle of a train journey, rhythmic music and sound. Visuals of the New Orleans 2005 flood.

TRAIN GUARD: All aboard the North Star!

PASSENGER 1: 'Why, the fact is Haley, Tom is an uncommon fellow; he is certainly worth that sum anywhere, – steady, honest, capable, manages my whole farm like a clock.'[23]

PASSENGER 2: 'Well haven't you got a boy or a gal that you could throw in with Tom?'[24]

TRAIN GUARD: Macon-Savannah!

PASSENGER 3: I wish my husband had not such queer notions about teaching that nigger to read.

TRAIN GUARD: Charleston-Petersburg!

PASSENGER 2: By Jupiter New Orleans is flooded, flooded with the likes of that thar gal!

---

22 Craft, p 22.
23 Harriet Beecher Stowe, *Uncle Tom's Cabin*. (Oxford: OUP, 1998[1852]), p 8.
24 Ibid.

PASSENGER 1: At that price Katrina is not to be sold, she is worth her weight in gold!

TRAIN GUARD: Wilmington-Richmond!

PASSENGER 2: Capital Sir, the deal is done!

PASSENGER 3: My husband complains I punish her too severely. But 'You know these niggers are just like black snakes; you can't kill them. If she wasn't tough she would have been killed long ago.'[25]

TRAIN GUARD: Baltimore-Philadelphia!

PASSENGER 4: Are you quite all white Sir?

MOJ: I, I, pardon?…

PASSENGER 4: Quite all white sir, are you quite all right? You look deathly pale.

MOJ: Good. No. Yes. Are we in the North?

PASSENGER 4: We are at Philadelphia.

MOJ: Thank my stars… (*MOJ collapses into sleep.*)

TRAIN GUARD: New York-Boston!

PASSENGER 3: Sir, we have arrived.

MOJ: Thank you Ladies (*MOJ tips her hat*), good day to you!

PASSENGER 5: Oh Aunt Martha, that gentleman is so delicate, do you suppose he resides here in Boston, I think I am quite taken with him.

PASSENGER 6: Uh not again Cecilia – Stop! 'There goes my Nigger Ned!'[26]

MOJ: At last I arrived in Boston, where I met an abolitionist, Lars Homer Esquire.

25 Harriet E. Wilson, p 47.
26 Craft, pp 31-35.

9 THE NORTHERN FREAKSHOW

On arrival North MOJ *goes to a white abolitionist's house – LARS HOMER. This later transforms into a scene in an abolitionist hall.*

LARS HOMER: 'But now…ancient friend, you must tell us about your troubles and satisfy our curiosity. Who are you and where do you come from?'[27] And for the love of God young lady how did you become dressed so?!

MOJ: I thank you for your kindness Sir but I would rather not discuss my past, I simply want to find a home, a job… My chief concern is the 'Fugitive Slave Law', I understand now all citizens, even here in Boston, are compelled to catch runaways and send them back as slaves?

LARS HOMER: Yes yes, but what is important in this moment is that you speak out! The testimonies of Negroes will be our greatest weapon in this impending war of North against South. The public will be crying out to hear a tale such as yours, think of the funds you could raise – just look at you!!!

We transition immediately to an Abolitionist lecture hall – house lights up.

Righteous Brothers, I am pleased to be the first introduce to you the runaway negro slave girl in her disguise as a white man – the incredible Moj! (*Applause. Beat.*) Everyone is waiting Moj.

MOJ: (*Hesitantly she steps up to the lectern.*) 'I was never cruelly overworked;'

The audience interject – prompted by cues on screen.

AUDIENCE: Oh…

MOJ: 'I was never lacerated with the whip head to foot […so] that I could not turn from one side to another; I never had my heel-strings cut to prevent my running away; I was never chained to a log and forced to drag it about, while

27   Paraphrased from 'Eumaeus Hut' scene, Homer, *The Odyssey* (Harmondsworth: Penguin, 1971), p 220.

I toiled in the fields from morning till night; I was never branded with hot iron, or torn by bloodhounds.'

AUDIENCE: Aaaah…

MOJ: 'On the contrary, [unlike so many about me] I had always been [relatively] kindly treated and tenderly cared for… But though my [own] life in slavery was comparatively devoid of hardships, God pity the woman who is compelled to lead such a life.'[28]

AUDIENCE: (*Yawns. Snores.*)

HECKLER: (*Heckling.*) Tell us what you keep in your breeches! (*Laughter.*)

The ABOLITIONIST *steps up trying to rescue the event from disaster.*

LARS HOMER: Gentlemen, gentlemen I am sure you will agree Moj is a unique…er…specimen, such as any circus in Massachusetts would be proud to display. She is biologically female. Yet in stance, manner, aspect and voice she is virtually a hermaphrodite!

AUDIENCE: Oooh…

LARS HOMER: A half-breed indeed in hue this mulatto is quite unblemished, quite virgin.

AUDIENCE: Mmmm…

Following sentences inter-cut with still images of MOJ *in white face on Antarctica.*

LARS HOMER: 'She' is as pale as a polar bear! As flawless as a snow flake! A near Antarctic alabaster albino! The lightest, whitest negro in the Milky Waaaaaaaaay!

SOUTHERN SLAVE CATCHER: Yep, but she'll always be a Nigger!

Beat.

---

28 Moj's words spoken here are from Harriet Jacobs, *Incidents in the Life of a Slave Girl* (New York: Mineola: 2001 [1861]), p 96.

LARS HOME: Sir, we are abolitionists, we do not use such language in this hall. What is your business here? (*Beat.*) Speak up man!

SOUTHERN SLAVE CATCHER: My business, is to obey the laws of my country – get her!!!

This transitions into a chase scene away from the abolitionist hall and to the port. Video of MOJ dancing on the Antarctic mountain. MOJ runs around the space and into the auditorium. She is sings/calls the African-American traditional 'Sinnerman'. The audience the responses (prompted by MOJ), marked in bold.

MOJ: Abolitionists! I need your help, I need your spirit! We gotta confuse the slave catcher. So we'll set up a rhythm. I'll call and you respond. (*Improvises with audience.*) ... That's good now let's put a little tone in it... (etc)

Oh sinner man where you gonna run to
Sinner man where you gonna run to
Where you gonna run to
All on that day
Well I ran to the rock
Please hide me
I ran to the rock
Please hide me
I ran to the rock
Please hide me Lord
All on that day

But the rock cried out
I can't hide you
The rock cried out
I can't hide you
The rock cried out
I ain't gonna hide you gal
All on that day

I said Rock!
What's the matter with you rock?!

MOJISOLA ADEBAYO

Don't you know I need you rock!
All on that day

So I ran to the river
It was bleeding
I ran to the sea
It was boiling
I ran to the sea
It was bleeding
All on that day

So I ran to the Lord
Please hide me Lord!
Don't you see me prayin!
Don't you see me down here prayin?!

But the Lord said
Go to the devil!
The Lord said
Go to the devil!
He said go to the devil
All on that day
I cried power! **Power!** Power... [29]

Repeat 'Power' to end. Disorienting lighting effect, song and movement become a possession.

10 TO ENGLAND

MOJ: In the confusion, I grabbed the money from the lecture ticket sales and jumped a ship from Boston –

MOJ pulls a huge white sail across the stage.

– to Liverpool. I made my last salute to the past, leaving behind me a nation on the brink of war with itself.
Across the amniotic Atlantic we set sail
on the day I was 30 rains
And I still dressed masculine
Felt safe

29 African-American traditional made popular by Nina Simone.

Having reclaimed my melanin (*White gloves off.*)
To England!
Where I would be free to write my life with ink in my pen,
No more the invisible man.

11 TO LONDON

On arrival MOJ meets WILLIAM BLACK[30] in a pub. BLACK speaks with a Scottish accent. Sound of a bawdy old nineteenth-century pub.

MOJ: From Liverpool, I made my way to London. (*Changes accent to cockney.*) And in a pub in Deptford made infamous by one Christopher Marlowe some time ago, I 'appened upon a sailor with a story…

BLACK: Pardon young lad, but there is something very familiar about you.

MOJ: I'm sure there isn't Sir.

MOJ afraid she has been spotted gets up to leave.

BLACK: What matter is there, would you rather blether about the weather?

MOJ: Excuse me Sir. (*Goes to leave.*)

BLACK: What calamity man? Sit yourself down. (*MOJ stops from leaving, and sits.*) You are an African, like me, correct?

MOJ: Yes, no. I mean I was, then I wasn't, and now in London it seems I am an African again.

BLACK: Are you in something of a state of funk Sir?

MOJ: Sir?

BLACK: Something has stirred you mightily I can see. Fear not fellow African, so as the magnet draws the metal, you've met your match. I'll let you into something. I was a woman once. (*MOJ stirs.*) Be at peace, the whole of England knows it! (*Reads newspaper.*) 'Amongst the crew of the Queen Charlotte…is now discovered to be a female African who

---

30 Based on the true life character, William Brown.

served as a seaman in the Royal Navy for upwards of eleven years… highly to the satisfaction of the officers'.[31] Eleven years in the Royal Navy, I served under Nelson himself!

MOJ: Your name?

BLACK: William Augusto Black! And yes, I am a true story!

MOJ: And I am Moj –

BLACK: And a woman too. I ken that. Our sort can spot each other a mile off. Don't worry yourself, you're in London now, take a look around you. This place is full of them.

MOJ takes a look around. Notices they are in a 'trans' bar!! They toast.

BLACK: So, where is home Moj?

MOJ: Home? I'll know it when I find it.

BLACK: Well, what's your business?

MOJ: I am seeking a vocation.

BLACK: 'A purse is but a rag unless you have something in it'.[32]

MOJ: Yes.

BLACK: And you want to see the world? Aye?

MOJ: Aye.

BLACK: And you know what you want to be free from?

MOJ: Yes.

BLACK: But do you know what you want to be free for?

MOJ: (*MOJ thinks.*) Alas, no.

BLACK: Then a seaman you should become! 'Tis the best job for an African woman by far.

MOJ: A seaman?

BLACK: But you can forget the Royal Navy, they won't let another slip through the net after me. No, if I had my time again I'd become a whaler of the Southern Ocean Moj, I'd

---

31 Internet source quoting 1815 annual register.
32 Melville, p 3.

catch myself an oil-filled dragon of slimy gold. Do you know there was a whale in the Thames about a year ago. If I had the strength today I'd follow that monster all the way to the South Pole. Take some advice from an old sea dog, become a whaler Moj, there's plenty of work in the big fish and lucrative too.

MOJ: I thank you for your advice William but –

BLACK: Call me Willy.

MOJ: Willy, thank you but I have no desire to catch a whale.

BLACK: You want to see the world don't ye?

MOJ: Yes, I suppose –

BLACK: Well for an explorer today, there's only two places left to conquer, it's Africa or the ice. And I can't see you in the heart of darkness somehow, half naked carrying an English man on your head. No, it's the Southern ocean for you lad. Unless of course you'd rather pick up tricks in Piccadilly,[33] or perhaps display yourself upon the London stage?! You'll end up stuffed in the British Museum in no time.

MOJ: But whales –

BLACK: Aye it's dirty work, but not as dirty as the slave trade and you can't very well be a pirate of flesh. And think of all a whale can give a man...

Dainty music of the aristocracy.

Whale bones sewn into ladies' corsets and stays, billowing hoops and loops for pretty cotton dresses, crinolines and struts for parasols protecting the skin of the delicate from the elements, sweet perfumes to cover the stench of the day, soaps to wash the day itself away, whalebone whips for ring masters and rebels and springs for the carriages of heroic runaways, wax to light the long dark lonely nights where a lover by candlelight poetry writes, and oil, oil my friend, massaged into a gentleman's gloves and boots, and oil, oil my friend, lubricating the machinery of industry and progress.

33 Thanks to Carole Jones for this line!

Music out.

The Western world must have something to burn! It's nature that fans the flames of change pal. Smoke and steam makes the dream! 'Whaling is imperial!'[34] Why shouldn't you have it all Moj?! Go get yourself a nice big white Moby Dick.

MOJ: I'm not sure Willy.

BLACK: Think of all the perks of the job! (*Naughtily.*)

MOJ: The ports, the…women…

BLACK: Women?! Quite the opposite! I'm talking of the sailors.

MOJ: The men? But I thought you —

BLACK: I'm not a fucking sapphic Moj! I'm a sodomite! Aye. I circumnavigated the circumcised and the un- son!… 'To the great satisfaction of the officers'! Remember me Moj, remember meeee!

MOJ: And so like Melville's Ishmael, 'having little or no money in my purse, and nothing particular to invest on shore, I thought I would sail about a little and see the watery part of the world'.[35] Into the heart of whiteness, to hunt the great leviathan.

12 AN INTERVIEW

A SAILOR on the deck of a whaling ship inducts MOJ. He speaks in a London accent.

SAILOR: Next! (*MOJ changes into sailor outfit.*) Now then my sooty little sailor friend, do you count yourself fit to chase 'with curses a Job's whale round the world' in a motley crew 'made up of mongrel renegades, and castaways, and cannibals'?[36]

---

34 Melville, p 100.
35 Melville, p 1.
36 Ibid., p 167.

MOJ: I should say Sir, your crew I am certain are no more savage than I have seen in fine suits on the streets of Massachusetts.

SAILOR: Very good then, welcome aboard The Lady May!

MOJ: The Lady May???

SAILOR: That's what I said. She is the finest vessel to ever round Cape Horn.

MOJ: Cape. Horn. Yes, she is surely the finest. We'll follow the stars. (*Wistful.*)

SAILOR: (*Slightly sarcastic.*) Yes, and a map.

MOJ: Yes.

SAILOR: We'll have larks with you I can see.

(*To the audience:*) Indeed, 'whale-fishery furnishes an asylum for many romantic, melancholy, and absent-minded young men, disguised with the corking care of the earth, and seeking sentiment in tar and blubber.'[37]

But first things first dreamer, one or two rules:

The following rules are acted out in a gestural movement sequence.

Never back the direction of travel on the bridge.
Never shake hands through an open doorway.
Before you hoosh throw salt over your shoulder for the devil sits on the left hand side.
Cover the top of your glass when you clink or else a sailor may die.
It's unlucky, it is, to have a woman on the ship – the ship is Neptune's fiancée, we don't want to rile her envy.
No whistling on deck or below – it summons the storm witch.
Never say rabbit – say hare.
Never say salmon – say red fish.
Never say pig – say swine.
It's good luck to have an albatross following the ship –

37   Ibid., p 140.

Stone a petrel, harpoon a whale, stab a seal, eat a penguin, but never ever shoot an albatross my friend. A dead albatross is more bad luck than a dead duck in your tea cup. And a piece of advice: it might prove wise to have the cross of Christ tattooed onto your back, then you'll never live in fear of the captain's lash.

Beat.

MOJ: (*Nervous, quiet.*) I am afraid I cannot remove my shirt Sir, I am...marked.

SAILOR: Well sooty, you'll just have to take care to behave yourself won't you. Now, your first job as a sailor will be to take care of the cats, essential work for keeping off rats in the kitchen which will be your second occupation.
Here
'Pompey
Scotty
Pinky and
Nigger
Pinky is not despised, we can afford to give him plenty of biscuit.'[38]
Two balanced meals a day sailor,
take care not to poison us
and make sure there are supplies enough.

MOJ: Yassuh. The common et cetera of domestic duties – these I know well.

SAILOR: Woooooowondrous passing excellent sailor! You'll have one more task, since we shall be all at sea on Christmas day, somewhere in the Antarctic seas –

MOJ: The Antarctic!

SAILOR: It would go well with you not to interrupt. (*Beat.*)
At Christmas it is traditionally the kitchen boy's job to organise the entertainment!

MOJ: Entertainment?...

38 In Ernest Shackleton, *South: The Endurance Expedition* (London: Penguin, 2002), p 248.

SAILOR: (*SAILOR is physicalising.*) Merriment! Revellry!
Gaeity!… You'll think of something! (*SAILOR gestures with a big toothy smile and waving the palms of his hands – like a black face minstrel.*) Castawaaaaaaaaaaaaaaay!

MOJ sings reprise of 'Full Fathom Five'.

13 A LIFE AT SEA

Dizzy with words MOJ goes below, physically affected by the rock of the sea.

MOJ: (*MOJ speaks to the audience, in secret.*)
The sea swells like labia.
Neptune would be jealous
Should he find me in my guise,
For I have stolen his lover.
I am stowed away
Vested in her bow,
She has tucked me under her skirts
And here I lurk,
Licking the glacier tongue,
Skimming the earth's epidermis,
Heading 66 degrees south.

I remember you, my love
The Lady May.
You rock my memory gently
I bed anchor in words and dreams…

MOJ lies back in her hammock, created by a lighting effect. There is voiceover of the following text underscored with music/sound. Visuals of the sea in good weather. MOJ on stage takes a book and reads. (All voiceovers appear in bold.)

'It was a clear steel-blue day. The firmaments of the air and sea were hardly separable in that all pervading azure; only, the pensive air was transparently pure and soft, with a woman's look, and the robust and man-like

sea heaved with long, lingering swells, as Samson's chest in his sleep.'[39]

MOJ falls asleep to visuals and voiceover. She wakes and sights an albatross.

MOJ: First albatross!!!

MOJ gets out of her hammock and watches the video of an albatross projected.

The spirits of drowned sailors
Or ancestor slaves in suicide
Jumping bravely
Into the ocean waves
Ascend into the albatross
Which soars the sky
In the shape of a cross!
Albatross
You like we
Are an endangered species!

Video of MOJ dancing and sea birds in the background. Voiceover and music/sound:

'Hither, and thither, on high, glided the snow white wings of small, unspeckled birds; these were the gentle thoughts of the feminine air; but to and fro in the deep, far down in the bottomless blue, rushed mighty leviathans, sword-fish, and sharks; and these were the strong troubled, murderous thinkings of the masculine sea.'[40]

MOJ works and speaks the following.

Weeks I laboured at sea, cooking, cleaning with only the cats for close company.
The weather worsened as we travelled further South.
The fog sealed us in like a cataract over an eye.
The surf frothed and raged as a slave catcher in chase.

---

39 Melville, p 478.
40 Ibid.

The frost bit into me with the bitterness of an unchained hound.
'The ice was here, the ice was there,
The ice was all around:
It cracked and growled and roared and howled,
Like noises in a swound.'[41]

Visuals of very harsh weather conditions, MOJ squinting in the snow etc. Voiceover:

Cape Valentine
Black Island
Protection basin
Glacier Tongue

Cape Horn
The roaring forties
Inaccessible Island
The bluff

Deception island
Port Circumcision
Enterprise Island
Mount Terror

And then, at last, the mainland, the black Antarctic mountain.

Visuals section including of the black mountain, and various other gorgeous visuals of Antarctic landscape – connected with the text below.

The sailors below at their
Christmas Eve hoosh,
I steal away
To survey
The rump of the black Antarctic mountain
On a never ending Sabbath day
Where the sun merely skims the horizon then rises again…

---

41 Samuel T. Coleridge, *The Rime of the Ancient Mariner and other poems* (London: Penguin, 1995 [1797]), verse 60.

To gaze
At the African giantess
Rising out of the ice
She might be my mother lost
She is
Like Cleopatra
In the cat's cream
Her hip dipped
Her buttock protruding
From her cool bath.

I want to lick the snow clean off the mountains

With visuals of a gorgeous snow-topped land:

South to me was Georgia
Now cotton has turned to snow
In the deep deepest south of the earth.
The chain which once bedded we
to rape, madness and Christianity
Has become the chain which beds my anchor
In the ocean free!

MOJ doubts herself.

But, how can this cold continent
On a ship of men and me
With a cat called Nigger for company
Be freedom for me?

Past Africa we sailed
Weeks ago
But there me they did not know
Oibo Oibo 2 bob 2bob Queen Victoriaaaah!!!
There I was a foreigner,
Foreign more so than in my master's house
Or in a London street,
Yet in this wilderness
I feel so very close
to home.

I see a lip of snow pouting over
A pink mountain. (*Corresponding visuals.*)

I see stalactites dripping like a woman in love.
(*With stalactite visuals.*)
I see a penguin as awkward as a minister of religion.
(*Visuals of penguins.*)
Penguins, ringmasters of the ridiculous
Descendents of birds who forgot how to fly.

And under all this white
Antarctica is a broken rock as Black as my great-
grandfather, (*Black rock still image.*)
Stolen for rum and bum and baccy.
Sold by a chief for a bottle of gin.
Now a sea-shackled skeleton, a shackle-ton.
Black
Yes
Black as the lips between my lover's thighs,
black as a Pharoah's eyes,
White is a cover up
Is a beautiful lie.
This place is not but white but orange and pink and blue!
(*Antarctica in all its colour.*)
Iceberg blue.
Inked
Like the letters
I write to you,
Supernatural epistles
Of love
Taboo.

Visuals of whale – MOJ sights the whale.

MOJ: Whaaaaaaaaaaaaaaaaaaaaaaaaaaaaaaaaaaaaaaaale!!!!! There
she blows! Boys and men there she blows!

SAILOR: Well done lad – get to work!

MOJ: (*Excited.*) 'There Leviathan,
Hugest of living creatures, in the deep

185

Stretched like a promontory sleeps or swims,
And seems a moving land; and at (her) gills
Draws in, and at (her) breath spouts out a sea'!!![42]

SAILOR: To work dreamer, prepare the harpoon!

VARIOUS SAILORS: (*Various accents.*)

– (*Cockney.*) Lower the boats!

– (*Irish.*) Lower away!

– (*Irish.*) Pull hearts alive!

– (*Mancunian.*) Pull, never mind the brimstone!

– (*Mancunian.*) Long and strong!

– (*Irish.*) The devil fetch ye, ragamuffin rapscallions; ye are all asleep!

– (*Cockney.*) That's it – that's it!

– (*Cockney.*) Start her, my silver spoons! Start her, marling-spikes!

– (*Mancunian.*) Pull and keep pulling, nothing more

– (*Irish.*) Burst all your livers and lungs!

– (*Cockney.*) That's the hump. There! There! give it to her![43]

Harpoon shoots, massive explosion, frenzy of bloody light.

MOJ: (*Playing the pastor, a kind of flashback.*): 'In that day, the Lord with his sore, and great, and strong sword, shall punish Leviathan… that crooked serpent; and he shall slay the dragon that is in the sea.' Isaiah 27.[44]

SAILOR: 'Haul in the chains. Let the carcase go astern!'[45]

MOJ: (*Low, stunned.*) Merry Christmas everyone…

It was a colossal death.

The whale beheaded

like a sphynx in the desert

her hieroglyphic skin shimmering on the slab

---

42 From John Milton, *Paradise Lost* quoted by Melville in 'extracts' to *Moby Dick*.

43 Melville, pp 195-203.

44 From the Book of Isaiah, quoted by Melville in 'extracts' to *Moby Dick*.

45 Melville, p 277.

Her trumpet herald ceased
Only the sound
Of pecking birds
Feasting on a steaming ruby sea.
I should have whispered to the whale
Instead of screaming bloody betrayal
'whale
swallow me
like Jonah
birth me in reverse.' (*MOJ is very upset.*)

SAILOR: Why so glum lad, what was your expectation? This is our business, (*He looks out to sea and notices.*) See the oil float on the water…

MOJ: (*She quotes William Black from earlier.*) 'The Western world must have something to burn.'

SAILOR: Aye aye! And so in celebration of our efforts the captain has decreed if the conditions are right this night we shall step foot on that great white wilderness before us, the Antarctic continent!! (*Big cheer from the SAILORS.*) A privilege even the great Captain Cook himself could not avail of. Moj, I trust ye have the festivities prepared! Come conquerers one and aaaaall!

SAILOR goes off.

14 TO ANTARCTICA

MOJ: And so we rowed out
To step foot on the unmarked Antarctic
A continent in exile.
A crystal desert
Of frozen tears.
'We stepped out gingerly'[46]
at first
Then playfully,
Like children in wonder on a moon of sugar.

46 Shackleton, p 94.

Our boots crunched beneath our feet
And it was all so beautiful and new.
I'll say 'this island's mine!' and remain a frosty Caliban
Caliban
Caliban!
'Has a new master
Get a new man!!!'[47]

SAILOR: (*Begins to strip to his pants and vest.*) And now in our cosy hut, the moment we have all been waiting for – our Christmas entertainment! Introducing our very own nebulous negro in surely the most southerly minstrel show ever – the kitchen boy Moj!

Pause. MOJ is empty. Then:

MOJ: So with whale blubber smoke smeared on my face
I played the tune
We all wanted to hear...

Black face visuals of MOJ. MOJ sings the Yoruba song we heard before, this time in its entirety.

Eiye n'sunkun
O n'beru f'ormor re
S'e b'oun lo fo lor
Wa iranlorwor fun ite eiye?
I daduro lo wa nsin ninu igin la
Ko le mpada lor le

'I am just going outside and may be some time'...[48]

MOJ exits. One image of MOJ naked on a whaling boat in Antarctica. Sound of blizzard and strong wind – big music. The audience must not think it's over. Costume change.

---

47 William Shakespeare, *The Tempest*, p 61.
48 Spoken by Captain Oates before his suicidal step out into the cold at the South Pole.

15 EPILOGUE

The ANCIENT returns. Video projection from the prologue plays again.

ANCIENT:

As Black people picked white cotton in the genocide fields
of Georgia
White faces blackened lungs in the emphysemic coal mines
of Tredegar
And The Canaries coughed up Africans
While canaries choked in the coal mines
To furnace the fires,
To power the factories,
To make pretty cotton dresses for the high-class ladies,
To make the women women,
And the men not
And Europe rich
And Africa 60 million futures lost.

As a starving baby belches oil in a village in the Niger delta,
A grown man drives a four-by-four in a town in Jamaica,
And ancient islands ossify in Nigeria and the Gambia
While a woman runs a sunken bath in a town in West
Yorkshire
And a girl pricks her finger in a sweat shop in Indonesia
Whilst the burn pumps an omen into the sky.
A little pin-prick of pollution
Opens a hole in our protection.
The earth's lungs are stretched
With the last gasps of a whale
And both the rich and the poor move closer to the sea.
And the cold heats
And the ice secretly retreats.
Salt water begins to rise,
Fertile land turns to a crust
As the DNA in a cell changes shape
Turning pale skin to cancer as the world turns close
To the sun.

And the wound is open.
And it begins
The drip
Drip
Drip.
Yet just as the machine removed the maker from the made
The humanity from the human
In the holocaust slave trade
We are removed from the feeling
That that unholy libation
of melting ice,
makes a
Sea
Change…

'Water, water everywhere,
And all the boards did shrink;
Water, water everywhere,
Nor any drop to drink.'[49]

End

---

49   Coleridge, *Rime of the Ancient Mariner*, verse 120.

THE SONS OF CHARLIE PAORA

'The World in Our Hearts':
The Sons of Charlie Paora

By Dr Valerie Kaneko Lucas
(The Ohio State University)

The *Sons of Charlie Paora* was created by actor and playwright Lennie James[1] in response to New Zealand director Samantha Scott and her South Auckland youth theatre group. They had seen James' BBC television drama, *Storm Damage* (2000), which was based, in part, upon James' own childhood. This account of the lives, struggles and missed opportunities of teenagers in a bleak, council-run children's home, so impressed the group that they invited James to South Auckland to create a new play, drawing upon their experiences as young men from immigrant families.[2] The young men, many from Maori and Samoan families, eagerly told their stories. As reviewer Kate Bassett notes: 'The issues of race and spiritual faith, aggression and forgiveness are sincerely tackled because James's inspiration came from listening to the company's own life stories.'[3]

The Sons of Charlie Paora explores the themes of the transition from laddishness to uneasy manhood, of the rights and responsibilities of those whom Paora loved as his sons versus those who are his blood relations, all viewed through the prism of a complex intercultural lens. Charlie Paora was a Maths teacher and beloved coach of the rugby first fifteen at Nga Tapuwai College, a school where the 'dumb, the poor, the low class island kids are locked down...to give Mangere some time off from the wild angry brown'. (201) As Paora befriends those whom others scorn as an underclass, he re-discovers a suppressed part of his own ethnic identity.

---

1   http://jerichowiki.cbs.com/page/Lennie+James?t=anon; http://www.tv.com/lennie-james/person/77394/biography.html; http://www.imdb.com/name/nm0416694/bio.

2   Paul Taylor, Review of *The Sons of Charlie Paora*, *The Independent*, 3 March 2004, http://findarticles.com/p/articles/mi_qn4158/is_20040303/ai_n12772936.

3   Kate Bassett, 'A Nice Try, Sincerely Tackled,' *The Independent*, 29 February 2004, http://arts.independent.co.uk/theatre/reviews/article71762.ece.

For Samoans Ezra and Semo, and Maoris Albie and Miro, Paora becomes an idolised father-figure. Semo fondly regards him as a man who 'had the world in his heart. That he put the world in our hearts'. (271) Excluded from his funeral by Paora's white wife, they decide to hold their own memorial celebration in Ezra's garage in run-down Mangere. Fuelled by beer and drinking games, the five young men, now in their twenties, veer from rosy nostalgia about rugby matches and victory celebrations to disturbing undercurrents of unfinished business and revelations about the lives they now lead.

Albie – jokingly dubbed 'Daddy No Bucks' – revels in family life with his partner Ripeka and three children. In contrast, Miro is an ebullient womaniser who boasts of his sexual prowess with a 'lily-white' English backpacker. A serial monogamist, he is a feckless father of 'five kids...from four chicks. There two...more that one mother says are mine.' (224) Ezra has returned after a three-year prison stint for attempted murder of a team-mate. Semo has given up the opportunity to enter professional rugby to protect his mother from her abusive husband. Jackson, the last of the group to arrive, is outwardly the most successful: he is soon to become an All-Black. Jackson's observations on their safe, small-town mentality is seen by the others as an attack upon Mangere and (by association) themselves. For although Paora may have lavished love upon his boys, they seem – even in their twenties – in a state of arrested adolescence. The simmering tensions and competitiveness within the group is galvanised by the arrival of Paora's own children. Sonny and Sarah.

Although Paora was idolised by his students, his own children have a different story to tell. Of an indifferent father who had little time for them. 'He really wasn't that good with us,' recalls Sarah. 'We didn't make him happy.' (265) She has accepted Ezra's invitation (and coerced her brother along) in an attempt to apologise for their mother's failure to invite the boys to Paora's funeral. Sarah's visit is motivated by the need to understand who these boys were and why they were so important to her father, and she makes awkward attempts to bridge the cultural divide. However, Sonny, brooding and aggressive, insults the lads and goads Ezra. Sonny sees Ezra as the usurper of his place as the true son, the blood relation and also as the cause for the family's financial ruin. Paora's devotion to Ezra estranged him from his real family and later cost him his job; it was Ezra, not Sonny, who was present at his father's deathbed. Sonny views Ezra as a rival who 'had him alive, held him dead and now you want the memory of him… You want to leave me out here with nothing. Not even what's mine to remember!' (264)

Ezra responds with a forgiveness ritual from Samoa: a *faatoeseaga*. Covering himself with a mat and prostrating himself before Sonny, he offers his body to the other's will. Sonny, perhaps wilfully misinterpreting the ritual in its most literal sense, sees it as a prime opportunity for revenge and declares Ezra will remain on the ground until he starves to death. Sonny, who both loves and despises his father, still longs for some form of redemption, a marker that he was, in some way, cherished by his father. And in this play, it comes through the power of story: to offer the dispossessed a means of reclaiming their past, whether it is as profound as Semo's father's self-loathing as colonised subject or, as seemingly trivial as Sonny's making guacamole. In the play's closing, Ezra tells Sonny the story of One Tree Hill – a story that will save both their lives.

Through the figure of Charlie Paora, the play explores the tensions of dual heritage. Although Paora was only one-eighth Maori, 'his soul was brown' (210) and the boys claim him as one of their own, according him the same respect they might to a Maori chieftain. Yet Paora's children claim him as white, and his marriage to a white woman as his attempt to transcend a Maori heritage which they associate with the underclass. Paora's story may be read as a metaphor for the dilemmas of dual heritage in a society which demands that the mixed-race person chooses between two mutually-exclusive worlds.

The play in performance

The London production of *The Sons of Charlie Paora* was realistic in its design elements, evoking Ezra's homely garage and yard, and creating a lush tropical atmosphere through strategic lighting. Actors were costumed in batik shirts, jeans, hoodies and casual summer wear. However, this realism was cleverly contrasted with the use of song and choreography, which often served as subtexts for the strong emotions which these young men would not, or even could not, articulate in daily life. In one particularly compelling sequence, Miro's sexually-charged dancing degenerates into the jitters and twitches of a drug addict. Their previous closeness as friends and team-mates were brought to the fore as the boys laughingly fell into step to a song from their college days, 'Candy Girl', or charged about, re-living the scrum that had made them district champions.

The Sons of Charlie Paora had its premiere at the Herald Theatre in Auckland, New Zealand in October 2002. It was produced by Massive Theatre Company in conjunction with the Edge Community Arts Programme. The director was Samantha Scott, with lighting design by Jennifer Lal and set and costume design by Tracey Collins.

Following its first production, the company performed *The Sons of Charlie Paora* at the Royal Court Theatre Downstairs in London from 25 February to 6 March 2004. In 2005, Massive Theatre Company toured the play to Gisborne, Napier, Wellington, Manakau, and Hamilton in New Zealand.

Examples of the critical reception of the London production:

'James's play makes the leap from anthropology into drama when it deals with confused, conflicting memories of the late Charlie, and when it takes on the resonance of the Prodigal Son parable. Samantha Scott's production, with its hakas, hip hop and choreographer recreation of rugby triumphs, also has a pounding ensemble vigour and catches exactly the mixture of realism and ritual that is part of New Zealand's multi-culturalism.'

Michael Billington, *The Guardian*, 27 February 2004

'Samantha Scott's production is charged with compensating vitality. The rugby players Max Palamo, Foma Taito, Joe Folau, Liston Rua and Jason Webb variously project emotion and vulnerability with relaxed conviction: they perform a Maori-Samoan rugby battle-dance as if it were drama, ballet and warfare all in one. They bring a far-off culture to life.'

Nicholas de Jongh, *Evening Standard*, 27 February 2004

'It views its subject from the perspective of a eulogy to a man who was metaphorically both a seer and blind… With its final message of redemption, this New Zealand import is ultimately an uplifting two hours with its combination of European style drama and Maori expression; there are dances and chants, fights and rugby.'

Philip Fisher, *British Theatre Guide,*
http://www.britishtheatreguide.info/reviews/charliepaora-rev.htm

Glossary

Haka: Maori traditional dance, involving war-like stamping and chanting. The New Zealand All Blacks perform their version of the *haka* prior to the start of a match.

Hangi: An outdoor cooking pit, using superheated rocks as fuel. Food is placed in wire baskets over the rocks, then covered with sacking and earth and cooked slowly.

Karakia: Maori prayers to bring everyone together. The karakia asks for the assistance of a superior being to offer spiritual protection to the participants of the powhiri.

Marae: A cleared area of land, usually rectangular in shape, often bordered with stones or wooden posts, used for ceremonial purposes.

Pakeha: A New Zealander of Caucasian descent.

Powhiri: Maori ceremony of welcome to visitors. Its elements are intended to ward off evil spirits and to unite visitors and hosts in an atmosphere of peace and friendship.

Rangatira: A Maori hereditary chieftain.

The Sons of Charlie Paora

by

Lennie James

Characters

EZRA

SEMO

ALBIE

MIRO

SONNY

JACKSON

SARAH

The Sons of Charlie Paora was first performed in October 2002 at the Herald Theatre, The Edge. Auckland, New Zealand. It was produced by the MASSIVE COMPANY (formerly AYPT) in conjunction with the Edge Community Arts Programme. The cast was as follows:

EZRA, Max Palamo

SEMO, Foma'i Taito

ALBIE, Joe Folau

MIRO, Liston Rua

SONNY, Wesley Dowdell

JACKSON, Jason Webb

SARAH, Kiri Lightfoot

Director Sam Scott

Set & Costume Design Tracey Collins

Lighting Design Jennifer Lal

Act One

SCENE 1

The space is in blackout. From the dark we hear a Maori song for the dead. The voices are all male with one female voice.

As the song continues a spotlight picks out the face of EZRA...

EZRA: (*Over the song.*) Charlie Paora...

CHARLIE's name is echoed by voices in the dark but the song is not broken.

... Charlie was five feet eleven and a little bit, but he said...he said he walked like six foot one.

EZRA goes back into the song. This pattern, of coming out of the song and returning, is repeated as each person speaks spread out across the space.

SEMO: Charlie Paora taught Maths and coached the first fifteen at Nga Tapuwae College... Nga Tapuwae... (*Smiles.*) ...

ALBIE: World famous in South Auckland! Nga Tapuwae where the dumb, the poor, the low class island kids are locked down... eight hours out of every 24... five days out of every seven, to give Mangere some time off from the wild angry brown...! (*Laughs.*)

SEMO: 'There's so much shit goes on down there they had to build a pond to hold it!'... That's how it's thought of. But it's not how it is, Mangere...

MIRO: Mange-re man, it was Mange-re when he said it. That was Paora's joke. 'If Mangere brings you down, make it Mange-re...and *vis ta vie* (*Pronounced 'vee-ta-vee'.*) – live your life!'

Laughter, but the song continues.

SEMO: He was our coach.

EZRA: He loved rugby.

SONNY: He loved that game, aye!

JACKSON: He coached the game for the love of it.

SONNY: He always wanted to, needed…to win…to be right! Actually he didn't even need to be right…just to win!

SEMO: He was the first good man I think I'd ever met.

MIRO: He was the best man this side of the shit ponds…

ALBIE: Either side.

MIRO: (*In Maori.*) Amen.

EZRA: He was like a father to me.

SEMO: And me.

SONNY: He was my father.

SARAH: And mine.

SONNY: Charlie Paora died two weeks ago on the 17th.

The song stops now and there is silence for a good few beats.

My sister called to tell me…

EZRA: I called his daughter. I didn't know how it was between them, so I didn't know who'd tell her if it wasn't me!

SARAH: (*Beat.*) I told my brother. Woke him to tell him…

SONNY: The telephone woke me, but not completely. I think most of me was still asleep…coz when Sarah gave me the news, I ran with it back into the dream I was having and tried to hide it there… It wasn't that I didn't hear her, I heard her…heard what she was telling me. I just couldn't wake up to it right away.

EZRA: I was with him…

SONNY: Paora died in the arms of somebody else's son… That's what I took back into my sleeping…but it wouldn't stay buried there!

SARAH: At least he wasn't alone…

SONNY: That's what she said, 'At least…'

SARAH: The phone rang nine times before he answered the second time. How could he sleep again after the news I just gave him? I held my tongue but, to beg him to come with

202

me to tell our mum. I didn't want the phone to tell her. I knew she'd be best hearing it where she could see the truth in our eyes.

JACKSON: My mum said Paora had a smile like Christmas morning.

SARAH: He was always busy with that smile!

ALBIE: My mum cried when she heard.

SARAH: Mine has just thought about crying.

JACKSON: Mine blessed his memory.

ALBIE: There was no blood between us but he called us his sons. (*Beat.*) I liked that that was what he called me.

JACKSON: I miss you Paora.

JACKSON walks out of the light and is gone into the dark.

SARAH: Me too!

SARAH looks across the dark to SONNY wanting him to say the same as her.

Sonny…?

But SONNY just walks out of the light. SARAH follows.

MIRO tells the story of what the Maori believe happens to you after death. Where you go and how you go there. He will tell it in Maori and ALBIE will translate…

MIRO / ALBIE: (*The translation.*) … And if his spirit was to bless me and stop at my house on it's journey to the north… I would sit him at the head of my table. He will not need to eat. He will not have come to drink. I will sit as close to him as I can get and we will arm wrestle and I will bring all of me and he will bring all of him and neither will gift the other a win. It must be taken. It must be won. Maybe we will sit together for days until his arm falls this way or my arm that… Then his spirit and mine will smile and he will leave. Win or lose we will part on a smile…

ALBIE / MIRO: … I wish that for you Paora. I wish that for you…

ALBIE and MIRO turn out of the light. SEMO speaks in Samoan and EZRA translates.

SEMO / EZRA: *(The translation.)* '... To everything there is a season, and a time to every purpose under the heaven:

A time to be born, and a time to die; a time to plant, and a time to pluck that which has been planted;

A time to kill, and a time to heal; a time to break down, and a time to build up;

A time to weep, and a time to laugh; a time to mourn, and a time to dance;

A time to cast away stones, and a time to gather stones together; a time to embrace and a time to refrain from embracing...

I have seen the travails, which God hath given to the sons of men... He hath made everything beautiful: Also he hath set the world in their hearts...'

Under SEMO and EZRA's words the lights come up on the space. It is a garage at the back of a single-storey Mangere house in South Auckland.

The wide entrance/exit through which you would park your car is opened front-on to the audience. There is also a door on the left-hand side towards the back of the garage. This door leads out to the garden area that runs behind and along the side of the garage. The garage is bare but for a table in the corner, a single bed, five chairs spread out and an old TV against the back wall.

There is a hangi pit dug in the garden. It is about a metre square and about half a metre deep and smoke rises from it as if something hot smoulders in its base. A large bucket stands to its side.

SCENE 2

EZRA steps into the garage carrying a sixth chair and a beat-box as if from the house. SEMO brings two crates of beer. EZRA sets the beat-box on the TV and plugs it in and selects a tune. SEMO waits for EZRA's tune… 'Everyday People' by Arrested Development kicks in from the beat-box.

SEMO: (*Nods his head.*) Fuck yeah, bro…

EZRA: Yeah?

SEMO nods his approval again as he puts the crates of beers on the table. As they speak they set up the garage for the evening ahead – moving the table into the middle of the room and the chairs around it, chatting as they go.

SEMO: Do you think I should say that about him?

EZRA: Say what?

SEMO: When they're all here I want to say that… That he had the world in his heart. That he put the world in our hearts…

EZRA: (*Beat.*) That's a good thing to say.

SEMO: Say it about him for me, bro.

EZRA: You should say it.

SEMO: If I can't say it in front of those boyz…say it for me.

EZRA: It's what you want to say about him…

SEMO: (*Cutting in.*) You don't think it's a right thing to say? You think I'm wrong about his heart?

EZRA: I don't think you're wrong.

SEMO: I was looking for something everyone would nod their heads to, agree with… I wanted something that everyone would know to be true an' leave it alone…

EZRA: Why leave it alone?

SEMO: (*Beat.*) Man, I'm stuck on me and Jackson now…coming here tonight!

EZRA: I know…

SEMO: I was doing okay, then you turned my head onto Jackson...saying he's coming here tonight.

EZRA: Tonight is about Paora.

SEMO: I want it to be that, for tonight to be about Paora, but me and that one, that... I'm stuck on him now!

EZRA: Tonight is about Paora.

A beat between them: SEMO *aware that* EZRA *is laying down the law and* EZRA *looking to see if* SEMO *has heard him.*

SEMO: (*Beat.*) I went to the book about tonight...

EZRA: You went to the book...?

SEMO: Fuck yes, an' that's been some time!

EZRA: An' it gave you that for Paora?

SEMO: Ecclesiastes 3:1 through 10... 'To everything there is a season...'

EZRA: Well that's one good thing that book's done!

SEMO: What's that?

EZRA: Don't matter...

SEMO: All the strategies an' stratagems, all the plays in life are in the book, Paora...

EZRA: I remember...

SEMO: ...Remember he used to say that?

EZRA: (*Under his breath almost.*) Fuck the book!

SEMO: Did I hear that?

EZRA: It's nothing...

SEMO: Fuck the book...that's nothing?

EZRA: ... It gave you shit to make Paora proud, but...yeah, Fuck the book! The deceivers who wrote it, the assholes that misinterpret it and those believers who think God'll love them more if they smell rich and stoke the myth...fuck them all!

SEMO: (*Beat.*) How you doing...?

EZRA: I'm good.

SEMO: You see me sitting here?

EZRA: (*Beat.*) I see you.

SEMO: … Before anybody else gets here… Tell me what you're saying?

EZRA: I'm good, bro… It's all good.

SEMO: I don't know, bro…

EZRA: … It's just…there's no redemption! You should know that up front. The book says there is but it lies!

SEMO: (*Beat.*) See when my dad brought us over from the island…

EZRA: Coz his mum was dying…

SEMO: He brought us with him to look after her house and carry her body home. (*Beat.*) Nine years it took her to die!

EZRA has to smile.

Nine years! But see some days she was closer than others and it got like a sport in our house. My dad put 20 dollars on the top shelf for anyone who saw my Gran go… I wanted it to be me, for the 20… Sit up nights with her, (*Excited child.*) 'Tell me another story gran!' Wear her out…for the 20 bucks. But it was my dad. He saw her go. (*Beat.*) I don't know how it was at the end of her but my dad wasn't the same after. That's how it took him. So I'm just saying, coz I saw it with my dad…coz you can see me sitting here… If you want me to carry some of it…?

EZRA: (*Beat.*) It wasn't that dark.

SEMO: You saw Paora die.

EZRA: Not as dark as you're tryin' to paint it.

SEMO: So who needs redemption?

EZRA takes a beat to figure out his answer, but he is interrupted by MIRO and ALBIE as they enter through the side door from the garden. MIRO is wasted. Drunk and wasted on top of that. ALBIE does his best to hold him in check.

ALBIE: Look what I found.

EZRA: Where?

ALBIE: The last chick on the list, bro. Four of them before I find
him with this valentine he's got over the back of Clover
Park. Two chicks before her started swinging just at the
mention of his name. One brought a knife out for my balls
coz he'd pissed her off with his!

SEMO: Did he forget tonight was the night?!

ALBIE: He remembered.

SEMO: Maybe he was best not coming!

*MIRO pulls ALBIE back to the door. MIRO is trying to take his
trainers off but can't focus on them long enough to manage
on his own.*

MIRO: Help my shoes off, bro.

SEMO: *(To MIRO.)* You don't have to start with that.

MIRO: It's respect. You should lose yours too...

ALBIE: *(To MIRO.)* Give me your foot.

SEMO: *(To EZRA.)* Tell them we ain't doing that tonight.

*ALBIE helps MIRO off with his trainers and then reels away
from the smell of his feet.*

ALBIE: Shit brother, I forgot about your feet!

*MIRO starts the Powhiri aimed at SEMO and EZRA. First the
Karakia.*

It's for the Marae.

SEMO: There's no Marae.

ALBIE: There's no Marae?

EZRA: There's no Marae.

ALBIE: ... Why not?

EZRA: Coz that's not how we were ever here, bro. The boyz are
coming here like they did in the day... The stones are hot
for the hangi, my mum's packed the food...waiting for us in
the house. We eat...

SEMO: We drink!

EZRA: … We laugh loud…

SEMO: We drink!

EZRA: … We remember ourselves and talk about how it was when Paora was with us.

SEMO: And we keep our shoes on!

ALBIE: We should give his passing respect.

EZRA: That what I just said. That's the respect we're giving him. Make tonight like it would be if he was here. That's what I think, bro… If you don't think that would respect him…?

MIRO: We cannot see a Rangatira go and not mark his passing as we should…

SEMO: A great-grandfather he never knew, that was all the Maori he was…

ALBIE: His name! He carried a Maori name! He protected it… We should see that we do right with his name…

SEMO: We're not here to bury him, bro. That's been done already…!

ALBIE: (*To EZRA.*) Were you there…?

SEMO: (*To MIRO.*) What respect are you talking about, the state you've carried yourself here tonight!

ALBIE: (*To EZRA.*) Were you there?

SEMO: Paora is dust… We don't need to be there to know that.

ALBIE: (*To EZRA.*) Were you there? Did you see him buried?!

EZRA: (*Answering for SEMO.*) No… None of us.

ALBIE: Not one of us!

A beat between all of them to mark what has been said. SEMO, ALBIE and MIRO all looking at EZRA.

EZRA: (*Beat.*) I think we should lay the hangi…if we want to eat tonight we should put the food on the stones. (*Leaving.*) Someone help me with what I've got to carry…

EZRA looks to leave but ALBIE stops him in the mouth of the garage with…

ALBIE: If nobody else, it should've been you, E-zee…

EZRA: *(Beat.)* She had a lot to think about, grieving for him and…

ALBIE: Who?

EZRA: His wife…

ALBIE: You think she just overlooked us in trying to hold down her loss? Is that what you're saying? You think that you weren't there by accident?!

EZRA: *(Beat.)* I think… I think my stomach's starting to think about getting hungry. If we lay the food now I'll be eating before it thinks it's starving…

And EZRA, avoiding answering, is leaving. MIRO, still staggered by whatever has him high, resumes the Powhiri. SEMO is immediately stepping in on him.

SEMO: Will I have to make you shut your arse up, bro?

MIRO: I don't care how small a part of him was Maori, Paora's soul was brown! And who's gonna remember that if it isn't us?!

SEMO: Miro if you make this back-house holy I'm gonna have to disrespect it…

And SEMO drinks from his beer.

MIRO: Be that on you.

SEMO: It's alright for you, you arrived fucked.

MIRO laughs.

Look at you…that's the state I'm heading for.

MIRO takes SEMO's beer and pours a drop on the floor by way of a blessing.

MIRO: One for Charlie.

Miro takes a drink from SEMO's beer.

The last time's been too long, bro.

SEMO: Four maybe five years…

They shake hands and pull themselves into a hug, but SEMO is immediately stepping back.

Feet…!

MIRO slips his trainers back on and SEMO takes him into a bear hug that lasts a few beats.

MIRO: You don't want t'squeeze me too tight, bro…

SEMO, sets MIRO down as quickly as he can.

(*Beat.*) So what's he said…?

SEMO: Who?

MIRO: E-zee, bro… That's some shit he's holding isn't it?!

SEMO: He says it ain't as dark as we're thinking…

MIRO: What was he saying when he said that?

SEMO: He said that… 'It ain't as dark…'

MIRO: What was he saying that about, see what I'm asking?

SEMO: Miro…you let him bring it when he's ready.

MIRO: Okay, yes…yes. (*Beat.*) Just tell me who did he say death looked like?

EZRA and ALBIE return, as if from the house, carrying a large wire tray/basket filled with tin-foil parcels of food.

MIRO and SEMO come through the side door to the garden to meet them and they all set about laying the hangi. EZRA and ALBIE place the wire basket of food into the hole and from the large bucket all the guys pull out wet sacking and begin to lay it over the food. Steam begins to rise. The guys talk as they work.

EZRA: (*To MIRO.*) What did you bring, bro?

MIRO: What did I what?

EZRA: Bring?

MIRO: What…?

EZRA: When you got the message about tonight… When you got that, I also said to say, bring something that Paora would like.

MIRO: If I'd known bro, I'd've brought this lily-white I got loving me over there in Clover Park… Paora would like this girl that Albie pulled me off tonight… English chick on a back-pack…

She's got one of those funny ways of speaking that you only hear in old time black'n'white English films, when their faces are black with coal and their speaking is white with breath you can see… Matlock she's from, used to be a mining town up in the north of England. She's meant to be back there three maybe four months ago now…but she just can't stop fucking me!

Laughter from the others. EZRA and ALBIE cover the wet sack-cloths with a tarpaulin and MIRO and SEMO seal down the sides with heavy stones or earth.

… She's on me like Friday night! This chick has… Respect to my sisters and all of that and I don't mean to take from their beauty, say anything against it, coz the brown girls I've known, the ones that've had a taste of me… They were beautiful women, I loved most of them but… I'm swinging-my-thing in a whole new complexion! White chicks bro, European chicks…y'got to get yourself a dip in that pool…

SEMO: *(Laughing.)* Fuck bro, you ain't changed a day!

MIRO: I should've brought her for Paora… He would've liked her.

ALBIE: To do what with?

EZRA: *(To ALBIE.)* What was she like?

ALBIE: There ain't much of her…

MIRO: She's 19 next birthday bro…and she loves me.

ALBIE: Only coz she don't know no better.

MIRO: She came halfway around the world to find me…

ALBIE: Smelt like jungle fever to me.

MIRO: That's not fever, bro…that's pheromones an' the juice I give off. They love it on me, that's what you were smelling…

EZRA: Probably couldn't tell eh, bro…past his feet!

Laughter. EZRA and ALBIE are at opposite corners of the hangi each with a container of water from the big bucket. SEMO is with EZRA and MIRO with ALBIE. SEMO and MIRO lift up their corners of the tarpaulin and ALBIE and EZRA throw the water in. Steam erupts out and the guys jump back before they seal the corners to allow the food to cook.

SEMO hands out a beer to each of the GUYS. Then lifts his in a toast.

SEMO: We are dogs…

All the GUYS bark out the 'Bulldog's grunt' (a part of the school rugby team's Haka).

ALL: Ko te puru toke…

Then they drink.

ALBIE: Bulldogs! That first big season…shit bros, remember that?

MIRO: The 42 and 2? Only two defeats all season… That was the best of us…

SEMO: We went clean the next season…no defeats, that was better.

EZRA: We knew it then. Knew we had it in us. Miro's right, that first season Paora had us, was our best…we took ourselves by surprise, bro…and never did that again.

ALBIE: Won twenty games back to back. When Semo ruled the number nine and *(To MIRO.)* you could run down more than pussy!

Laughter.

EZRA: Like the wind, dude…down that wing, you'd go like the wind.

ALBIE: The wind would come second. Do you remember?

MIRO: I can still go like that...

Laughter.

If I went back into training... Look at me! Look at me! Just coz you boyz are twice what you were doesn't make me past my best! Look at me...!

EZRA: Dude being active ain't the same as being fit. An' living on junk and juice, keeps the weight down...but it don't make you the Leautua [God] you were.

MIRO: Do you want to put the clock on me?

EZRA: No...

MIRO: Put the fucking clock on me... I'll bet you!

MIRO searches in his pockets for money but doesn't come up with any.

... If I had any I'd bet good money that if I'm not as fast over my best hundred, I'm not far off. Let's put the clock on that! Put it on!

MIRO has wound himself up into a state. It hurts him that the GUYS don't believe what he is saying.

Put it on!

EZRA: My mistake, bro... If you say so, you still go like the wind!

MIRO: Like the wind...

SEMO: (*Quietly.*) ... Out of my arse!

Laughter. MIRO, in a real rage, squares up to SEMO under the laughter but ALBIE gets in the way. ALBIE talks the rage out of MIRO, close to his ear as he holds him away from SEMO.

ALBIE: It's all good, bro. It's all good... Fact is that first season would never have been ours without you... The first time Nga Tapuwae had ever been there. No team had ever made that school proud like we did! Remember the whole college stopped for a day to pat our backs? Mr Reed told everyone to down their books, kick back their chairs...and take the rest of the day to celebrate us, what we'd done. The top team in the district… 42 and 2!

EZRA: That was when Nga Tapuwae dug its first pit…for us!

MIRO: But the wood was short.

ALBIE: You remember that? They were right on the food but wrong on the wood and the irons weren't as hot as they needed to be…

MIRO starts to laugh.

But Paora stepped up remember, took…who?

SEMO: Me and Jackson…

ALBIE: Went in search of wood and came back with plenty. Two or three trips they made. Everyone was so happy that no one asked where they got it. The irons got hot and when the hangi was laid we danced on the pitch to 'Candy Girl' and 'Billie Jean'…

SEMO: Till Mr Scott, the caretaker, started bitching…

ALBIE: … Scotty was marching across the lower field red like fire screaming for, (*As Scotty.*) 'The mongrels who'd stolen the lower school gates! They've nicked the bloody fences on either side too, the bastards!'

Laughter.

You remember Scotty…with his big head? The biggest head God ever put on a man!

MIRO: And the shortest legs!

ALBIE: (*Laughing.*) So short he had no room for knees!

SEMO: (*Laughing.*) The lower school gates were never closed anyway…

ALBIE: That's what Paora said, 'A gate that never closes…

ALL: …Is a waste of good bloody wood!'

Laughter.

MIRO: I was taking Mrs Rolston for a walk somewhere quiet when Scotty's noise killed the mood…

ALBIE: Try and stay with me here, bro… I'm trying t'tell you why the hangi's laid tonight… It's for Paora, because he loved his food slow cooked and poor…

MIRO: That's what you brought for him?

ALBIE: Dug the pit before I went out looking for you…

MIRO: *(To EZRA.)* What did you bring for him?

EZRA: I made guacamole.

MIRO: You made it?

EZRA: I made it.

SEMO: It weren't shop bought and then tipped into one of your mum's bowls and mashed up to make it look home-made?

EZRA: I made it!

MIRO: You didn't pay one of your sisters to make it and say it was you?

EZRA: I made the guacamole! From everything you need to make it to it being made, that was all me…my hands, I made it to Paora's recipe chopped and mashed… I made the guacamole!

MIRO: Awesome!

SEMO: Sweet…!

And MIRO and SEMO shake EZRA's hand to show how impressed they are.

MIRO: One serving for Charlie.

ALL: One serving for Charlie…

They all take a drink.

MIRO: *(To SEMO.)* What about you, bro…?

SEMO: What about me, what?

MIRO: What did you bring for him?

SEMO: We were asking about you…

MIRO: So it's me and you don't have nothing for him?

SEMO: No it's just you…

MIRO: What then?

SEMO: It's not for now.

MIRO: What is it?

SEMO: Maybe you should go and get something to bring back here and shut your mouth!

MIRO: I will, but tell me what you've got so I don't get the same.

SEMO: You ain't going anywhere and coming back with what I got.

MIRO: What the fuck is it, bro?!

SEMO: I told you, it's not for now!

MIRO: (*To others.*) Why isn't he saying?

ALBIE: Leave it let it be.

MIRO: Do you know? Does everybody knows what he's got for Paora except me!

ALBIE: I don't know!

MIRO: Why the fuck not?

EZRA: Bring it down, bro…my mom's ain't far!

MIRO: You know…?

EZRA: It's up to Semo what he does with what he has…

ALBIE: (*To SEMO.*) Mo tell him what you've got before this starts him up again, please!

SEMO: Don't bring please into this, bro…

MIRO: So you PI's can know, it's alright for you…but the Maori boys have to sit and wait?!

SEMO: That's right!

MIRO: Fuck you!

SEMO: No, eat arse…fuck you!

And MIRO tries to get to SEMO again. This time SEMO is calling him on and EZRA has to hold him back from the fight.

JACKSON: That is always the way. Get too many brownies in one place and sure as shit they get hungry for blood…

A silence as all eyes turn to JACKSON. Then from JACKSON to SEMO.

Is that you Semo?

SEMO: Don't I look like me?

JACKSON: (*Beat.*) How you doing…?

SEMO doesn't answer. He just stands and looks at JACKSON. The GUYS are unsure how to get past SEMO to greet JACKSON so all are silent and standing still.

The stand off is broken by MIRO. He begins the Bulldog's Haka. This Haka is part Maori (led by MIRO and ALBIE) and part Samoan (led by EZRA and SEMO). It is a celebration of the different make up of the team as well as a battle cry.

The GUYS execute the Haka with all they have, making the audience the opposing team. When they end the stage goes to black.

SCENE 3

The lights come up with 'End of the Road' by Boys II Men playing on the beat-box. JACKSON, ALBIE and EZRA are sat at the table. SEMO has dragged the large bucket of water, that held the sack-cloth, into the garage. He is putting the remaining beers into it to keep cool. MIRO is sleeping it off on the bed.

JACKSON has a pack of playing cards and is dealing them out into a large spiral shape on the table.

JACKSON: … It's why I was so late coming over here. I'm not the last though am I?

EZRA: More or less…

JACKSON: Just the five of us?

EZRA: That's all I could reach.

JACKSON: (*Beat.*) That's what he said, aye...us five? The rest of them were there to throw the ball for us to take the game seriously... That's what Paora said, aye?

SEMO: Yeah, none as seriously as you, bro...

EZRA: (*Beat.*) Walker, Maka and Franky Darling have all lost themselves in Oz somewhere. Kepa's around, but I hated him around us back then... I couldn't see the point of him around us now. Jonesy's got another two to serve on a eight-year lock-down, but he sends his love...

They lift their bottle to Jonesy.

ALL: Jonesy...

EZRA: ... Vitale, Blue and Davey all found themselves dead sometime between then and now!

JACKSON: Fuck, Davey now...?

EZRA: Got the wrong side of the booze...

ALBIE: Found him next to a woman that wasn't his, she couldn't remember him from the night before so the body stayed no name till someone heard his wife bitching him from over in Flat Bush...and put two-and-two...

EZRA: That's the life.

ALBIE: That's the life...

JACKSON: (*Beat.*) And Billy Jay?

EZRA takes a beat too long to speak and ALBIE saves him from the answer.

ALBIE: You're still looking fit't'fuck there Jacks...

JACKSON: (*To EZRA.*) Did you ask Billy here?

ALBIE: Someone said they saw him around somewhere...

JACKSON: Billy Jay should be here tonight, aye...

ALBIE: How was he gonna do that?

JACKSON: BJ'll feel Paora as much as any of us.

ALBIE: Do I need to draw you a map?!

JACKSON: A map...?

ALBIE: So you can find your way off fuckin' Billy Jay!

JACKSON: *(To EZRA.)* Was it that bad?!

EZRA: That was too far a reach, bro…!

JACKSON: … I'm sorry I didn't get back down here for you then. *(Beat.)* I heard five years?!

SEMO: He walked after three…

JACKSON: I'm sorry I wasn't down here…

SEMO calls over from the bed next to MIRO.

SEMO: He wouldn't have wanted you…

EZRA: I didn't want anybody… That's what Mo's saying.

SEMO: Don't think he is…!

EZRA: *(To JACKSON.)* I stopped everyone coming down to see me. I kept my family out, Semo came once and I begged him never again…but none of you boyz, so so it's done… Those were my years to do and I did them…

JACKSON: Paora…?

EZRA: *(Smiling at the memory.)* But for him… But for him Wendy's burgers and homemade guacamole…!

Both try to laugh at this.

JACKSON: Did he take any care of Billy Jay too?

SEMO walks over to the table.

SEMO: *(To JACKSON.)* How's your mum? You're asking about everyone else an' we ain't asked about you…

JACKSON takes a moment to take in the manoeuvre that has just happened. ALBIE and SEMO are, both physically and verbally, protecting EZRA from JACKSON's questions.

ALBIE: How's your mum?

JACKSON: *(Beat.)* … I went over to see her… I was saying that's why I was late getting here, I went by to see her. She's still over there on Tennessee…

SEMO: How is she?

JACKSON: … My mum? I was over with her just now…
(*Laughs.*)

EZRA: What's the joke, bro…?

JACKSON: I don't know, maybe it's not funny but she's just in
that one room over the under-house… It made me laugh
seeing her sitting there, living there in that one room with
the light on. The rest of the house is dark. I said to her it's
like the rest of the house is dead. All the life's moved into
that one room, by the kitchen… She's not even leaving it to
sleep these days. My brother's made something for himself
under the house, never goes into her from what she says…

EZRA: How is he…?

JACKSON: He has to work a little for it. If he wants a life, he's
just got to…y'know…

ALBIE: So everyone's good then…?

JACKSON: I just looked away for second, a second…turned back
and they're living like ghosts…

EZRA: It's been three years!

SEMO: (*Almost to himself.*) That's a long time in the life.

JACKSON: (*Beat.*) I came around Wickman Way on the way over
here. What is it about that corner? Coffee coloured brothers
stand there…getting mean drunk and making more noise
than they're worth. (*Beat.*) You ever remember anybody ever
stood up straight on that corner? Knew I was home when
I saw them guys walking staggered and all the words they
said to me…blurred.

ALBIE: What did they have to say to you?

JACKSON: Just how they remembered me… But I thought
they'd be the guys they were, aye. Y'know from when
we'd catch one to buy a bottle for us… Wiki, Big George
Waitu…and the fella lost his nose bitten off by David Mina.
I thought it'd be them, but half the guys there were younger
than me at school!

EZRA: You feeling old?

JACKSON: I remember Big George and those guys being old, when they come to mind...they're old, close to death...just using cheap wine and a fist-fight to feel like living!

EZRA: What are you getting yourself ready to say?

JACKSON: (*Beat.*) In my mother's house! (*Beat.*) You know the number of times I said I'd bring them out of here? My second year in Wellington, the club said they'd bring her out if I wanted. Find somewhere for them close by me, jobs. But she wouldn't come and my bro wouldn't come without her. They'd rather sit out their days in a dead house in fuckin' Mangere!

SEMO: Stop the clock! Who was timing that? Who was timing?! How long he'd take t'start bitch-mouthong Mangere? How long?!

JACKSON: Look at the turnout, bro! Look at what's left of us to remember Paora and tell me again about Mangere!

JACKSON reaches for his beer and continues to deal out the cards.

MIRO: 'Mange re'...

MIRO's sleepy voice comes from the bed by the music.

EZRA: You landed back with us Miro.

MIRO looks up and is immediately elated to see JACKSON. He rushes over to him as best as he can manage.

MIRO: Jackson Burns is that you?!

JACKSON: How's that short-term memory, bro?

MIRO pulls JACKSON into a big hug and drags him over to the music.

MIRO: I was just dreaming about you... You were the guy. I was trying to remember who it was, in my dream...in the dream I was having I was trying to tell someone who it was use to dance with me... I was trying to remember you and then... who do I wake up and see? Remember how we use to go...?

MIRO speaks as he fishes out a CD and puts it into the beat-box. All the guys yell their appreciation as 'Candy Girl' by New

Edition blares from the box. MIRO and ALBIE are immediately dancing. It is a dance from their memories, a routine that was born out of this track. MIRO remembers it best but ALBIE, then JACKSON and then EZRA soon catch up and are soon all in step.

Only SEMO doesn't dance. He downs his beer watching JACKSON dance with the other guys.

The track plays on as the lights dip to black.

SCENE 4

'Candy Girl' stops as the lights lift out of the black. The GUYS have positioned themselves around the table. All have a drink or are getting one. There is general chatter out of which we hear...

EZRA: Give me a name.

A beat as all the GUYS are thinking.

ALBIE: 'Little Big Paora'.

This has the GUYS nodding and applauding.

EZRA: ... I'll take that.

ALBIE: Gimme a name.

Another moment's thought.

MIRO: 'Daddy No Bucks'...

SEMO: 'Super Sperm'...

MIRO: 'Kissing Cousin'!

There is laughter all over the suggestions as ALBIE protests.

ALBIE: She ain't my cousin, bro...

MIRO: Look again, Bro...look again!

ALBIE: She is a cousin... (*Laughter.*) ...but, but...but it's third or fourth and so far removed that the blood is as related as not!

EZRA: Take a name, bro...

MIRO: 'Daddy No Bucks'...

223

ALBIE: OK…that's me. It's the closest to the truth!

JACKSON: How many you got now, Albie?

Shouts of protest, from EZRA *and* SEMO *and pointing with elbows.*

SEMO: The brother's been named. That's 'Daddy No Bucks' you're talking to…

JACKSON: How many children do you have 'Daddy No Bucks'?

EZRA: No…nah-nah-nah! Down in one, bro… The game's on.

JACKSON downs a bottle of beer in one and EZRA opens another and sets it on the table next to him.

JACKSON: *(To ALBIE.)* … How many?

ALBIE: Three… Mere is nearly seven now, Rongo's five and Marama's eighteen months.

JACKSON: All with Ripeka?

ALBIE: Don't confuse me with Miro. Yes with Ripeka! Who else?

JACKSON: Why, how many you got Miro?

MIRO: *(Beat.)* Give me a name.

JACKSON: How many?

MIRO: Give me a name.

ALBIE: 'Seven Off Five'!

JACKSON: You got seven kids?

ALBIE: 'Who Let The Dog Out'…

Laughter and the GUYS bark out the remainder of the song.

MIRO: I've got five kids…from four chicks. There's two…more that one mother says are mine but…five for sure.

JACKSON: Jesus H Christ, bro…

MIRO: Is that the name you're giving me?

Laughter.

JACKSON: 'Lock Up Your Daughters'…

SEMO: 'Lock Up Your Mothers'!

THE SONS OF CHARLIE PAORA: ACT ONE

ALBIE: 'Lock Up Your Brothers'!

Laughter.

MIRO: It was just a taste! I just tried that once to know it weren't me! Just once!

Laughter.

EZRA: It's 'Who Let The Dog Out'…

The GUYS bark the tune.

(*About barked tune.*) That too. (*To MIRO.*) That's you. Semo?

SEMO: Gimme a name.

A long pause as the GUYS think.

MIRO: (*Beat.*) 'Eachy-Beachy-Big-And-Bouncy'…

Laughter

SEMO: Is that it?

JACKSON: 'Jamoa Jammy Dodger'…

SEMO: What's that? Jammy what?

JACKSON: Jammy Dodger… It's a biscuit. They've got them in England…

SEMO: I'm a biscuit, now?!

JACKSON: Jammy… It's like lucky. Jammy, these London boys I hooked up with…for them jammy was calling someone lucky…

SEMO: Where's d'you see the luck around me?!

JACKSON: Alright, I'm just saying what… (it is)…

SEMO: (*Cutting in.*) Saying what?

JACKSON: (*Beat.*) Is it now…?

SEMO: Do you want it to be now?!

ALBIE jumps on SEMO naming him.

ALBIE: This is my 'Samoan Soul Brother'!

225

SEMO: I'm taking that from Albie, coz I don't know about 'jammy'...!

ALBIE: Taking what? Taking what from who?

SEMO: Taking it from... Where's my beer?

And SEMO downs his beer looking at JACKSON.

Just you then bro...

JACKSON: Just me...

SEMO: (*Beat.*) 'All Black And Brown'!

There is a long beat between SEMO and JACKSON that the other GUYS allow to stand.

JACKSON: You heard about that?

SEMO's take's a deep drink of his beer.

ALBIE: Is that true?

EZRA: That's what the whispers say...

ALBIE: (*To JACKSON.*) You got the black jersey, bro...?

JACKSON: I haven't been named yet...

MIRO: But...

JACKSON: But...the club says they see no reason...!

MIRO: Fuck!

ALBIE: That about says it, bro...fuck!

EZRA takes JACKSON's hand to congratulate him.

EZRA: That's what you brought for Paora?

JACKSON: I thought so, yeah...

EZRA: Proud...

ALBIE: (*In Maori.*) Amen.

JACKSON: I ain't got it on yet.

ALBIE lifts his beer in a toast. The GUYS lift theirs to join his. All except SEMO.

ALBIE: Paora should be alive for this... A Bulldog is gonna be in the Blacks.

The GUYS, *except* SEMO, *bark out the Bulldog's grunt.*

MIRO: Ko te puku!

MIRO / EZRA / ALBIE: Ko te puku toke!

SEMO: We should name him before we drink to him.

JACKSON: Maybe we shouldn't drink to it till I've got it on.

EZRA: What did your mum say?

JACKSON: I'm not sure she heard me.

EZRA: Did you tell her? Or was it like you just told us?

JACKSON: (*Beat.*) Give me a name…

EZRA: Shit bro, why you want to take the joy out of this…

JACKSON: Give me a name.

SEMO: 'Does His Shit Still Stink'!

ALBIE: … And the last of the joy just took a cab!

JACKSON: No…leave it, I'll take it…this night I am… 'Does His Shit Still Stink'…

And MIRO *leads the toast.*

MIRO: For the jersey he wears…covers all our backs!

The other bottles are lifted to meet his, all except SEMO'*s.*

EZRA: My Samoan Soul Brother?

SEMO: What, Little Big Paora?

EZRA: Are you gonna make me say it…?

A beat and then SEMO *lifts his beer to meet the others.*

MIRO: Game on…!

And MIRO *goes to the spiral of cards dealt out on the table. His hand hovers over the card at the outer edge of the spiral. He closes his eyes trying to sense the colour of the card.*

Black or red…black/red/black/red/black…black!

MIRO *turns the card. He guesses right, eg six of clubs…*

(*Celebratory.*) Yes!…

EZRA: Six swallows. All to one or spread out…

ALBIE: Picture cards are on you, down in one, yeah?

JACKSON: That's still the rule, bro.

MIRO: My six...'Samoan Soul Brother' two, 'Does His Shit Still Stink'... two and...'Little Big Paora'...swallow two for me, bro.

JACKSON, SEMO and EZRA all drink from their bottles swallowing twice. The lights in the garage drops out but stay up in the garden.

SCENE 5

Running into the garden to the side of the garage are SARAH and SONNY. SONNY carries a bottle of whiskey and SARAH a box (cake size) covered in a plastic bag.

They are both out of breath as if they have been running for a while. SONNY paces this way and that for a good few beats trying to calm his breathing. When they speak their voices are hushed.

SONNY: *(Hushed.)* Oh man, we are so wrong to be here, so wrong! This is wrong, wrong...wrong! Why did I say yes to this?!

SARAH: We're here now.

SONNY: Nothing good, nothing...nothing good is gonna come out of us being here.

SARAH: We were invited.

SONNY: Why would he do that? That's why I said yes. I know now, I remember! I wanted to know why he would invite us down here...at this time of night!

SARAH: It wasn't this time of night. It wasn't meant to be. It's this time of night because I had to wait for you to be brave enough...

SONNY: You don't think you need to be brave! You need to be brave!

SARAH: We didn't have to be so late...

SONNY: Sun up or night falls… Did you see anybody else looks like us from Walmsley Road to here?

SARAH: We're here now.

SONNY: Have you seen anybody else pale like you, that wasn't me, for the last half hour or so? Anybody?

SARAH: Stop it Sonny…

SONNY: One other body white like us…?

SARAH: Yes!

SONNY: Where?

SARAH: I saw a few driving in their cars.

SONNY: And which way were they heading?… Out! The opposite way to us! Night drops and most white folks, that ain't you, head out of this side!

SARAH: You've said that now.

SONNY: And tell me for what again…?

SARAH: You know what.

SONNY: I don't know.

SARAH: Yes you do.

SONNY paces around the hangi pit.

SONNY: What does he wants with us… Coz if it's just to eat dirt food and… (*Stops what he was going to say.*) … He can fuck off with whatever he's got planned!

SARAH: Ezra…his name is Ezra and he invited us, Ezra did.

SONNY: I know his name.

SARAH: I'm making sure.

SONNY: I'm not in the mood, Sarah…

SARAH: I know you're frightened.

SONNY: I'm not frightened… Of what?

SARAH: I know you are…

SONNY: And you're not? If I didn't come with you, would you have come on your own?

229

SARAH: When you're ready we should say we're here…

SONNY: Would you have come here if I wasn't with you?

SARAH: You're not here for me, Sonny…

SONNY: I'm not?

SARAH: No…

SONNY: (*Beat.*) What, you're here…? Why are you here for me?

SARAH: (*Beat.*) Ezra invited me to bring you…

SONNY: If it's about him…? You should've said that before because if it's some shit about him…

SARAH: Ezra…

SONNY: I can say his name!

SARAH: … Say it then.

SONNY: I'm going if you want to come with me.

SARAH: Ezra… Say it and prove me wrong about being here!

SONNY won't or can't say the name.

… Ezra who was there, where you should have been…

And SONNY is walking away. SARAH calls him back but still trying to keep her voice down.

(*Calling.*) Sonny don't! Sonny…? Sonny please!

SONNY has gone. SARAH thinks about following. Then sits in the dark at the back of the garden.

SCENE 6

The garage busts back into life as the lights come up. The GUYS are laughing loud and a good few beers further along in their game. The drink has reminded them of the fun they use to have together.

JACKSON is at the table. He reaches straight for a card calling it just before it turns.

JACKSON: Black…

The card is black, eg two of spades.

You have both of those 'Daddy No Bucks'!

ALBIE: Shit bro, I'm getting close to my limit…

ALBIE takes two reluctant swallows from his bottle.

MIRO: Let's have some music on this…

EZRA goes to the beat-box as SEMO reaches for a card. SEMO puts his finger on the card and waits for the music.

SEMO: Let the music tell me.

All eyes turn on EZRA. They all await his choice.

MIRO: Pressure, bro…

EZRA selects the track. As the intro to 'Pacific Colours' by Jamoa Jam kicks in SEMO calls the card and flips it.

SEMO: Red my boyz…red hot!

The card is red. The ten of hearts. SEMO holds the card up to JACKSON.

Take them all 'Does His Shit Still Stink'…

JACKSON: All of them to me…? Again?

SEMO: I don't need to get you drunk to fuck with you, Jacks…

JACKSON: So you're not fucking with me yet?

EZRA pulls SEMO into dancing and singing 'Pacific Colours'. SEMO smiles back at JACKSON as he goes.

SEMO: (*To JACKSON.*) That's ten on you and don't piss your skirt over it!

JACKSON empty his bottles and half of another one with his eyes fixed on SEMO.

ALBIE reaches for a card.

MIRO: (*To JACKSON.*) That'd bring me down… Tight as you two were, shit…that'd bring me right down!

JACKSON: Tight as who…?

MIRO: You and the Samoan Soul Brother used to be in step. Like one body with two heads…you see one of you the other was right next to him…always!

ALBIE: I remember you like that…

MIRO: That's how they were…

ALBIE calls the card…

ALBIE: Black…

It is red. The four of diamonds. He takes four shallow swallows from his beer while the others are busy.

MIRO: I just think it'll have to be you.

JACKSON: Be me what?

ALBIE is beginning to feel the drink now.

ALBIE: 'Little Big Paora'…you're the next pick.

JACKSON: (*To MIRO.*) Be me what?

MIRO: If you and Mo…

Without being told MIRO drinks from his beer and continues without missing a beat.

… You should want to…

JACKSON: Should want to what…?

MIRO: Tight as you were.

JACKSON: Back further than I can remember…

ALBIE: That's bullshit, bro!

MIRO: (*To JACKSON.*) You should want to get back next to him…

JACKSON: Let me say it… (to you again)

EZRA comes out of the song with SEMO to make his pick. JACKSON stops speaking at the sight of him.

EZRA: (*To JACKSON.*) What?

JACKSON: Nothing… Miro's making mischief is all…

EZRA: That's 'Who Let The Dog Out'…

SEMO and ALBIE bark out the rest of the song as they dance now to 'Pacific Colours'.

JACKSON drinks from his beer.

MIRO: Before this night is out…you two should take a few steps back towards each other…

A silence. JACKSON stops his chase as he finds himself in the middle of the garage facing SEMO.

SEMO: What have you got him saying for you?

JACKSON: I'm trying to shut him up.

SEMO: Shut him up saying what?

JACKSON: His landing-gear's not quite down…

SEMO: You lot think I should make more noise on the jersey?

JACKSON: It was Miro's mouth you heard.

SEMO: I think you've been gone so long you've forgotten how to be around us…?

JACKSON: Just get it said…!

SEMO: Get what said?

JACKSON: Whatever it is you're biting your tongue not saying.

SEMO: (*Beat.*) Tonight is about Paora.

MIRO: Fuck Paora!

All the GUYS turn on MIRO as one.

ALL: 'Shut Up Miro!' 'Miro don't!' 'Fuck you!'

MIRO: I say fuck Paora and fuck you two for not getting over yourselves!

EZRA: Miro, stop your mouth!

ALBIE: (*To MIRO.*) Come here!

MIRO dutifully walks over to ALBIE. SEMO steps slowly up to JACKSON picking his words.

SEMO: (*To JACKSON.*) How fast you doing the hundred in?

JACKSON: (*Beat.*) 11.2 and some…

SEMO: That's what's got you the shirt…

JACKSON: Y'got to be able to play a bit.

SEMO: Yeah…?

Then there is a silence between them, the rift still not healed.

ALBIE: (*Beat.*) If you fellas wanna go for tongues I'll turn the boys away!

Laughter.

SCENE 7

The lights come up in garden. SARAH is standing alone listening to the laughter coming from inside the garage.

SONNY walks back to the garden.

SONNY: (*Beat.*) I was worried about you on your own here... Or I was too scared to find my way back to the car, don't know which!

They both try to smile at this.

SARAH: (*Beat.*) I'm sorry...

SONNY: You don't have to be.

SARAH: I am...

SONNY: (*Beat.*) Do you even know the last time I spoke to him? Do you!?

SARAH: I don't...

SONNY: Well that about says it! (*Beat.*) I told him to go to hell. We had words, he called me up after something or other and I told him, 'Go to hell.' Said something about the fucking cheek of him...calling me about anything and told him to go to hell! He said...he said, 'That was more than likely!' (*Beat.*) The last words from him to me...

They stand in silence for a good few beats.

SARAH: We're here now...

SONNY: You think Charlie had something for me at the end, don't you...?

SARAH: I don't know.

SONNY: But that's what you think.

SARAH: I don't know.

SONNY: He didn't!

SARAH: We're here now, Sonny…

SONNY: It was probably all for them… (*Beat.*) I know what you hoped, but Charlie didn't wake up at the last and remember about me!

SARAH: (*Beat.*) At the funeral… At the funeral… Mum was like the years they'd been split were just days…

SONNY: (*Cutting in.*) Are you going to beat me with not going again?

SARAH: There wasn't a sound coming from her. It was weird. She was like in grief, every part of her was crying except for her eyes, bone dry…but the rest of her was wracked with weeping. Somewhere she'd made a decision about how she was going to deal with the day…and the effort in doing it, the pain of it all, stopped her mouth and shook her body all the way through. I held on to her, thought she might let go onto me, but she wouldn't cry… Everybody tried, words of condolence… Auntie June, teachers from Nga Tapuwae college (?), family, family friends…people she hadn't talked to in years…didn't know some of them…

SONNY: You said all this to get me here and I'm here…

SARAH: Auntie June said that it was Mum's love for Charlie. That's what she was not crying out…her love for him. (*Beat.*) But I'm not sure…

SONNY: What was it then?

SARAH: I barely thought about Dad for a minute at the funeral… I was busy holding Mum up and making excuses for you! Making sure everybody knew where to go after the church and had a ride to the crematorium, had enough to eat back at the house…didn't drink too much and holding Mum up and making more excuses for you…

SONNY doesn't have a comeback for her now.

If it was about her loving him she would've left some room for him… She would've let those guys be there and she…she would've made you show your face! She would've decided something else about that day and let it be about Charlie…!

SONNY: That's what you're doing here?

SARAH: Thanks for walking me down…

And SARAH doesn't wait for SONNY. She steps into the doorway at the back of the garage.

SCENE 8

As SARAH steps into the doorway the lights come up on the garage. The GUYS are re-enacting a game they remember. A particular try that won a particular game.

ALBIE has his arms over the shoulders of SEMO on one side and EZRA on the other. They are as if in the scrum with ALBIE as the hooker and SEMO and EZRA as the props. They use a rolled-up jumper as the ball.

ALBIE drops the 'ball' at his feet as if it were the put in. SEMO and EZRA grunt and step forward as if forcing the opposing scrum-line back. ALBIE hooks the 'ball' out.

ALBIE: Go, go…go! The scrum is won. I won the hook against the put in! We're in our own 22. It's the last game of the season. We've won every game up till now…

SEMO peels off from ALBIE and takes up the number nine position at the back of the scrum. He comes up with the 'ball' and marks out a weaving run, palming off a few tackles, but running on the spot.

SEMO: *(Over his run.)* … We are 19:15 down with maybe two minutes to play at most. There's not been a whitewash season in maybe 20 years and never one out of Mange-re… Only a try'll win it. I go past one, go past two…

All the guys are running on the spot now as if backing SEMO's run. The image should be of the five GUYS being the entire fifteen of their school team.

EZRA: I'm running out on his left ready for the off load…wide open waiting for the ball to come…we're still at our own

38. Does the bastard ball come? No! The bastard ball goes down in the tackle with the bastard who wouldn't release it…

And SEMO *goes down under a heavy tackle. He falls with his back to the opponents, shielding the ball. He sets the ball back for* ALBIE *(now acting as scrum half).* EZRA *and* JACKSON *are over* SEMO *as if holding the opponents back and forming a ruck.*

ALBIE: It's a ruck just our side of the halfway line…

ALBIE reaches in for the 'ball' and acts out what he is saying.

… Scum half fakes left but spin passes behind himself out to the right…

By the time ALBIE *releases the pass* JACKSON *has come out of the ruck and is behind* ALBIE *to receive the pass.*

ALBIE spins the 'ball' out to JACKSON. *He catches it on the run. Jumps one tackle, palms off a second as he tells us…*

JACKSON: The ref's looked at his watch once already. The next time the ball goes dead the game is done, the season is done. I come over the halfway line with their forward sniffing me out from the left and the back line stepping up tight in front and to the left… There's one pass, one…one chance…with seconds to go…

As JACKSON *speaks* ALBIE *and* EZRA *have run up between* JACKSON *and* MIRO *to make the back line.* JACKSON *releases the pass. It goes over* ALBIE *and* EZRA *to* MIRO.

MIRO: It's a looping pass, missing out the centres… I had to pick it up on the run…their inside centre's on me. He's got the feeling he's got the tackle… I spin out once I've got hand to ball…then it's just me and the wind!… Ttttrrryyyy!!!

As MIRO *spins away from the tackle and starts to run the other guys all step back as they shout* MIRO *on. The effect should be to show* MIRO's *speed and the distance he runs before he… Touches down for a try!!!*

And SEMO *whistles for the end of the game and the* GUYS *scream like the crowd as they run to mob* MIRO.

… That's us, district champions…

ALBIE: … Second year in a row!

SEMO: Unbeaten…from the first game to the last, unbeaten!

EZRA: That night the Bulldogs roared! Roared straight through to the next morning and beyond…carrying Paora up high all the way!

ALL: Ko te puku! Ko te puku toke…!

The Bulldogs' grunt is stopped by SARAH *stepping into the garage.*

A long awkward silence. The GUYS *try to look as sober as they can.* SARAH *waits for something to be said.*

EZRA: Hey.

SARAH: Hey…

And silence again. Then SONNY *walks in behind* SARAH. *He tries to meet the eyes that all look at him but can't. He just stares down at his feet.*

EZRA: Guys, these are Paora's kids…his son and daughter! (*To* SARAH.) These are the guys…

SARAH: I remember you, most of you…

The GUYS *nod their greetings or step up to introduce themselves, shake hands. Everything said now has a growing sense of awkwardness. The silences, the gaps where everyone waits for the next thing to be said, become more and more painful.*

MIRO: Miro…

SARAH: Sarah…

ALBIE: Hey Sarah.

SARAH: You're…?

ALBIE: Albie.

SARAH: I didn't know if that was you or… Jackson.

JACKSON: You're the first to make that mistake.

ALBIE: And the last, bro… God willing!

JACKSON: I'm Jackson, how are you?

SARAH: I'm good, y'know…

> *SEMO is next in line. SARAH smiles at seeing him.*

You're Semo…

SEMO: Yes I am.

SARAH: You haven't changed a bit.

SEMO: No I haven't…

SARAH: (*Smiles.*) It's good to see you…

SEMO: You too.

> *ALBIE reaches a hand out to SONNY.*

ALBIE: I'm Albie…

> *SONNY shakes his hand barely looking up from his feet.*

What's your name, Bro…?

> *And SONNY spits out a laugh.*

SONNY: Fuck!

ALBIE: (*Trying a joke.*) … What's that short for, bro…?

SONNY: Short for, 'fuck you'!

> *And ALBIE takes a beat to see where that came from in SONNY.*

(*To ALBIE.*) You don't know my name?! (*To SARAH.*) That's how little they've ever heard about me!

EZRA: He didn't mean anything by it.

ALBIE: (*To EZRA.*) What the fuck, bro…?

EZRA: Guys this is Sonny. (*To SONNY.*) We've been going at it a bit so don't take it wrong if we're a little off-centre.

SONNY: I won't then.

SARAH: Sonny brought something for your table…

> *SONNY lifts the bottle in his hand.*

SONNY: Sarah said you asked her to bring something for Charlie. So I brought his poison…

SONNY hands the bottle to EZRA who hands it on to MIRO.

MIRO: Bushmills… Kia ora, this was only ever good times… only ever. A glass for Charlie…

ALL: A glass for Charlie.

EZRA: *(To SONNY.)* … Can I get you one?

SONNY: No…

SARAH: He'll take a beer…

ALBIE opens a beer and hands it to SONNY. SONNY is slow to take it.

ALBIE: My mistake…

SONNY: Nah, I was just… I just needed a beer.

SEMO: *(To SARAH.)* Beer good?

SARAH: Beer's good, yes…

As SEMO opens the beer for SARAH. MIRO steps in closer to SONNY, cutting right across the atmosphere.

MIRO: See we've been on the spiral game. All of us have a drinking name. I'm 'Who Let The Dog Out'… *(MIRO barks out the rest of the tune.)* …

SONNY: What are you saying to me?

MIRO: 'Daddy No Bucks', Albie there…maybe he thought 'Fuck', short for 'Fuck You', was what you were bringing to the game.

SONNY: My name is Sonny!

MIRO: That ain't your disposition though is it, bro…?

ALBIE: Miro we're finished with the game.

MIRO: Game over.

SONNY: Yes it is…!

A silence.

ALBIE: (*To* SONNY.) I never knew mine to miss him, my dad, but… I don't know what it would do to me, losing a father…but we all feel a little of what you've lost in Paora…!

SONNY: Just a little though, aye…

ALBIE: (*Beat.*) More than you made it sound there, but yeah, I guess just a little…

SARAH holds out the the plastic bag, with the cake box inside, to EZRA.

SARAH: (*Beat.*) I brought this. It's a pumpkin pie…

EZRA: Yeah…?

SARAH: It's a special of my mum's…she made it actually.

EZRA: Did she…?

SARAH: Gave it for me to bring for the… We were chatting and I said you wanted us to bring something for my dad…

EZRA: Okay…

SARAH: … I said that to her when we were chatting. She wanted to know where we were going and I said we were coming here…and I was looking for what I was going to bring and I told her what I was looking for and she set about making this. It's a pumpkin pie.

EZRA: I've never had that.

SARAH: My dad loved it…loved how my mum made it she said.

EZRA: And she sent that for us?

SARAH: She did, yes.

EZRA takes the pie.

EZRA: A piece for Charlie…

ALL: A piece for Charlie.

EZRA puts the pie on the table. Another silence.

SARAH: I'm sorry about the funeral…

ALBIE: Well if the pie's good enough Sarah, you're forgiven!

SONNY: That's not why she made it!

ALBIE: Is she not like that...?

SARAH: Not like what?

ALBIE: Like someone who'd stop us from seeing Paora buried and then bake her guilt in a pumpkin pie!?

SARAH: I don't know why she did that, stopped you coming.

ALBIE: Yes you do!

EZRA: (*To SARAH.*) It's okay...

SARAH: No it's not!

ALBIE: No it's not! It was out of spite...

SONNY: (*Stepping up.*) Which one are you?!

SARAH: Only family went on to the crematorium, except for the priest... (*To EZRA.*) Wish he hadn't. He didn't know Charlie...pissed me off saying how we should remember him...!

MIRO: What did she say?!

ALBIE: What the hell?!

MIRO: You made Paora ashes?!

SARAH: What do you mean?

EZRA: Was your dad buried or burnt?

SARAH: My mum heard him say once, remembers him saying... that was what he wanted...

SEMO: She knew that for sure?

SARAH: She must have...

JACKSON: If it was his wish...

MIRO: No!

ALBIE: That's why we should've been there! That's why! To make sure he was put in the earth where he was meant!

MIRO: How would the sky know when to cry?

SONNY: What the fuck have we got wrong now?

MIRO: The earth deserved him!

SONNY: The earth deserved him, did it?

ALBIE: (*To SONNY.*) Was it raining?

SONNY: Was it, when?

ALBIE: Was it raining?!

SONNY: I don't know!

ALBIE: You don't know?

SONNY: I don't know, I wasn't…

ALBIE: (*To SARAH.*) Was it?!

SARAH: I think it might have…or it threatened to.

ALBIE: It should have rained. Whether the day was sunny or no. It should have rained. The wailing should have made the sky sad and the earth grateful…

MIRO: It always rains when a Maori dies…when a Maori is given back! It's what they tell the children, about the rain and the Maori's last journey.

SONNY: It can't rain every time.

MIRO: (*Angry.*) It's as true as truth…!

MIRO and ALBIE sing/chant a Maori lament. JACKSON bows his head in prayer.

SARAH: (*To EZRA.*) We didn't know if he would've wanted…

SONNY: Don't apologise to them again, Sarah!

SARAH: My mum said it's what he'd always said…

ALBIE: It wasn't up to him, that's what you lot don't know… He wasn't alone in the life…

EZRA and SEMO bow their heads joining JACKSON as MIRO and ALBIE continue their lament for PAORA.

SARAH and SONNY back away unsure what to do.

Blackout.

End of Act One.

Act Two

SCENE 1

Lights up on the area of the garage around the music. SONNY busies himself checking out the music and drinking his beer. He barely acknowledges the arrival of EZRA. EZRA stands, just out of SONNY's space, waiting.

EZRA sees the CD SONNY is thinking of putting on.

EZRA: Is that what you're into?

SONNY: I like this track I'm after…

EZRA: These are memory music. I got them out for the boys, from when we had time together… Public Enemy, man… just ripped at us! Heard nothing like it…getting away with saying what they were saying. It opened it all up…and it made you dance, ripped us up! You ever listen to what was being said… Chuck D, man…the last great angry black man…

EZRA reins in his enthusiasm seeing SONNY's cold response.

(*Beat.*) I mean he put it right in front of the backbeat…what he was saying…

SONNY: Small talk…is that what this is?

EZRA: You're not ready…?

SONNY: I'm just… What am I? I'm thrown…that you think there's small talk to be had between me and you.

EZRA: Like I said they're memory music. Shit that mattered.

SONNY: I just like the track and… I'm just in the mood!

SONNY presses play and 'Fight the Power' by Public Enemy plays. SONNY sits down with his beer on the other side of the music to EZRA.

(*Over the music.*) Are you going to tell me?

EZRA lowers the music a touch

EZRA: Tell you what…?

244

SONNY: You invited us here...?

EZRA: I told Sarah what we had planned for tonight and said she was welcome if she wanted to come.

SONNY: And that's all the invite was?

EZRA: (*Beat.*) What else...?

SONNY looks at EZRA. Then he ups the music again and they sit listening to the track for a good few beats...

The lights open up to include the rest of the garage. SARAH *and* SEMO *watch the dumb show being played out between* SONNY *and* EZRA.

SARAH starts to help SEMO *clearing the cards from the table. On the chairs and around the table are cutlery, plates, a large bowl of guacamole, bread... etc...*

SEMO: I'm alright with this...

SARAH: I'm good, thanks for asking.

SEMO: You are?

SARAH: Is that what you asked me?

SEMO: What?

SARAH: Am I alright...?

SEMO: No...

SARAH: You didn't?

SEMO: I said I'm alright with this, clearing the table.

SARAH: Right. (*Laughs.*)

SEMO: Everybody's been asking you if you're alright...

SARAH: The last couple of weeks, everybody...yes! I hear it said now when it isn't and answer out of habit, 'I'm good, thanks for asking...'

SEMO: Like you've been hypnotised into it... If they ask it enough and you say yes enough...

SARAH: Maybe that what's been done. (*Laughs.*) ...

SEMO: What?

SARAH: You just reminded me. My dad gave up smoking once. He was still with us at home then. I think they thought him smoking might be the problem between them. I think they hoped it was… Between my mum and dad…

SEMO: You mum doesn't smoke?

SARAH: Never has… My dad was on close to 40 a day and my mum was always on at him and what he was doing to us kids. So he gave up… Got himself hypnotised. You know how that works…they give you a suggestion, when they've got you under…they plant a suggestion in your subconscious I suppose. It's a bad taste or something you hate…that scares you. When you wake up and a cigarette is there you taste the bad taste or feel the hate or the fear. (*Laughs.*) With Dad the hypnotist or whoever planted that every time he had a cigarette or thought about having one he was being unfaithful to his wife, my mum… And it worked for a good month or so, but then something went off between them or it just got uprooted in his head because every time any one offered him a smoke he'd start saying, 'No thank you I'm married!'

Laughter between them.

… And it'd get worse. He'd see someone light up and think that they were being unfaithful to their wives or husbands. He pulled a cigarette out of my uncle's hands at a barbecue and nearly hit him for cheating on my Aunt May in front of everyone…! (*Laughs.*)

SCENE 2

The lights spread out further to the garden. JACKSON, MIRO and ALBIE are sharing a smoke. The strains of Public Enemy reaches them and plays under the scene…

JACKSON: They were invited…?

ALBIE: You're asking me?

JACKSON: Did you know about them…that they were meant to be here?

ALBIE: I didn't know until they were here!

JACKSON: It makes sense.

ALBIE: Does it?

JACKSON: Wouldn't you want to know...?

ALBIE: You think that's why E-zee hasn't said anything? Saving it for them...?

JACKSON: Makes sense.

MIRO: He met death... Awesome! Ezra was in the room with death. I want to know about that. (*Beat.*) There was an old queen... A royalty queen some way back in England...

ALBIE: What is he saying now?

MIRO: ...On her deathbed. Time came and death arrived...and she stood up to meet him. Got out of bed onto feet she hadn't stood on for months and told death, 'Welcome, charmed I'm sure.'... It was that virgin one they had with the red hair. (*Beat.*) You ever think what you'd say? When you knew death'd come for you...? What would you say?

ALBIE: I'd give him directions to your house.

Laughter. EZRA has come to the side door.

EZRA: You guys should come in back together.

MIRO and ALBIE head back into the garage past EZRA. JACKSON stops EZRA at the door to share the end of the joint.

JACKSON: E-zee, how's it, bro...?

EZRA: It's what it is, y'know...it is what it is.

JACKSON: Seems like...

JACKSON follows EZRA back into the garage. The others are milling around, chatting, the beat-box still plays Public Enemy, beers are being opened.

EZRA: We're gonna do something about remembering Paora. (*Beat.*) Anyone can start...

A long silence.

SARAH: *(Not confident.)* … Ezra said he thought you'd all bring food. Charlie loved his food…

SEMO: He'd love yours too if you let him.

A silence. (Who's next?)

SARAH: I remember his smile… That it made my mum giggle, when he had his smile on and smiled at her…

A silence.

EZRA: I thought we'd bring what we'd bring if…as if he was gonna be here. So we've got the green stuff…

Cheers from the GUYS.

SONNY: That's what someone brought to the table?

JACKSON: Guacamole…?

SONNY: Yeah.

JACKSON: Ezra did…

And SONNY is laughing. It is a bitter laugh, but he is enjoying it. The others wait for him to finish.

It is SARAH's arm on SONNY's shoulder stops his laughter.

SARAH: You okay?

SONNY: Yeah…

SARAH: Don't drink too much, eh…

SONNY: *(To EZRA.)* Why? Why would you bring that for him?

EZRA: The story? *(Beat.)* I got it from your fridge. I was looking for tomato sauce for my takeaway…

SONNY: This was at my parent's house?

EZRA: Right. You were away at school. *(To SARAH.)* Don't know where…

SARAH: Mum's mum if there was a game on.

EZRA: We were round to watch a game, yes… Paora had the whole team there so he had a reason to shout shit at the set. I was in the fridge looking for sauce and there was none. Just this green stuff in a bowl. I took a finger taste, liked it…spread it on my Wendy's and loved every bite I bit…

SEMO: How'd you even guess it was meant for your mouth, bro?

ALBIE: (*Agreeing.*) Shit didn't even look like food, still doesn't…

SONNY: (*Cutting over.*) And you told him so?

EZRA: Did I what?

SONNY: You told Charlie how you liked the taste…?

EZRA: Gave him a bite and he had to agree…it was the shit!

SONNY: And that was it?

EZRA: That was it.

SONNY: That wasn't it!

EZRA: That was it…

SONNY: That's not why you brought it to the table tonight!

EZRA: (*Beat.*) It's not all of why, no…

SONNY: Why then?

JACKSON: My mum'd say Paora had a smile like Christmas morning!

But SONNY is still going after EZRA.

SONNY: I'm right aren't I? That was you wasn't it…?

EZRA: (*Beat.*) That was me.

SONNY: Beat a team mate half to death in my mother's front room… That was you wasn't it?!

EZRA: That was me.

SONNY: Attempted murder! (*Ezra nods.*) Five years for you and Charlie, for pulling you off before it was murder, lost his job.

EZRA: That was still me…

SONNY: And this guy, this nearly dead guy…? Billy Jay, he did what?

EZRA: It doesn't matter!

SONNY: To you or to him?!

EZRA: It doesn't matter…because he didn't deserve what I did to him for it!

SONNY: I hear one side of his face is frozen and his brain can't make one of his arms work!

EZRA hasn't any reply to this.

But every last Sunday of every month Charlie would drive over to Paremoremo prison, bring you two Wendy's quarter pounders, with cheese…spread thick with homemade green stuff. He called it the green stuff…said it was what guacamole meant in the Spanish. (*Beat.*) He did that for you didn't he?

EZRA: Yes he did.

SONNY: Every last Sunday of every month until your time was served!

EZRA: I told him not to come again every time he showed up!

SONNY: Then that's the measure of you then isn't it?!

SARAH: You should stop now, Sonny…

SONNY: Cost him his job…broke him from his wife and family…

SEMO: That blame ain't his!

SONNY: …But every last Sunday he'd mash out the green stuff for Ezra's burgers and make that drive!

A silence now. Everyone waits for what SONNY will say next or what EZRA will say in return. Neither has the words.

SONNY turns away from the table and heads out into the garden. SARAH goes after him. The lights drop in the garage on all the GUYS except EZRA. He watches SARAH leave and stays looking at the side door as the scene plays out in the garden.

SCENE 3

SONNY is pacing the garden again. SARAH watches him for a few beat.

SARAH: I want you to stop it now.

SONNY: Do you think he has any idea, the shit he's caused?

SARAH: I want you to stop it...

SONNY: I bet he thinks he owns the grief that's ours too! That's why he wanted you to bring me here. So he could loan my father's memory for the night.

SARAH: Stop it! I want you to stop it! I want you to find some other noise to make that isn't raging!

SONNY: You saw how he was...

SARAH: And how you were and it's enough now! I've got to say this to you because...coz you're never going to see it on your own, without me telling you, making it clear but... My dad is dead! Mine too...and you and Mum and them in there are taking up all the space around that and...and I want you to stop it!

SONNY: *(Beat.)* I'm sorry.

SARAH: Don't be sorry, just leave me some room not to hate Charlie!

SCENE 4

Back in the garage. Lights up and EZRA is still looking to the door out onto the garden.

SEMO: *(To EZRA.)* You think they're coming back?

EZRA hears the question but he doesn't answer. He just keeps looking at the door.

JACKSON: *(To MIRO.)* So shit, Miro... Seven kids!

MIRO: You say it like that's a lot.

JACKSON: Scratching two off doesn't make it much less.

Laughter between them.

MIRO: I had two, actually it was three in one year. Three different chicks… So they just sort of crept up on me.

JACKSON: And it took till seven to figure out what was causing them?!

Laughter.

MIRO: That wasn't all me, brother. I'm like I've always been. I don't lie to a soul and I'm honest to myself… I'm a fiend, a succubus, I'm a dog! That's been my name around here for a good while now… Every skin knows me well enough not to make a mistake with me, thinking I'm something else…

ALBIE: You're a suck-my-what…?

MIRO: A succubus. A scoundrel… I'm a demon. I love to make love. I've got that about me…and women fucking know, bro, they know! I tell you, bro if I was to make love to you now…

JACKSON: Y'not going to are you?!

MIRO: (*Shouting.*) It was just a taste! I don't mean I'm going to or want to… I'm saying if I did you'd think I was a freak, a devil, like I said…but you'd come back for more!

JACKSON: I don't think I would.

MIRO: Yeah you would!

JACKSON: No!

MIRO: Yeah.

SEMO: I definitely wouldn't but Albie might!

ALBIE: I wouldn't go there with yours!

SEMO: Yeah you would.

MIRO: You'd all come back…

SEMO: Is that all you've got for the table?

MIRO: Might be. (*Beat.*) My memory of Paora, what's in my head about him right now… That Saturday, two Saturday's before we were supposed to go to Wellington for the try-outs, he was working us, trying to give us a little extra to see us through. I'm still carrying the night before and he's

ragging me all over the field. Turns on me and tells me…
I'm not good enough. 'You're not good enough!' Told me the
trip down would be a waste coz I didn't have it in me. Told
me to look at Mo to see what I had to be. And if I didn't
see some of me in Mo I should go find something else to be
serious about…

SEMO: (*Beat.*) He ran that one on all of us. He just put you
down for you to step over it…

MIRO: He meant it with me.

JACKSON: That's just what you heard.

MIRO: He meant it!

*SONNY has put on a CD, 'As Yet Untitled' by Terence Trent
D'Arby. It grows slowly as MIRO speaks.*

Thing I'm saying is… He was never wrong. Paora'd say you
can run under 11 and you'd do it. Your legs'd die trying but
you'd do it…because Paora wasn't ever wrong!

ALBIE: You think he was wrong about you…?

MIRO: I didn't stop to find out… That's the weight he had over
me and maybe he should've done better with it. I don't
know… I got what I've got. Might not be what he saw in
Semo but around here, the devil in me…it's twice as good
as nothing! If they gave a black jersey for it, bro… I be first
on the team sheet! So…fuck Paora, I came here to say that,
I wanted to say that… Just that… FUCK PAORA!

*(Optional ending to scene: It is as if he has heard himself say
that for the first time and it pulls him up short.*

*MIRO's silence gradually reads to the other GUYS. MIRO downs
the remainder of his bottle, steps away from the GUYS and tries
to lose himself in the music.*

*The music begins to envelope the whole space and the
audience. The GUYS stop where they are and let the track
play for them.*

*And MIRO is dancing. At first it isn't even that. He is moving,
trying to shake off the words and the feelings he let out to the*

GUYS *or maybe he is saying it now. Saying it in movements that he could not express in words.*

MIRO's *dance is about sex. He never lets go of his beer bottle as he translates the euphoria and the vacuity of the sex he has. About hiding his disappointment in himself.)*

At the end of the track all the lights drop to black except a single spot on EZRA.

SCENE 5

As EZRA *rattles through the map of his neighbourhood another spot picks out* SEMO. *He adds his voice overlapping* EZRA's *running through the streets he knows in Mangere. Then another spot find* ALBIE's *and a last spot joining* MIRO *to the others. All overlapping.*

The effect should be a wall of voices mapping out Mangere, street by street and bringing the map to life with faces, names and incidents from the streets they know so well.

EZRA: *(Quickfire.)* ... Man I stay in Mangere. I stay in Robertson Road... The first on the left, if you go down is Ashley and when you turn down the other street, down there is a dead-end street, that's Halswell Street... on the right of that is Mervan Street, on the left of that, further down is Lyncroft... On the main road along there, that's Bader Drive. *(SEMO starts.)* If you go down, you turn right, you get to Wickman Way...goes on to Garus and down along to McNaughton...

SEMO: *(Overlapping.)* I play for Manukau Rovers, our club is on Viscount Street, next door to Viscount Primary School. Our 1st 5-8 lives on Ventura Street, which is off Elmondon Street. Also off Elmondon Stree is my street Watchfield Close. *(ALBIE starts.)* The corner of Bader Drive and Cessna Place is our number 8. They've rebuilt their house after it was burnt down in a fire. He lost his younger brother. He was a good player, but now he's the best in the team, I suppose that's what happens in the life. Off Bader is Mascot Avenue where our to try scorer lives – Arona Fealii our winger, our wind. If I put a clock on Miro and Arona… I'll put good money on Arona.

ALBIE: (*Overlapping.*) We're on Portage Road, turning right onto Woburn… Ripeka's screaming blue murder in the back… I'm telling her, 'I can only go as fast as the cars in front!' When we hit Raglan everything stops! (**MIRO starts.*) Nothing's moving. I don't know what's holding up the traffic, just too many fucking cars in Mangere… Ripeka's ripe man, busting! Just back from the turn off onto Buckland that leads up to Massey, which then leads up to Middlemore Hospital, where we need to get…but we ain't making it!

MIRO: (*Overlapping.*) Man I know where they all stay… Jenny stays five houses down from the McKenzie shops, second window on the left of the front door… Lucy lives on McNorton (*EZRA cuts over.*) just off McKenzie Road. She stays in the brick house next to the alleyway…if you walk through the alleyway you get onto Buckland Road and straight across the road next to PIC Church is Elaine's place. Elaine mmmmmmmmm…! Stay on Buckland Road, go towards the big roundabout…

EZRA: (*Overlapping.*) … That's the power of the joke! In Paremoremo Prison I also met up with Eric Seme of McKenzie Road. Four years he'd been in Parry before I met up with him on my fifth month. (*SEMO cuts over.*) Funny how four years hadn't changed him one bit. He looked exactly like he did four years ago. I mean his jokes were the same and his…you know everything was the same! The same as the last time when we rank at the the club rooms near Walter Massey Park! The same as the last time I saw him in Mangere…

SEMO: (*Overlapping.*) … Through Robertson Road onto Buckland, next on the left is Wickman way… Number 24 is where our half back stays. It's a three-bedroom house, but that family must have like ten kids. (*MIRO cuts over.*) At the end of Wickman Way is Tennessee… Number 41, next to Jackson's house, is Toby our Captain. He lives with his grandma. Mind you she's never home, always playing Housie down at the Bingo Inn.

MIRO: (*Overlapping.*) ... Straight through and left at the small roundabout by the town centre and then left down the Fresian Road... There on Fresian lives Mele. She lives at the house with the home-made stone wall...you know the ones that all the Tongans have these days. Man, I can go on and talk about my world here in Mangere...

ALBIE: (*Overlapping.*) ... She can't hold Rongo in any more, he's ready for his birth...right there on Ragland by the church. I get Ripeka out on the drive (*SEMO cuts over.*) and we're into the breathing and the pushing, she's losing her mind with the pain...

SEMO: (*Overlapping.*) ... Every day she stops by to tell me about her winnings and how all the wives are living in Mangere...

MIRO: ... I'm at the centre of my universe here and everyday I find something new... Yeah, someone new!

EZRA: ...And that taught me how to grow. Don't you say anything against Mangere.

ALBIE: ... I didn't even see where they came from...out of the cars, from the houses, the shops but one brother's on the phone trying to bring the hospital to us...coats are rolled up for pillows for Ripeka's head and one lady's talking my son out into the world. Right there on the road, man...rush hour in Mangere! Don't you say nothing against it!

When SEMO speaks now the lights snap up and the voices fall into order. SEMO, EZRA, ALBIE and MIRO are all arguing with JACKSON.

SEMO: Fuck, it's just like that. I know everybody, man... I know my whole area and it's...it's safe man.

ALBIE: Why would I want to go and move somewhere I only know the person who lives right next to you?

EZRA: You might know everywhere where you're going, you may know the streets and everything but, fuck... I know everybody in all the streets around where I live...

JACKSON: I'm happy for you man, but that's not what I said…

ALBIE: That is exactly what you said. You told Miro to get the fuck out of Mangere.

JACKSON: You don't think Miro should see something other than these streets and the name he's made here?!

ALBIE: Why?

JACKSON: Because he'd do good to measure himself against something more than Mangere!

ALBIE: You've been out from home too long, out for too long!

JACKSON: Don't tell me that! Don't you tell me that!

ALBIE: You looking in like that fella (*SONNY.*) and his skin. There's nothing down here but coconuts and mongrel Maoris… That's why they build the shitponds so close, to keep the flies off our food…!

JACKSON: When did I say that, bro? When did I say that?! Miro did you hear me say that?

MIRO: I haven't heard you say how glad it is to be home, bro…

JACKSON: Well, coz…

ALBIE: Coz he ain't glad.

JACKSON: Glad of what? You boyz get out of Mangere for any time, anytime at all, you'll see what wrong this place does to you. I have carried my brown arse from one side of the world to the other. It's like the fella who went up in space and looked down for his home town, then saw his city, then his country, his continent and finally his world. You got a Mangere state of mind and it's tiny…!

ALBIE: You wanna come down from out the clouds bro and sniff the flowers! Coz where ever you take your brown arse you're still a coconut!

SEMO: I walk out there in Pakuranga and I'm a big brown guy and the pakehas are crossing the street rather than walking past me for fear of what I might do to them. I walk my streets and people stop me to ask after my mum and share their lives…

257

JACKSON: There's the Mangere state of mind. That's what brought you back home from Wellington…

ALBIE: (*To SEMO.*) Oh now brother Jackson's gonna bin your life because it isn't his!

SEMO: (*To JACKSON.*) You don't have the first idea why I came back from Wellington…

JACKSON: I know, your mum called you home…

EZRA: Mind your step there, bro!

JACKSON: I'm just saying there's more… If you're not scared of what it might do to you…there's more.

ALBIE: But that don't make it better…more is just more, it ain't always better… That's just fucking rude! You don't like Mangere? Fine, but don't shit on it, bring it up to what you want it to be… Don't just run off somewhere else and hide from it… Make round here where you want to be…

JACKSON: As long as you live your life here, Mangere will decide it…!

SEMO: That's what you think it did to me isn't it?

JACKSON: I think when we went down to Wellington to try out you were more likely than me. I brought the news of the jersey for Paora. That's what I had for the table, that's where Paora said I could go, I went… And I know what he would've said. He would've looked at you and wished you where I was standing…

SEMO: My mum is my heart…

JACKSON: That's why you came home. It's not why you stayed. So shut that shit up about your heart and your mum…it's tired!

The GUYS leave a beat for JACKSON's words to land.

Then SEMO is flying at JACKSON. The guys try to pull them apart but SEMO is fixed on hurting JACKSON.

The lights drop to black in mid-fight.

SCENE 6

The lights come up in the garden alone. Out there are EZRA, ALBIE, JACKSON *and* SONNY.

ALBIE *is removing the stone or the earth from the tarpaulin that covers the hangi.*

JACKSON *is pacing now. Walking off his anger from the fight. He feels his hands from the punches he has thrown and thinks about going back into the garage and* SEMO.

EZRA *guards the door back into the garage.* SONNY *is close to them silently smoking a joint.*

When ALBIE *speaks he is talking to* JACKSON.

ALBIE: You have to find whatever it is that decides your life. (*Beat.*) That's what Paora said to me… I went to him to say I wasn't going down with you and Semo to Wellington… Ripeka was late, too late to do anything other than have the baby. She'd been dressing baggy for months and I had my head on Wellington so I didn't put two-and-two…

EZRA: We put money down that you'd run.

JACKSON: Let me back in at him!

JACKSON heads back for the garage. EZRA *steps in his way.*

EZRA: That's said and done now man…

SONNY holds out the joint to JACKSON. *JACKSON refuses it and sets off pacing again.*

JACKSON: That's the shit that set my mouth running in the first place.

ALBIE: (*Beat.*) Anybody bet on me staying?

EZRA: … No!

ALBIE: I didn't know what Paora was saying to me. I had it figured out what I was saying to him… I never knew my dad and I didn't want that for mine. No idea what I was meaning but it was all I had to say… Heard his words again when Mere was born, all made sense… From her first breath, she decided my life… Her and Mangere. I love this place bro. I found myself here and I love it. (*To JACKSON.*) There's shit in this life, bro...but that ain't all there is... That's why Mo threw himself at you...don't fuck with what decides a brother's life...

And EZRA joins ALBIE in pulling back the tarpaulin. Steam billows out of the hole as the lights switch from the garden to the garage.

SCENE 7

SEMO is in the garage with SARAH and MIRO. SARAH is tending to a cut on SEMO's face with a napkin and a cup of water.

MIRO lies on the bed, his head close to the beat-box and Dido's 'Thank You' playing out softly.

SEMO: It was the second or third day... I phoned home like every day. I'd asked about everyone, said all I had to say...then I heard it in her voice. She never told me, never asked me to come home... I asked after my dad and there was something in her voice. She tried to hide it from me but it was loud when I heard it... I was on my way home the day after that...

SARAH: (*Beat.*) Were you right?

SEMO: Right about what?

SARAH: I remember those three days you spent with us... That's where I remembered you from.

SEMO: Paora caught me on my way back from Wellington.

SARAH: Held you for three days.

SEMO: You want to know if I was right?

SARAH: I listened at the door. He'd take you in the study so it was just you and him...shut us out. I listened at the door.

SEMO: He tried to talk me back down to Wellington. They'd called to say I'd be selected if I went back... Jackson was and I would've been.

SARAH: You were the better... I could hear Charlie saying so.

SEMO: Jackson fought with me to stop me coming back… Said shit that was best not said. Called me a fool. And I said everything I could to kill the best-friends we were, so he'd be glad to see the back of me and let me go…

SARAH: She didn't call you home…

SEMO: No she never did. But my dad… I have love for him. I have good love for him, but I couldn't leave my mother in his house without me. There was a way he was back in Samoa that he can't be here. His generation can't find much to be men with here… Work degrades them if they've got it and makes them worthless if they haven't. Men like my father…that's what they live on, worth and respect… I saw my dad take a fall once. Crossing a road, he tripped on something sticking up and hit the ground so hard he lost about a minute of himself. He woke up to see me, nine or so I was, crying for my daddy I saw bleeding. (*Beat.*) He grabbed me to him and whispered hot into my face, 'Dry them tears before they shame me!' (*Beat.*) He drummed it into me, worth and respect, worth and respect and then sent me off to look for it in the game… That's where brown boys find what their fathers couldn't find for themselves. But the more you get, the more worth, the more respect for the son… The more it shows the father what he hasn't got, is never going to get… Some days that's hard to take. My dad loved me, proud of me but…some days it was hard for him not to burn at what I was given and he wasn't… Some days my mum might catch some of his disappointment in himself. When I was away from home he could get like that with her! When he couldn't find worth he would turn on her… (*Beat.*) She is my beauty…and I couldn't leave her to him!

SARAH: (*Beat.*) Were you right…?

SCENE 8

The lights again switch from the garage to the garden.

ALBIE and JACKSON are removing the sacking from the hangi. EZRA and SONNY remain by the door.

EZRA: Why'd it bring all that shit out, that I made guacamole for Paora... Why?

SONNY: You don't like me much do you?

EZRA: Tonight is all I know of you. I don't know you...

SONNY: No you don't... *(Beat.)* That's not odd to you, that it should be like that? That Charlie would let it be like that?

EZRA: Is this still about the green stuff?

SONNY: The green stuff was mine! This is something pathetic... This is something I wish I didn't give a fuck about but...you call it the green stuff and I want to put my fist in your face! *(Laughs to himself.)*

EZRA: You wanted to hit me long before then.

SONNY: I came home from school with it in a bowl. We'd made it at Home Ec. We laughed at what it was called because he couldn't say it properly...we settled for green stuff. I got back the day after you guys had been in our house and it was gone, finished. He'd eaten it he said...loved it he said and wanted me to teach him how to make it again.

And here comes SONNY's empty laugh again.

... It was a good time. It was a good time that I remember clearly with my dad... Teaching him what he didn't know... laughing! He said it was the best cooking coz nothing needed fire! *(Beat.)* It was a good time... Then he gave it to you!

SONNY is quite calm when he says to EZRA...

What the fuck did he see in you...coz I can't see it! Are you one of those that didn't have a dad of your own?

EZRA: I don't know...

SONNY: You don't know?

EZRA: I don't know what he saw in me...

SONNY: Because, as I said... I can't see it!

EZRA: Maybe I just wasn't you!

SONNY: Fuck you!

EZRA: He looked at me, didn't see you...and that was enough! Maybe if you'd come to him when he called you to...he wouldn't have been right about you!

SONNY: What the fuck do you know?!

EZRA: I know that...

SONNY: You know shit!

EZRA: I know Paora didn't shut the door on you so fast as you shut it on him!

SONNY: And that's all that is written, how Charlie told it...?!

EZRA: That's what I know...

SONNY: (*Cutting in.*) No you don't! That's not how you'll set it down. No you don't! (*Beat.*) You ain't gonna make Charlie's fucking lie the truth!

EZRA's rage is up to match SONNY's now.

EZRA: He called me after you sent him to hell... Is that a lie? Is it?!

SONNY: ...

EZRA: DO I LIE?!

And something in EZRA hits SONNY as a sudden revelation.

SONNY: (*Almost calm.*) You want it all don't you? Don't you...?

EZRA: ...

SONNY: You had him alive, held him dead...and now you want the memory of him. You selfish fuck!

EZRA: That...that's not it!

SONNY: (*Cutting in.*) ... No! No you don't! You don't have the right! How do you think you have the right?!

EZRA: ...

EZRA and SONNY look at each other. Each seeing the other's almost naked hurt for a moment.

SONNY: You want to leave me out here with nothing. Not even what's mine to remember...nothing!

EZRA: Tonight is about Paora...

SONNY: (*Beat.*) I hope that lie keeps you warm! Hope it does you good...

EZRA seaches for the next thing to say. A silence screams between them. EZRA hasn't the words and SONNY has said it all. EZRA leaves.

SCENE 9

The lights switch back to the garage and SEMO and SARAH.

SARAH has finished seeing to SEMO's cut.

SARAH: Were you right...?

SEMO: ... What is it you want to be right about?

SARAH reaches into the plastic bag she brought and brings out a framed photo of her mother.

SARAH: I brought this for my dad...

SEMO looks at the picture.

SEMO: Jeez, she's all you, aye...?

SARAH: You think?

SEMO: You're all her more like...

SARAH: (*Beat.*) All him! Her life was all him... She was his wife, then his ex-wife...and now his widow. That's who she is now... Charlie Paora's widow. I think she prefers it to his ex-wife... I invited her to come with us, to come here. I think she started making the pie to hide from me asking her again. (*Beat.*) She made three...

SEMO: Three...

SARAH: Three pies... They kept not coming out good enough. It's how she stopped herself coming... She couldn't come with a shoddy pumpkin pie. I blazed at her for being silly, shouted at her... I've never shouted at her. She was always, has always been... I am safe in my mum. She has always done that for me... I've just got to be with her, see her looking at me...hear her call my name and I've always felt... I've never shouted at her! (*Beat.*) She cried... See she didn't at the funeral... (*Almost laughing.*) It took a soggy pumpkin pie.

SEMO: Not you shouting at her?

SARAH: I don't feel safe with her anymore. That's not what she gives me, not anymore. That was about him... I'm just getting to this as I say it but... I felt safe from Charlie with my mum. He really wasn't that good with us. We didn't... Oh fuck! We didn't make him happy. (*Beat.*) That's what she was hiding from us, keeping us safe from that... When he was happy, it wasn't us...!

SEMO's cut is tended to.

SEMO: Thank you...

SARAH: I don't know if I'm right what I just said...

MIRO: You could make me happy...

SEMO: Miro don't you ever turn that shit off?!

MIRO: It's off bro, I don't mean it like that... I was sitting all twisted up coz...and forgive me that I'm saying this but... I don't miss Paora! I think you should've buried him right but... He wasn't the best of men to me. He made us guys want to love him, made himself so big around us none of us could measure up. So fuck loving him...fuck love. I can make you happy. If it's happy you're after, I can do that for you...

SARAH: (*Beat.*) Thanks for the offer.

MIRO: It's there if you change your mind...

Something in the way MIRO says this makes SARAH give him a hug. MIRO holds her tight but it isn't sexual, he just needs to be held.

(*To* SEMO.) Tell me now...?

SEMO: What?

MIRO: What did you bring for Paora...?

SEMO's answer is stopped by ALBIE *and* JACKSON *coming into the garage carrying the food from the hangi.*

It goes straight onto the table and the GUYS *set about it.*

SARAH: This smells delicious. Who do I thank?

SEMO: Albie's the hangi man...

SARAH: (*To* ALBIE.) Thank you.

ALBIE: You're welcome...

EZRA walks to the middle of the stage carrying a piece of cloth, a mat or a covering.

He gets down on his knees, then bends forward, prostrating himself in front of SONNY *and covering himself with the mat.*

No one speaks for a good few beats as they begin to notice what EZRA *is up to.*

SONNY: (*To* EZRA.) What are you doing?

EZRA, his head bowed to the floor and his body covered, says nothing.

What is he doing?

And SONNY *walks away.* EZRA *stays where he is, not moving and not speaking.*

MIRO: (*To* EZRA.) Hey bro, you take some bad lamb?

No answer from EZRA.

ALBIE: E-zee, you alright bro...?

MIRO: What the fuck is this...?

JACKSON goes to EZRA *to see if he is alright.*

SEMO: Don't touch him!

SARAH: What's the matter with him?

SEMO: Nothing...

JACKSON: What's this about, Mo?

SEMO: I think he's asking for forgiveness. I think it's called a faatoeseaga…yeah, a faatoeseaga. It's from Samoa…if you have wronged someone, this is how we ask for forgiveness. (*To SONNY.*) He has given himself over to you, your will…

SONNY: Mine?

SEMO: Yours…

SONNY: For what?

SEMO: For whatever you want. It is you he wants forgiveness from. Until you take the mat…you own him. He will not eat unless you give him food to eat. He will not drink, unless you give him drink to drink… If you beat him he will take it without fight. He is yours to do with as you will…

SONNY: What does he want me to forgive him for?

SEMO: I don't know. He thinks you know.

SONNY: I don't know…

SEMO: He thinks you do…

SONNY: (*To EZRA.*) What the fuck are you playing at?

SARAH: Sonny don't!

SONNY: I didn't start this!

SARAH: Let him get up… Ezra get up.

SONNY: It's up to me isn't it?

SEMO: It is, yes…

SONNY: Then he stays where he is!

ALBIE: (*To SEMO.*) When did he come up with this?

SEMO: This is what I'm seeing him doing…

ALBIE: Why does he want forgiveness from him?

SEMO: It between Ezra and Sonny…

ALBIE: (*To SONNY.*) Why does he want this?

SONNY: You know.

ALBIE: I don't know.

SONNY: You know, you all do!

ALBIE: I don't know. Miro, you know?

MIRO: I don't know.

ALBIE: Jacks…?

JACKSON: I don't know.

ALBIE: Sarah…do you know?

SARAH: I don't think we should do anymore of this.

SONNY: Is this why you brought me here?

SARAH: No…!

MIRO: It's easily stopped. Get your brother to let Ezra off the ground…

ALBIE: *(To SONNY.)* None of us know…

SARAH: Sonny, stop this now. Give him what he wants and stop this now!

SONNY: *(To ALBIE.)* He knows… *(To SEMO.)* He can't talk to me?

SEMO: No. .

SONNY: He knows, doesn't he? He knows what he's asking?

SEMO: I think he does.

SONNY: Then he can stay there till he starves because I am not letting him up!

MIRO: Let him up.

SONNY: No! He won't have that from me!

MIRO: Let the brother off the ground!

SONNY: Or what?

MIRO: I'm not the guy you should say that to. I'm the last guy in the room you should say that to!

And MIRO is stepping in on SONNY. SEMO steps in between them backing MIRO away.

SONNY: Anything you do to me I will do to him. *(To SEMO.)* I've got that right, yeah…?

SEMO nods as he sits MIRO as far away from SONNY as he can.

SEMO: (*To MIRO.*) He didn't bring this on, Ezra did.

SARAH goes to SONNY and tries to make her words as private as possible.

SARAH: (*Beat.*) When?

SONNY: When what?

SARAH: When are you going to stop this?

SONNY: He just said it… I didn't bring this on…

SARAH: Do you mean to starve him?

SONNY: I'm thinking seriously about kicking his arse first… I'm thinking very seriously about that! (*To SEMO.*) Do I have to be around the whole time he starves…?

SEMO's answer is a cold stare at SONNY. SONNY goes to the CDs.

SARAH: Think again about this!

SONNY: Why, it's what he's down there for!

SARAH: And they're just gonna let you do that?

SONNY: (*To SEMO.*) This is just between me and him? What happen between us you can't do anything about.

SEMO: He is there for you. No one will disrespect that!

SONNY: Good. I think I want to dance now…!

And SONNY presses the button to play 'Jump, Jump' by House Of Pain. SONNY dances. It becomes a manic, warlike dance around EZRA on the floor.

All the others watch in silence.

SONNY ends the dance landing a kick on EZRA. All the GUYS step up to him but are held back by SEMO.

SEMO: No!

JACKSON: Look at you…!

SEMO: Let it be!

JACKSON: (*To SONNY.*) You come in here, bitter as a fucking lemon...you eat his food, drink his beers, play his music and now you're gonna spit on him in thanks...

SONNY: I hadn't got there yet but... (*He spits on EZRA.*) ...

Again the GUYS go for him and again SEMO stops them...

Y'know, you should be down there with him...you're just as bad.

JACKSON: You can kiss my brown arse for all the forgiveness I need from you! What have I done to you?

SONNY: That you don't know says it all. You...his fucking team! The time he gave you he never gave half to us... Less than that. (*Beat.*) And God forbid any of you could play his game! Then there wasn't enough of him to give to you. Whatever you did! Beat a boy half to death in his front room and he's there every day of the trial and every last Sunday of the month! Piss on a dream he's given you because why...? Because your dad didn't love y'mum enough not to beat on her...

SEMO turns at this but holds his rage back.

...and he brings you into his house and loves you for it. Get some girl pregnant you barely know and disappoint him and he buys you a pram...like a fucking reward! The worse you lot were the more he gave... Whatever the cost...a job, a wife...kids. I didn't give him one moment of concern. I did as I should have done... But he wouldn't have noticed, didn't notice...because he always had his back to me looking after you lot!

SEMO: And then he goes and dies with one of us...

SONNY: Yes he did!

SEMO: And that was us too!

SONNY: Yes it was!

ALBIE: I bet you hate the day he came to Nga Tapuwae...

SONNY: He didn't give a shit about who he was from until you fuckers reminded him. Woke up all that brown in him. He couldn't have married a whiter woman in my mum... He was trying to breed the Maori out of his line till he's down among you lot, you're calling him Paora and hanging on his every word... Then he's looking at us, like the biggest mistake of his life...! (*To SARAH.*) It was never going to be me... There with him, with Charlie...at the last. It was never going to be me!

SARAH: Sonny, please...

SEMO: ... To everything there is a season, and a time to every purpose under the heaven:

A time to be born, and a time to die; a time to plant, and a time to pluck that which has been planted;

A time to kill, and a time to heal; a time to break down, and a time to build up;

A time to weep, and a time to laugh; a time to mourn, and a time to dance;

A time to cast away stones, and a time to gather stones together; a time to embrace and a time to refrain from embracing...

I have seen the travails, which God hath given to the sons of men... He hath made everything beautiful: Also he hath set the world in their hearts...

A silence in which ALBIE, JACKSON and MIRO all nod at what SEMO has said.

MIRO: (*Beat.*) A little something for Charlie...

ALL: For Charlie...

SEMO: (*To SONNY.*) It's for the table... So you'd know. Whatever you saw him do to you...that's what he did for us... He put the world in our hearts. (*Beat.*) If you don't know the weight of that, if you can't see the consequences...then we'll take the time out to teach you...

SONNY: Fucking teach me! Teach me what?

SEMO: He put the world in our hearts...

SONNY: I don't care!

SARAH: Sonny!

271

SONNY: *(Beat.)* I want him *(EZRA.)* to speak to me!

SEMO: I speak for him…

SONNY: If he wants anything from me… I ask him a question and he answers. He tells me the truth and he has what he wants…

SEMO: That's not how it works…

SONNY: Then that's where he'll stay and rot. He can stay there for the worms an' he will never get anything from me!

SARAH: *(To SEMO.)* Tell Ezra to get up…!

ALBIE: He won't…

SARAH: Then lift him up, make him! One of you, any one of you…stop him doing this to Sonny! Ezra stop this!

JACKSON: It's Sonny doing this…

SARAH: Jesus you fucking boys! You boys! You jump around here making noises like men but you're boys…all of you. You're frightened to be men! It doesn't matter what Sonny forgives or doesn't forgive Ezra for… Look how sad it is how he's asking like he is!

SARAH waits for the GUYS to take in EZRA on the floor.

If your eyes were open you'd help your friend off the ground… You'd lift him up and help him figure out who he's going to be without my dad to hide behind or live up to… If one of you could see what it's all been about this evening…

ALBIE: Get off the ground Ezra!

EZRA doesn't move. ALBIE gets down next to EZRA whispering in his ear.

(To EZRA.) Sarah makes a point there, bro… This is looking sad now. Let's get up now…you don't need nothing from this pakeha pain-in-the-arse! Come on, bro… Let's get back up!

SONNY: No you don't! No you don't! He doesn't move until he has answered what I ask him…!

A beat. All eyes on SEMO. *He must decide to break tradition and allow* EZRA *and* SONNY *to speak directly.*

SEMO rips the mat from EZRA *and hands it to* SONNY. SONNY *can't or won't take it.* SEMO *gives the mat to* SARAH *and walks away.*

SEMO: (*To* SONNY.) Then ask him...

And now SONNY *can't. Now, with all eyes on him, asking reveals too much of his pain.*

ALBIE: What are you asking?

SONNY just stares at EZRA.

JACKSON: Is he gonna ask him?

ALBIE: Ask him or give him what he wants!

SONNY steps in closer to EZRA *but the question still won't come.*

MIRO: Tick-tock, bro?

SARAH: (*Beat.*) He wants to know... He wants to know if Charlie...

SONNY: How was he at the end?

EZRA is still and silent on the floor.

SARAH: Did Charlie have anything for him, for Sonny...

EZRA stands and looks at SONNY. *They stay looking at each other for few beats.*

SONNY: (*To* SEMO.) Tell him I want the truth...and I'll know it when I hear it!

EZRA: (*Beat.*) No...

SONNY: No...?

EZRA: He phoned you.

SONNY: He phoned me...

EZRA: You told him to go to hell.

SONNY: He said, more than likely...

EZRA: He called me.

SONNY: He called you…

EZRA: First time in weeks. There was always extra in my
mum's cooking and I'd take some for him. Semo's mum
too. I'd take him eats, we'd talk over the days, remember
faces…forget names. He'd cry for Bushmills…and some
days we'd have it and some days we wouldn't… But not for
weeks.

SARAH: Who'd feed him when you didn't?

EZRA: (*To SONNY.*) He called you…

SARAH: At the end…

EZRA: He just complained that his arm was hurting and then
he fell forward. We were laughing at a memory…and he
stopped the laugh holding his arm and fell forward…

SARAH: What did he have to say then?

EZRA: We went back to laughing. He was on the floor now,
in my arms, on the floor now…holding him…and he was
laughing at what they were gonna call One Tree Hill now…
It really tickled him, what to call One Tree Hill now the
mad Maoris cut the one tree down…

SONNY: That's what he said about there?

EZRA: He was laughing at some memory there. He didn't share
it all with me and then… He was just, all of a sudden, I had
all of his weight in my arms…!

SONNY: (*Beat.*) He said One Tree Hill?

EZRA: Yes he did…

Silence.

SONNY turns and leaves. The others watch him go.

The silence holds for a good few beats and then…

Blackout…

SCENE 10

In the darkness we begin to hear the voices singing 'Knowing You' by Jamoa Jam.

When the lights come up it is a spotlight picking out the faces in the dark as they speak...

SONNY: I pissed myself dancing with this girl. School disco, the last dance... I'd waited all night for the records to slow down... Shirley Austin was my world! I waited all night to dance with her. Music's down, she's said yes to me holding her and stepping around, but I need to piss. But I can't miss this dance with Shirley, so I fight it and dance and fight it and breathe her in and fight it and steal a kiss...and then lose it. The kiss made me forget to clench and as the piss ran so did I. (*Beat.*) Charlie found me on One Tree Hill. He waited at the school and then came looking. He just sat next to me, up the top, saying nothing... We said nothing for ages. When I looked over at him, his smile started laughing and he had a wet patch, just like mine spread over the front of his trousers. (*Smiles.*) That's One Tree Hill... where we wet ourselves until we laughed...!

JACKSON: Under the collar of the jersey. When I wore the black I had names stitched into the collar... Five sons and Paora. Miro was right. It was on all our backs...

ALBIE: And if his spirit was to bless me on its journey to the north, the next spirit north would be mine. But I would still welcome that last time with Charlie. That's the life, that's what Mangere does... It can take your spirit at anytime... anytime in the life. (*Beat.*) I told Mere that, wanted her to love the life all the same. I took her onto my lap...held her in my arms and I told her it all...as much as I thought she would understand, what my heart carried. I wanted her to know how my life was decided... How she decided it, how Mangere did...!

SARAH: I thought about that night, dreamt about it... Be doing something, something mundane...where your mind would wonder and I'd be back in that night...thinking I was there to forgive Charlie Paora. I thought that's why I was there, to bring Sonny and forgive Charlie... I wasn't, looking back on it I wasn't... I was just there to see if there was anything left of him to carry...!

MIRO: I never saw the boys again. After that night, they never saw me... I never saw them... It was something Jackson said... That there was more. That Mangere didn't have to decide... I put one foot in front of the other and when I stopped walking I was somewhere else... Mange-re and *vis ta vie*... Live your life!

SEMO: I brought the book to his table. I went to it to find something to say...and it told me, '... To everything there is a season, and a time to every purpose under the heaven...' I try to tell that to my team. The Nga Tapuwae first fifteen. I try to coach the game for them like he did. I try to put the world in their hearts...

SONNY: Skin the tomatoes, scoop out the seeds and chop into small pieces... Halve the avocados and remove the stone. Peel the skins off and squeeze the lemon juice over now to stop them turning brown, then mash... Add that to the tomatoes, grated onion and the garlic, stir in the chilli powder and the Tabasco and season to taste! (*Beat.*) That's it...the green stuff, cooking without fire!

EZRA: Charlie Paora was five feet eleven and a little bit...but he walked like he was six feet one. On his last breath, let me tell you what he said, at the end...he said, 'There is no redemption, Ezee!' Before I felt the weight of him in my arms he said that and... 'It ends with me. It's already been said...' (*Beat.*) He was wrong! If he never was before, at the end...he was wrong about the life. That's why I gave his son One Tree Hill, something that his father had for him. Told him that's what Charlie said at the last. I wanted to make Charlie right with him... Because Charlie Paora was only five feet eleven and he was wrong about redemption and wrong about where it ends... Where I go now, I know it's not already been said...

And all the voices are back into 'Knowing You', singing: 'In this world of sorrow and broken dreams', etc.

Blackout.

BROWN GIRL IN THE RING

Giving an Account of One's Self: Valerie Mason-John's *Brown Girl in the Ring* (aka *Sweep It Under The Carpet*)

By Professor Gabriele Griffin
(University of York)

> "I" has no story of its own that is not also the story of a relation – or set of relations – to a set of norms. (Butler 2005: 8)

In describing the genesis of *Brown Girl in the Ring*, also known as *Sweep It Under The Carpet*,[1] Valerie Mason-John states that it emerged from a workshop with the American actress and director Lois Weaver for which, '[Weaver] instructed us to bring a picture of our family'. (Mason-John 1999: 99) For Mason-John this was a difficult request: as she had been raised in a Barnardo's home, and had had an only intermittent and very difficult relationship with her biological mother (Mason-John 1999: 8-10), her sense of what her family was, was thus clearly compromised. She decided that 'instead of falling into negative mental states about not having a biological family, I looked at a picture of a jigsaw puzzle showing a group of white French aristocrats at a ball and decided this was my family. After all, as a Barnardo child I socialised regularly with the royal, the rich, the famous, at parties and events thrown annually.' (Mason-John 1999: 99)

This statement brings together the four key elements that inform *Brown Girl in the Ring* as a theatrical piece. The first is the notion of identity as relationality (accounting for oneself *through* family and *to* others – here the workshop director and, more extendedly, eventually, the audience). Indeed, according to the Background Notes to the play and its stage directions in this volume, the play is set to create 'the atmosphere of a [regal] court in preparation for the press conference' at which the central character is given one hour to account for herself

---

1 An earlier version of the play *Brown Girl in the Ring* based upon her performances of the piece was published in a volume of writings by Valerie Mason-John with the same title in 1999 (see references, page 429). In that volume Mason-John details the history of the making of this play which originally was called *Sweep It Under the Carpet*. The revised, unpublished version of the play I received in late 2007 also bore that last title. I thank Deirdre Osborne of Goldsmith's College, London, for making that revised version available to me prior to its publication in the current volume.

and prove to the world that she is the Queen. The second key element relates to normative ideas about family as biological entity or 'genetic fiction' as Donna Haraway (1997) has called it, and the problem for an individual asked to provide an account (in this instance, an image) of herself when she has no normative account to provide. The third concerns the transformation of the need and desire for a family, into a fantasy family, that simultaneously offers a critique of prevailing notions of family and an expression of the desire for distinction – in Pierre Bourdieu's terms (1979) – in the form of belonging to an elevated/'ideal' family as discussed in Sigmund Freud's (1909) 'Family romances'. The fourth is the metaphor of the jigsaw puzzle as an emblem of fragmentation, incompleteness and construction. This metaphor is both what gives the play its shape and serves as the vehicle for critiquing the race politics that structure ideas about family and belonging. I shall briefly discuss each of these in turn, utilising Judith Butler's *Giving an Account of Oneself* (2005) in particular, as the underpinning theoretical frame.

In *Giving an Account of Oneself*, Butler argues that 'there is, as it were, a sociality at the basis of the "I"' (75), which manifests itself in the dialogic relation between other and self, there from the beginning. This makes both a sense of the self and of the other possible, and without it neither self nor other are sustainable. That sociality of the self finds expression through the narratives of self and other of which we avail ourselves. *Brown Girl in the Ring* constitutes the dramatisation of a narrative of self, where the self – drawn both from the playwright's own life experiences but also from historical models of mixed-race children born into aristocratic families – is less a particular individual and more an emblematic figure of a particular kind of experience. That experience is one where connection, lineage, belonging and identity are denied. And that denial requires a constant effort from the self, both to construct and maintain itself.

Briefly, *Brown Girl in the Ring* is the monologue of Regina, the 'brown' girl in the ring, accounting for herself as she struggles 'with the unchosen conditions of [her] life' (Butler 1999: 19), of being a mixed-race girl whose family denies her existence: 'My poor Mamama never spoke again and Dadada castrated himself. I was packed off to relatives.' (306). This disavowal of relation produces a fragmentation of the self, indicated in the stuttering speech of the challenged speaker, and theatricalised in the play through the use of the jigsaw puzzle metaphor and the shift between different versions (child-adult-imaginary friend) of the self – the central character Regina. Mason-John describes this as 'the psychosis that many black people go through when growing up in a white culture' (Background Notes, 288). The figure Regina thus becomes emblematic of the ways in which people (whose belonging and identity is disavowed) are not only required to produce an account of themselves, but also struggle to establish and maintain that account – of an identity that is always precarious, provisional and under threat – through the pressure to conform to dominant narratives. That pressure itself of course points to the very relationalities that are disavowed. Thus to insist that there is no African blood in the Royal family, for example, is to suggest the possibility of its presence that then needs to be disavowed.

Brown Girl in the Ring, in theatricalising that struggle, explores fragmented selves and multiple relationalities, and challenges linearity and sequentiality:

- of different selves (the child self of Regina, the central and single character; her imaginary friend Lizard, portrayed through hand movements and changes in voice; the adult Regina); of different temporalities (past-childhood, present-adulthood, different historical moments);

- of selves and others not present on stage who challenge the selves actually portrayed;

- of the relation between performer and audience.

The sociality of the self, a condition of theatre which assumes a performer and an audience, is also inherent in the fact that a mother gives birth to us, and conventional cultural narratives assume the continued primary relation between mother and child. The disruption of that relation and therefore of the conventional narrative – as in Mason-John's own case but also in the case of the central character of her play, Regina, who claims to be the Queen and the black child of an aristocratic mother – creates the need to (re)invent onself. In the play, Regina is 'sent to the family psychiatrist, who suggested I re-create my family picture'. (Mason-John 1999: 106)

Such re-creation raises the question of quite what account or image one might create. Butler, summarising Michel Foucault, argues that '[t]he subject forms itself in relation to a set of codes, prescriptions or norms and does so in ways that not only (a) reveal self-constitution to be a kind of *poesis* but (b) establish self-making as part of the broader operation of critique.' (Butler 2005: 17) The codes or norms prescribe certain narratives as possible, whilst suppressing others. The demand for re-creating a family picture born of the suppression of the 'true' story of Regina's belonging – itself a violent intervention in the construction of, and an assault on, the self who is asked to suppress what is 'true' – is indicative of the norms that govern permissible narratives of self. Here the conjunction of race and class figures as a violent terrain in which only certain permutations and heritages are acknowledged.[2] In her portrayal of a black or mixed-race child being born into an aristocratic family, Mason-John drew on historical cases such as 'the French Queen Maria Theresa [giving] birth to a black child' (Background Notes, 288). However, and in ironic parallel with the experiences of the character Regina, the media responded to this historical implication with incredulity, thus reproducing precisely the fantasy of the logic of 'pure lineages' the play itself challenges: 'The media found it hard to believe that the Royal family had African blood […] the *Sunday Times* […] proved me right. I was called a political activist by this paper. I say I am a writer and performer who is interested in miscegenation, interested in family secrets and taboos.' (Background Notes, 288) The media's response echoed Mason-John's experiences of travelling with a friend and finding that 'nobody ever believed we came from England, they just looked and nodded, dictating Americano, Africano, no blacks from England'. (Mason-John 1999: 100)

During her travels, Mason-John was variously mistaken for: 'Joan Armatrading, Grace Jones and Tracy Chapman', and at one point, fed up with all this, she apparently 'forged Whoopi Goldberg's name'. (Mason-John 1999: 100) Here a lineage opens up of affirmation (being (mis)taken for a black singer or filmstar), distinction in the

2   This disavowal of certain heritages within royal families, which may occur for many reasons including miscegenation, illegitimacy and disability, was recently dramatised in Stephen Poliakoff's (2003) two-part drama series for BBC One, *The Lost Prince*, which documents the disavowal in public of King George V and Queen Mary's youngest child John who was epileptic and had learning difficulties. See http://www.bbc.co.uk/pressoffice/pressreleases/stories/2002/12_december/16/lost_prince.shtml.

Bourdieusian sense (being (mis)taken for someone more exalted/ famous), and belonging (all the referents are black) which in its own way is as problematic – because imaginary and born of a, presumably white, imagination that refuses to distinguish between different black people, instead constructing them as 'all the same' – as Regina's alignment in *Brown Girl in the Ring* with a white aristocratic family.

One way to respond to the struggle for self implicit in all these assumptions, ascriptions and disavowals of identity and belonging – that constantly needs to be fought by those who do not fit into the dominant narratives of self of a given culture – is to extend real-life experiences into 'a phantasy in which both [...] parents are replaced by others of better birth'. (Freud 1909: 223). Thus, 'chance occurrences' in real life such as 'becoming acquainted with the Lord of the Manor or some landed proprietor [...] or with some member of the aristocracy' (Freud 1909: 223) are worked into a phantasy, a family romance, of exalted parentage to produce an account of oneself that constitutes a form of wish fulfilment rather than an attempt at deception or an outright lie. This is precisely the mechanism Mason-John describes (Mason-John 1999: 99) in discussing the genesis of her play, with her decision to use the jigsaw portrait of an aristocratic family as her family picture, for Weaver's workshop. In the play that phantasy is married with historical narratives of the disavowal of a black presence in the European Royal lineage which provide a further real-life basis for the central character's assertions of her identity. The Background Notes invite the audience to decide if the Queen's account of herself – namely that she (despite being black) is the Queen – is 'plausible' or whether she is 'raving mad'.

Here a key factor in the sociality of identity and belonging emerges, namely, the notion that the affirmation of identity and belonging requires the other, here the audience, to believe the account one gives. The very fact of being asked to, or feeling compelled to, give an account already suggests the potential for not being believed, for disavowal of what is asserted. As Butler puts it: 'The "I" finds that, in the presence of an other, it is breaking down'. (2005: 69) Mason-John dramatises that potential in the fragmentation of the central character, her slippage between past and present, child, imaginary friend and adult self, of which she increasingly loses control, reverting in the penultimate scene to her child self, against her will.

Mason-John also makes use of a number of formal, theatrical devices to the same effect. Thus, the use of dance, song – especially the song 'Brown Girl in the Ring' – of repetition, of key phrases such as, 'sweep it under the carpet', of fragmentary language, incomplete sentences, changes in linguistic register, the reproduction of (child's) play within the play – such as peek-a-boo which directly addresses the question between what you can and cannot see or avow/acknowledge – all these contribute to the sense of ambivalence concerning identity and belonging that is at the heart of this play.

The most prominent of these devices is probably the jigsaw which is both a stage prop and a metaphor to suggest fragmentation and dis/avowal. The stage directions require scattered jigsaw pieces on the floor which, together with an incomplete jigsaw picture of the Queen's aristocratic family (one head is missing) and a red carpet, form the pared-down, central, on-stage materialisations of the dilemma of belonging, as dramatised in the play. This condensed semiotic indicates the play's preoccupations with how one lives one's identity and articulates one's sense of belonging, with psychic structures and their precariousness, rather than with the issues that inform the more conventional realist plays that have characterised British theatre, including work by Black playwrights. *Brown Girl in the Ring* thus belongs to an experimental tradition of theatre that includes works such as Ntozake Shange's (1974) *for colored girls who have considered suicide when the rainbow is enuf...* or Caryl Churchill's (2002) *A Number*.[3] Its experimentation is grounded in its focus on the psychic impact of having to account for oneself in a context where one is likely not to be believed or where one's assertions, indeed one's identity and belonging, are in question.

The play itself does not resolve this problematic even though the central character, according to the stage directions, walks off as the Queen: '*She has proved her point. She is THE QUEEN.*' This is evident in the media's responses discussed above to the first production of the play. The question is, to whom she has proved her point: herself, the audience...? The play, in maintaining that question, thus gestures, not least formally, towards the unending task of those marginalised by

---

3   I reference this play because it too has one actor playing multiple versions of self, and raises questions of accounting for oneself, albeit in a very different context. Formally, it is particularly the fact of one actor playing multiple versions of self and the specific use of language that align this play with experimental theatre.

dominant discourses, to account for themselves – again and again – to prove their identity and belonging, and towards the need for recognition and acceptance of their account by the other.

Brown Girl in the Ring

by

Valerie Mason-John

Brown Girl in the Ring

Background Notes

This script was developed with Talawa Theatre company and a half-hour version was part of their Zebra Crossing season. I was given the opportunity to develop this script, and in 1999 a full one-hour version was produced by the Oval House Theatre, and then toured nationally. This production was directed by Paul Everitt.

This play was inspired by the fact of African blood in the European Royal Family. For example, Queen Sophia Charlotte – married to George III – was of Afro-German descent.

When Louis XIV's queen Maria Theresa gave birth to a black child, the doctor explained her malady to the King by saying, 'The [black] servant must have looked at your wife'. The King is reported to have said: 'The servant must have given her a very penetrating look indeed'. Apparently this child was locked up and never publicly exposed to the world, though there is supposed to be an existing picture of her in France.

No family is of one pure blood, and the Royal family definitely do not fit into this brief. I was interested how some white people do their utmost to deny any link to the black race, and how some of them will simply 'sweep it under the carpet'. This play is also influenced by the mental psychosis that many black people go through when growing up in a white culture.

When this play was performed, the media found it hard to believe that the Royal family had African blood. A journalist from a reputable paper said: 'What our Queen, the British Queen? Unbelievable,' and hence did not cover the show. However, the *Sunday Times* went off and did its research and proved me right. I was called a political activist by this paper; I say I am a writer and performer who is interested in miscegenation, interested in family secrets and taboos.

As a writer I have taken this one small fact of African blood in the Royal family and have explored it in the genre of fiction, to create a story about a Black woman who claims to be Queen. Due to her childhood – being denied her biological right to parenting by her biological parents because of the colour of her skin – this character has developed a multiple personality. The three main personalities I dramatise are: the Queen, the Queen as a young eight-year-old child and the eight-year-old child's imaginary friend Lizard, who is depicted by the shape of her hand. However, at the character's most vulnerable moment she does become a chimpanzee at the zoo and also has flashbacks of her African ancestors who were paraded at circuses for people to view.

The subtext for the actor to work with is:

This is a story of a black woman who claims to be Queen. She is a throwback from the European Royal families. She has called a press conference to tell the world her story. It's the first time she has had access to tell her story and so it's as if she is in her Royal Court, or at the House of Lords or House of Commons. She has one hour to prove to the world that she is the Queen. The Queen is not mad. This is for the audience to decide. Is the Queen's story plausible, or is she raving mad?

Director / Actor Notes

There are certain parts of the script that can be revised to give the production a contemporary feel. For example, the show opens and ends with a Queen delivering her speech. These speeches, especially the opening one, can be revised to include the current political and social affairs in the media.

For example, the Queen's speech currently refers to the famous Clinton and Lewinsky tapes and to MP Ron Davies who was found cottaging on the notorious Clapham Common. These cases are outdated now.

The Queen is evicted to Broadwater Farm, the famous black housing estate which had riots; if the play were staged in another country you might want to draw a parallel.

Also there are references to commodities that may appear dated, and so do use more contemporary commodities. For example when the Queen is distressed by requests from her African descendant, people would be asking for iPods, Playstations, etc. Also if performed in another country be aware of cultural references – may need to unpack a little, and perhaps refer to the popular lagers of the country when the Queen is disturbed by her sons impregnating the Redstripes, the Carlsbergs, etc.

However, it is important not to change references to the champagnes, as this is an integral part to the play, hence alluding to the alcoholism in the Royal family, but also to the French link to the British Royal family and of course humour.

In other words, play with the Queen's speech and cultural references, while keeping to the integrity of the script, and not changing the filling of the script, as this is relevant no matter what year it is performed in. Just pay attention to referencing and those words or expressions that only an English audience would understand.

There are three characters, played by one actress – although the production could have two actors: one who plays the Queen, and another who plays the eight-year-old child and the imaginary friend Lizard.

THE QUEEN – she is extremely proud of her white European ancestry, but embarrassed by her African ancestry. This causes a huge conflict for her. She wants to be rid of it, as she believes it is because of her colour she is not believed to be the Queen. This conflict causes great distress and she often reverts back into an eight-year-old child who was humiliated because of her colour. The Queen is always at the centre of attention and in control of her court until she regresses into an eight-year-old child. She is embarrassed by this as she is in the public eye and doesn't want the world to see this. However when she regresses she is unaware of her public. There is an ease and naïve innocence; her sadness is her loneliness, and having no other children to play with.

YOUNG REGINA is the eight-year-old child – she is always in her own world. There is no conflict for the child, as she believes everything she has been told, to the extent that she is not black. The child is also connected to ancestral memory, and at times it is as if she is the black child in the circus and the audience have come to view this peculiar specimen.

LIZARD is the imaginary friend, which takes form in the eight-year-old's hand. The hand contorted with two fingers always pointing at her is Lizard. Lizard is her confidant, her only friend, and her conscience. Lizard is the child's conflict: he makes her see reality. Lizard is the young child's Royal wave; as the Queen she has a proper wave, and sometimes we see the conflict between Lizard and the Royal wave being played out.

Characters

REGINA
{
THE QUEEN

YOUNG REGINA

LIZARD
}

Brown Girl in the Ring was first produced at the Lyric Hammersmith in 1998 and then in a longer version produced by Talawa Theatre at Oval House Theatre, in 1999, with the following cast:

REGINA, Valerie Mason John (aka Queenie)

Lighting and design Crin Claxton

Director Paul Everitt

Producer Jennifer Dean

The theatre is set in traverse, creating the atmosphere of a court in preparation for the press conference. The audience enter to the sound of chatter. And a male voice calling out: 'Order, order, order'. On stage is the jigsaw throne, with jigsaw pieces either side of it. Leading from the throne is a Royal red carpet. At the end of the carpet are three more jigsaw pieces scattered either side. There is a picture suspended in mid-air at the end of the carpet. It is a picture in jigsaw form of REGINA's aristocratic family from which she descends. There is gap in the picture where a jigsaw piece is missing, it is the head of the black descendant in the white royal family. On the floor there is a backdrop of a slide portraying a white royal-looking family. There is a head of someone missing in the picture.

REGINA is dressed in a ballet dress with several petticoats underneath and bloomers; she is wearing ballet shoes, a white courtier (Victorian) wig. And jewels fit for a queen. She enters from the opposite entrance of the audience. The soundtrack of the 'Dance of the Sugar Plum Fairy' from The Nutcracker *begins to play. She arrives in a puff of smoke.*

Lights come up, and REGINA is giving a Royal wave to the imaginary crowds who have come to view her. She begins to approach the throne, balletically walking up the red carpet, and offering her Royal waves to the crowd. She reaches the throne, and turns to face her court, scanning everybody who is present. It is the first time she has had the opportunity to claim her place on the throne. She picks an ancient scroll from the throne, sits, unties the ribbon, and unravels this auspicious document. She begins to give her New Year Speech.

THE QUEEN

My Lords, ladies and members of Clapham Common, I Regina the Second, state that 2001 was an horribulus anus year. My husband and I visited the old British Empire, only to find the natives were bored of trading their land for our Bible. They were vociferously protesting for the rise of our dear Lord, God, Almighty himself, before being further annexed to war, hunger and poverty.

Pause.

However I am pleased to announce the reinstatement of the House of Queers, with the guarantee, that there shall be no hereditary Peers. The Right Honourable Ron Davies shall be my first life-long Queer.

Pause.

My Government intends to govern for the benefit of the cabinet and let the rest of the nation suffer. My ministers shall be allowed to climb the social ladder with the help of the Mandelson Foundation. It will allocate loans of one million pounds for the purchase of cottaging on the Queen's Common.

Pause.

My Government's first priority is to raise the standard of our prisons. The West Indies have been named as the new penal colony. Taxpayers' money will be invested in floating banana prisons in order to keep the locals happy.

Pause –

My Government has introduced a new bill containing measures to raise the standards of the Metropolitan Police. Equipped with band aids, bandages, boxing gloves, ropes and truncheons they will be licensed to kill properly. Undesirables will be kept of the streets by the new BIG UP Laws (Blacks in Great Britain Under Persecution).

Pause.

My Government has established a Department for International Development. It will publish a black paper setting out the Repatriation and Reparations Scheme. In brief any alien who agrees to return their native country for ever, will be allowed to take one stolen artefact from the cellars of my museums as compensation.

Pause...

Indeed my Government's second priority is the education of the new generation. Each home will be issued with one computer, and children will be expected to sit in front of itt for six hours minimum a day. Money saved by this new creative scheme will be used to improve the standards of public and private education. There will be no need for state schools in this country again.

Pause…

My Government shall also raise the British standard of participation in all national and international sports conventions, by barring all white children from sports education. It will agree to finance coloured schools if they only teach sports science. This will ensure a suitable and high quality education of the negro.

Pause…

The central economic objectives of my Government are to ensure opportunities for all, by keeping employment high and stable. A car fitted out with a mobile phone, laptop and fax will be classified as a tax-free office. If more than one person is found in this type of office, it will be called a Clinton Sex Shop, and they shall be prosecuted under the Lewinsky Tape Acts.

Pause…

My Government will seek to restore the confidence in the monarchy and integrity of the nation's political systems by upholding the highest standards of patriarchy and patriotism. Such social deviances within the 21st-century modern family have forced my servants to introduce stringent laws.

Pause…

Microwave weddings held at registrar offices shall no longer be legal. Couples will be able to marry if they agree to divorce after two years, and remarry each other within the following year. Homosexuals will be allowed to marry if they are able to biologically produce a child between two women or two men. These laws will be the beginning of the new family.

Pause – she stands.

We must try to be more of a family. There are model farms, now model villages, even model factories. I Regina the Second must be a model family for the nation to look upon.

She drops her speech.

I pray that the lies of the Almighty God rest upon your cheeks. As your Queen of the British Empire I am proud to introduce the new law of the land.

She gives a Royal wave, smiling at her audience, allowing them to see how happy she is. REGINA begins to greet her court; she approaches her court, keeping a good distance between them and herself. Offers her hand at a distance and greets them with a short phrase; before anyone can answer she is off greeting someone else – this is timed to the music.

So pleased to see you,
Was it difficult for you to arrive here,
Wonderful weather isn't it,
Of course you must be used to it,
That's a rather wonderful jacket you're sporting,
What a lovely hair do you have,
So delightful that you could make it,
And who are you?

THE QUEEN scans the crowd

Have the photographers arrived yet?

Camera lights flash. The soundtrack of 'The Dance of the Sugar Plum Fairy' is still playing. THE QUEEN, aware of this auspicious occasion, does a ballet to the music, showing herself of to the world. After all she is still Queen now, she pivots on tiptoes, turning around and around alone in her own world. She comically prances balletically back to her throne; she turns and becomes aware of a picture at the end of the carpet. THE QUEEN balletically runs to the other end and catches sight of a goblet resting on a jigsaw piece.

She picks it up and runs backwards to the throne, collapsing in a heap on the throne. (This is timed with the end of the 'Sugar Plum Fairy' soundtrack.) There is a change of light. THE QUEEN composes herself. With the goblet still in her hand she calls in an austere attitude for her gentleman in waiting.

Waiter, Waiter, Wait…Wait…

And on the abrupt impulse of 'Wait…' she sits back into her chair. She calls one more time, as she speaks she continues to move throughout this whole monologue in high stylized fashion, with the exaggerated upperclass English aristobratish voice. She speaks as if she is in conversation with the waiter – who is in fact not visible to the audience. Although the waiter appears to be insulting, REGINA is not fazed by it. In fact it all goes above her head. Important to leave space between each line so the audience can imagine what the waiter is saying.

Wait!

And the champagne goes flying out of her hand.

Oh how stupid of me. Sweep it under the carpet.
At long last.
Yes most perfunctory.
I'll have caviar…and rice and peas.
I said caviar… and rice and peas.
How dare you question me.
No I'm not mistaken.
Caviar…and rice and peas.
I had hashish for starters.
Oh and would you be so kind to switch the air
conditioning on, before you return to your menial tasks?
I beg your pardon?
Oh used to the heat, yes yes of course Australia was
absolutely marvellous last month.
Aborigine?
No No, you don't understand I am as English as Her
Majesty,
My title is Regina.

REGINA begins to regally wave, until she hears the next insult.

Not Vagina, Regina.
Exotic, um lychees will be absolutely divine for dessert.

Black Pudding, how preponderous I had that for breakfast.
W! O! G! My poor poppet you do seem to be losing it.
I'm most definitely not a Western Oriental Gentleman.

She leaps from the throne looking for chips on her shoulders.

Chip, chip, chip. On my shoulder? Which chip? On my
Shoulder, chip.
But it only rains cats and dogs in England.
Now scarper, enough of your verbal bowel syndrome.
I have friends to attend to.
Now where was I? (*An internal reflection.*)
We must try to be more of a model family, let's clone our
sheep, The Duke of Edinburgh, the Duchess of York, the
Earl of Scotland, the Princess of Wales, the Windsors,
Balmorals, the Tudors, the…

REGINA slowly regresses in her throne and begins to sing in an eight-year-old's voice.

YOUNG REGINA

There's a brown girl in the ring
Tra la la la la
There's a brown girl in the ring
Tra la la la la la la
Brown girl in the ring
Tra la la la la
I look like the sugar
In the plum plum plum

REGINA speaks in an eight-year-old's voice:

My mummy says I'm special
She says I look like the
Sugar in the plum plum plum.

REGINA with her shoulders shrugged, swings her legs playfully and impulsively (surprise element) jumps off the throne and rolls onto the carpet. REGINA bends her head back and raises her two hands in front of her eyes, contorting her fingers into an irregular shape. She begins speaking to her imaginary friend.

What do you think Lizard?

LIZARD

> Sticks and stones will break your bones
> But names will never hurt you.

YOUNG REGINA

> Sticks and stones will break my bones
> And names will never hurt me.

REGINA jumps on to her feet and says:

Really Lizard, really Lizard.

She begins to play hopscotch, up to ten and back down again, stumbles but manages to keep her balance on the floor. She engages with LIZARD again.

Look what I've found.

She begins to play with her petticoats – counting how many she has

One, two, three, four…

Slowly becoming aware of the audience – she becomes THE QUEEN again.

THE QUEEN

> My shrink says they're good for catching the flies with.
> Oh indeed he cost me Buckingham Palace.

With this retort she walks to the picture, pauses for a moment and then turns towards her throne. THE QUEEN is melodramatic with this next piece of her story. It is absolutely awful for her to remember the Queen Mother's death.

The dear old Queen Mother, appalled by my fate of an eviction order to Broadwater Farm, was found choked to death on a chicken bone, pickling away in a bathtub of Gordon's Gin.

THE QUEEN begins to approach her throne, holding court while she talks and walks.

Anthropologists fascinated by this primitive ritual, have placed her in the Commonwealth Institute for the study of the octoroon, a a a quadroon, a a a half
coon, sweep it under the carpet.

THE QUEEN arrives at her throne, turns, and reminds her court of its purpose.

Of course my Lords, Ladies and Members of Clapham Common, you're all here to observe the family's heirloom.

She takes a regal pose while still seated on the throne. THE QUEEN begins to pout a little as if she were having her photo taken. She picks up an antique mirror beside the throne. She looks into it and has a fright. She is shocked as if for the first time she has noticed her black skin – through fear she begins to shrink herself in the throne by becoming smaller. Then suddenly she breaks out into song, singing like an eight-year-old.

YOUNG REGINA
There's a brown girl in the ring
Tra la la la la
There's a brown girl in the ring
Tra la la la la la la
Brown girl in the ring
Tra la la la la
I look like the fly
In the milk, milk, milk.

By the end of the song she is crouching in her throne, still clasping the mirror. She looks into it again, and then slowly begins to rise to standing position. She is regal. And the camera flashes begin to flash again.

THE QUEEN
Henry the Eighth
Mary Queen of Scots
Elizabeth the Second

THE QUEEN is so proud to mention her lineage that she becomes intoxicated by her story and begins to slip up and mention the black ancestors to her disgust.

Kunte Kinte
Chicken George
King George the Sixth
Martin Luther King

Malcolm X
Muhammad Ali

THE QUEEN is able to get back to her white lineage – and metions the next with pride. But sadly it doesn't last long.

Queen Victoria
Marcus Garvey
Bob Marley
Charlotte Sophia
Sweep it under the carpet

THE QUEEN throws the mirror to the ground in disgust. She tries to compose herself. She is angry with herself for revealing the African blood. But she has no choice.

Now you see
I descend from a Royal lineage of Africans who were
captured and brought to France in the 16th century.
Indeed they remained very proud. So much so that they
couldn't quite understand why my Great Great Grand
Dadada was affected by the paler complexion. Lily Whites
so to speak.
The poor man brought a curse upon the family by
impregnating a Daz White a, a, a, Snow White a, a, a, Lily
White, Alabaster white, And that was the last we heard of
the natives.
Sweep it under the carpet. (*This is said with humour and
while sweeping her petticoats up too.*)
My Great Great Grand Mamama from the Dom Perignon
family was married off to the family queer, and packed off
to England to raise her predicament in secret. They also say
my Great Great Grand Mamama, Maria Theresa, Queen
of France, ate so much chocolate while big with child, gave
birth to a girl as black as the devil.

The QUEEN guffaws as if to hide a chuckle.

So when my Great Grand Mamama turned 18 she was also
betrothed to the next family queer in line, in the hope of
erasing the primitive strain.

She sweeps her petticoats up, masking her face. As she sweeps them up she playfully says:

Sweep it under the carpet.

She becomes the young child again. YOUNG REGINA *calls for her imaginary friend* LIZARD *in a child's voice – still hiding behind the petticoats.*

YOUNG REGINA
Lizard, Lizard, Lizard,
You can't see me
Boo.

She pulls the petticoats away from her face and continues to play with the petticoats.

You can't see me
Boo.

REGINA *jumps off the throne and begins to sing in a child's voice as is she were in flight.*

There 's a brown girl in the ring
Tra la la la la
There's a brown girl in the ring
Tra la la la la la la
Brown girl in the ring
Tra la la la la
I look like the currant
In the hot cross bun, bun, bun.

REGINA *begins to observe her court with the fear of an eight-year-old. It's as if she has flashbacks from her ancestral past. She is the black specimen on show at the circus.*

THE QUEEN *tries to compose herself. She wishes that the last few embarrassing moments hadn't have happened.*

THE QUEEN
Sweep it under the carpet.

The lights begin to flash – THE QUEEN *is affected – it's as if the paparazzi have caught her in the act – she tries to shield herself from the photographers – she freezes, blocking her face – and regresses into the child, engaging with* LIZARD.

YOUNG REGINA (*The persona of the child has taken over the adult Queen.*)

Smile at the people Lizard, go on, give them a wave, go on wave Lizard, wave Lizard, Show them how happy you are Lizard, go on Lizard, let the people see how happy we are.

She exposes her face, and awkwardly recieves the attention. Embarrassed she begins to sing in a child's voice.

Ring a ring a roses
a pocket full of poses
a-tissue
a-tissue
we all fall down.

REGINA collapses in a heap on the floor and begins playing with LIZARD.

Ah wogga matter, are you all white, nigger mind, go black home and eat your coon flakes and you'll be all white in the morning. You will Lizard, you'll be all white in the morning.

Still in her own world she stands and begins to play with LIZARD contorting her hands and arms moving them awkwardly

Eany, meany, miney mo,
catch a nigger by its toe,
if it's clean let it go,
eany, meany, miney mo.

She scans the crowd and notices the amusement and hilarity on their faces. She composes herself by internally reflecting.

THE QUEEN

Now where was I?

Slowly she comes back into the reality of the court, and becomes THE QUEEN. With authority she walks to the picture, turns to the throne and continues as if nothing has happened.

Yes by some idiosyncratic malfunction my great grand Mamama amd the family queer produced a fine specimen of a daughter, red curly hair and green eyes.

She takes up a ballet pose.

They named her The Pink Lady.

The soundtrack of Gaîté Parisienne *by Offenbach begins to play.* THE QUEEN, *so proud of this fact, begins to balletically waltz while telling her story.*

She looked so respectable, she was married off into a notable family. The Lansons of Monte Carlo. And between the two of them they produced four boys and one girl. My Mamama, she is claimed to be the most beautiful lady in Champagne.

REGINA *pivots showing herself off, as if she were her Mamama.*

Accepted back into the Dom Perignon family, she was brought back to France, and betrothed to my Dadada Moët Chandon.

Takes a ballet pose for her father.

She begins to move quickly as if she were at the masquerade.

Oh indeed it was a splendid wedding, masquerading for seven days and seven nights, and in the fall my Mamama fell pregnant, and in the summer she gave birth.

She pauses, and looks at the picture as if seeing it for the first time – she recoils.

Throwback!

Gasps.

Throwback!

Gasps.

Throwback!

Turns back to the picture with her head to the audience and on each phrase she turns her face to the audience. Building up into an African frenzy:

Throwback, throwback, throwback, back, back, back, Waiter I'm technophobic.

Throwback, throwback, throwback,
No I wouldn't prefer reggae music,
Back, back, back, back
I was quite happy listening
to Handel's *Messiah*, you toe-rag

Reaching a climax in her movement she spins, and the movement brings her back to her senses.

Now where was I?

She pauses as if she were going to burst into song she takes up the pose of the Royal wave, breaking into LIZARD, and back into the Royal wave. The conflict of QUEEN and child becomes apparent. The hand contorts from the royal wave into the shape of Lizard several times. THE QUEEN is trying hard to keep all her faculties intact.

YOUNG REGINA
Lizard

She breaks into a wave.

Lizard

She breaks into a wave.

Lizard

This last time she takes hold of her hand (LIZARD) and tries to control it by keeping it at bay – she walks towards the throne while speaking to LIZARD as an eight-year-old.

We must try to be a model family – let the people see how happy we are.

She sits on the throne with relief – and continues her story.

THE QUEEN
Well out popped my twin brother, blond hair and green eyes, Laurent Perrier Chandon.

Takes a ballet pose for the brother.

And five minutes later out...

THE QUEEN lets out an horrendous scream – she stands with eyes closed and arms stretching up to her chandeliers.

Hallelujah, Hallelujah, Hallelujah
Hallelujah, Hallelujah, Hallelujah

She opens her eyes and sees that her court is still seated.

Waiter, my guests are still seated,
Why aren't you standing?
Rise up you fools, Rise up you fools, Rise up you fools
I said rise up.

The sound of Handel's 'Hallelujahs' blast out, REGINA acts as if she were a conductor conducting her court to stand. THE QUEEN engages on an official walkabout – only this time not speaking but walking down the aisle offering her hand to be kissed – at the part of the music 'King of kings' she returns to her throne – and nods to the crowd (audience) to sit down. And as the music begins to fade she sits giving her official Royal wave. Still waving she says:

And out popped my twin brother blond hair and blue eyes and five minutes later:

The wave subtly changes into LIZARD and grabs her mouth she struggles forcing herself of the throne and says:

And out popped me.

REGINA bursts into hysterical laughter, so much so that it ranges from hysteria, into the macabre. She laughs for several minutes trying to speak at the same time. This revelation is the most important part of her story. They could not sweep her under the carpet. This fact is both hilarious and horrifying. The laughter is so much that she can hardly get her next word out.

My poor Mamama never spoke again.

She still continues to laugh.

And my Dadada castrated himself.

She still continues to laugh, but at the same time trying to compose herself, while laughing she returns to the throne and collapses on it as if she were exhausted by the whole drama. Her laugh fades out and she appears quite pensive and sad, reflecting on her past.

And I was packed off to relatives – the Bollys of Ascot.
They were very kind to me, they civilised me, taught me
etiquette, deportment lessons, elocution lessons. But the
problem began when they sent me to the family doctor, for
my apparent skin condition. He in turn sent me to the
family psychiatrist, who suggested I re-create my family
picture.

She gets up from her throne and walks to the jigsaw pieces.

*REGINA takes hold of one jigsaw piece on the floor and looks
at as if it were a mirror.*

So that night I tore out a page from the Bollys' album,
and where there were heads cut out, I pasted in
pictures like me from a native book I acquired as a
child. Strange that.

*REGINA places the jigsaw piece over her head, as if she is the
picture on the jigsaw.*

I woke up to Mrs Bolly passed out on my bed and Mr
Bolly screaming 'Sweep it under the carpet, sweep it
under the carpet'.

REGINA drops the jigsaw piece.

Sweep it under the carpet.
Baffled by the whole affair, I pulled the covers over my head
and woke up the next morning under an Axminster. Now
you see, Now you see, Now you see.

REGINA turns to the jigsaw piece, taking hold of it.

The music of Handel's Messiah *('Breaking the bonds asunder').
She tries rubbing the colour of the jigsaw and of herself. She
struggles in a frenzy, and becomes angry with* LIZARD. *She
stands, still rubbing at her skin, and calls for* LIZARD, *as if she's
telling* LIZARD *to stop.*

*While speaking and pointing to the audience her hand posture
changes, and she contorts her hand into her imaginary friend
LIZARD. She speaks to him:*

YOUNG REGINA
What do you think Lizard?

One banana, two banana three banana four, five banana, six banana, seven banana more.

Lights dim, and REGINA *moves in stylized chimpanzee movement, playing around and making chimpanzee movement. Lights slowly come up and* REGINA *makes the transition into a sophisticated aristobrat. She plays at being an adult.*

She is most vulnerable: her story has been told – and what next? She is only able to be the child.

Mr Bolly says I de de scend from the apes. He says if I go to the zoo I'll see lots of animals who are like me. Mrs Bolly says I'm different, I'm not like the rest.
I think she means the Chimpanzees at the zoo.

The chimpanzee.

In her deepest vulnerability she becomes a chimp. YOUNG REGINA *thinks it's a game. But to the audience this is proof of her blood-line. Ape to human.*

REGINA *makes chimp noises, moving in chimp style of the throne. When she begins to speak, she falls back into an eight-year-old's voice.*

REGINA *in her child's voice says:*

Lizard, Lizard, stop it
Lizard, Lizard, Lizard,
What do you think Lizard?

LIZARD
  Odd girl out
  Just remember to shout.

YOUNG REGINA
  But I am shouting Lizard, I am shouting, I am, I am, I am

REGINA breaks into song again, doing a humorous skit.

There's a brown girl in the ring
Tra la la la la
There's a brown girl in the ring
Tra la la la la la la

Brown girl in the ring
Tra la la la la
I look like the alien
From Mars Mars Mars.

Hey Lizard let's play
Tell me when to stop

REGINA puts her two index fingers together and slowly begins to separate them. Suddenly she stops, freezes into position, and visually makes contact with the white members of the audience.

Ding dong, ding dong,
Your nose is this long.

REGINA chases LIZARD onto the throne, she explores it like a child bouncing up and down on it and humorously bursts into song doing a short skit.

There's a brown girl in the ring
Tra la la la la
There's a brown girl in the ring
Tra la la la la la la
Brown girl in the ring
Tra la la la la
I look like the golly
On the Jam jar jar jar.

She is naively very proud of this. REGINA stands om the throne, bends her head back and raises her two hands in front of her eyes, contorting her fingers into an irregular shape. She begins speaking to her imaginary friend again:

My mummy says I can't be Snow White, or Sleeping Beauty
but I can be the Big Bad Wolf or the Ugly Duckling.
What do you think Lizard?

LIZARD
    All black girls
    Have got the best curls

YOUNG REGINA
    But I'm not black Lizard,

I'm not, I'm not,
I'm coloured, so there.
We're all coloured
My mummy says I'm coloured so there.

She says I'm coffee-coloured
Just like Nescafé.
She says I'm special
So there.
Coz coz Santa brought me down
The chimney on Christmas day.
My mummy said when I was a baby,
I ate all the carrot tops,
Which made my hair go curly, wurly, wurly.
I'm not black Lizard.

YOUNG REGINA jumps of the throne and begins to respond physically to what she is saying.

My mummy named me after the Queen,
She did Lizard, She did,
She wants me to walk like her,
Talk like her,
Live like her,
I am the Queen, I am the Queen, I am the Queen.

REGINA struggles with LIZARD and her Royal wave.

I'm not black Lizard!!!!!!

And then she breaks into a Royal wave, this is repeated several times, until LIZARD forces REGINA into her seat.

There's a brown girl in the ring
Tra la la la la
There's a brown girl in the ring
Tra la la la la la la
Brown girl in the ring
Tra la la la la
I look like the mould
In the cheese, cheese, cheese.

The adult (QUEEN) begins to emerge again.

THE QUEEN
Sweep it under the Carpet.

Sits in throne. But her mental states are quite jarring. Under pressure to to prove that she is in fact THE QUEEN, her story becomes jumbled.

Now you see I descend from a royal sewage of Gorgonzollas oh indeed they remained very strong, until they were mistaken for gorillas.
Sweep it under the carpet.
My blue blood comes from an erroneous lineage of Cheddars, a, a, a, the Bries, a, a, a, the Stiltons, a, a, a, Cambozolas and that was the last we heard of the Gorgonzollas.
Sweep it under the carpet.

THE QUEEN sweeps herself around the throne, landing upside down, and speaking from this position.

Indeed I am the only sane, surviving member of the Royal family. Oh yes.

She swings her legs around and leaning on the throne she continues to speak.

I was found, conducting on the number 69 bus, while rapping the National Anthem of course.

REGINA gets up from the throne and entangles herself in the petticoats rapping the National Anthem. The QUEEN becomes melodramatic again. She has remembered an important part of her story. But it is excruciating to retell it and reveal some of the embarrassing bits about her family.

Oh Indeed, it was the same year that poor Prince Charlie was incarcerated in a lunatic asylum, after being spotted stalking my bus, naked, waving the crown jewels above his head, screaming 'Long live the Queen, Long live the Queen, Long live the Queen'.

THE QUEEN physically responds to this story within the context of the dying swan. Music is playing from 'The Dying Swan'.

He never ever recovered from the death of the Royal Family, who died after expectorating LSD, sent by well-wishers, while meeting on the eve of the millennium at Windsor Castle, to discuss the future of the Monarchy.
Sweep it under the carpet.

THE QUEEN balletically references the dying swan. The music fades out and there is stillness. A spot light on the crumpled-up QUEEN. After a few seconds an eight-year-old voice begins to sing. She raises herself up and sits on the floor cross-legged.

YOUNG REGINA

There's a brown girl in the ring
Tra la la la la
There's a brown girl in the ring
Tra la la la la la la
Brown girl in the ring
Tra la la la la
I look like the brown
on the tin foil foil foil

THE QUEEN emerges again.

THE QUEEN

Sweep it under the carpet.

The QUEEN stands and moves to her throne, sits and composes herself for the camera.

Indeed one month of shitting on the throne, has left me penniless.
Descendants of my Great, Great, Gran Dadada, have sprung up like weeds. Letters from Africa are requesting mobile phones, BMWs, Nike shoes, Ray Bans, Kentucky Fried Chicken, weave-ons and S-curls.

REGINA moves off the throne and becomes quite frantic as she walks up and down. There is music in the background. As if each request hits her in the face. She can't bear to reveal what has happened to her current family. She can hardly say the words 'Redstripes', 'Tennants', 'Carlsbergs'.

My four sons have caused a major embarrassment, by impregnating the Redstripes, Tennants and Carlsbergs with their 'Sperms'. Their children have been given the title the Special Brews of London.

I've had no choice but to set up a trust, Her Majesty's Posse, for the welfare of their 'Seeds'.

Sweep it under the carpet.

A smile of relief emerges. She takes hold of her petticoats in both hands and becomes Jesus Christ on the cross offering her petticoats as the blood and bread as the body of Christ.

Indeed my dear brother Laurent Perrier Chandon, has saved the day by inspiring the popularity of the church. He has introduced Rizlas [cigarette papers] as the body of Christ, and brandy as the blood of Christ.

Now you see I am the Queen, descending from a Royal lineage of Africans, a, a, a, Palm Oils, a, a, a, Moët Chandons, a, a, a, Cassava Leaves, a, a, a, Gorgonzolas, a, a, a, Maggi Sauces, a, a, a, Special Brews, and that was the very, very, very, last we heard of the natives.

Sweep it under the carpet. (*As if to get rid of her mistakes she has just revealed.*)

She sweeps her petticoats over the face and speaks.

Now where was I?

THE QUEEN becomes sombre. It is as if there is an integration of all her personalities. There is music in the background.

Hello, Hello, Hello, Hello
Lizard, Lizard, Lizard
My shrink says I need an electric shock.

She pulls her skirt down, revealing a statuesque regal manner, and begins to move in a hypnotic manner. She sits opposite the throne at the other end of the red carpet near the picture.

I took stock.
My shrink says all negroes are manic,
I didn't panic.
My shrink says I need a rest,
I failed his test.
My shrink says, negroes just don't seem to have brains,
I didn't complain.

My shrink says I should be grateful,
I was resentful.
My shrink says all negroes are aggressive.
I let him live.
My shrink says I've got a chip on my shoulder,
I began to smoulder.
My shrink says I am depressed,
I was distressed.
My shrink says I should be thankful,
I was disdainful.
My shrink says I need education,
I asked for segregation.
My shrink says I've got marijuana psychosis,
I smoked his prognosis.
My shrink says I belong in the gutter,
I began to mutter.
My shrink says I shouldn't be seen,
I reminded him I am the Queen.
My shrink says I'll end up scrubbing floors,
I didn't speak any more.

REGINA becomes quite child-like, begins to act out of character, looking under the throne, behind it, in front of it.

Sweep it under the carpet.
Sweep it under the carpet.

YOUNG REGINA
What do you think Lizard?

As she speaks she mimes the words too.

LIZARD
I think
Your shrink
Stinks.

She speaks again in her child voice.

YOUNG REGINA
Sweep him under the carpet Regina.

LIZARD pulls her nose and drags her under the throne.

There's a brown girl in the ring
Tra la la la lah
There's a brown girl in the ring
Tra la la la la la la
Brown girl in the ring
Tra la la la la
I look like the patient
behind bars, bars, bars.

She is both the child and adult, this image represents enslavement, institutionalisation and the ridicule of black people.

LIZARD speaks to her through the bars, LIZARD represents the shrink, all the people who have oppressed her.

LIZARD

Smile at the people REGINA, wave at the people Regina, show the people how happy you are.

THE QUEEN

Now you see,
My shrink says,
I need pills,
I pushed him off the hill.
Sweep it under the carpet.

Music from the music box – 'Für Elise' – blasts out and REGINA begins to dance as a ballerina, oblivious to the audience. She is playing at being an adult. She moves to the throne. Sits back on it. And clearly is THE QUEEN:

As your new Queen of England I am sworn under oath to carry out the wishes of the late Queen Elizabeth herself. She has requested that the Fayeds be written out of history, and Dodi be referred to as the imaginary consort of the late deluded Princess of Wales.
That if Michael Jackson becomes the shade of the English pink rose, he may be classified as an authentic British subject.

315

That any books published alluding to the delicate male
friendships of the late Prince Andrew be banned and passed
off as a mere cock up.

That a statue of Queen-size dentures be erected in
remembrance of Princess Anne.

That any entry in the *Guinness Book of Records* referring to
the divorcee Princess Margaret be edited.

That my Great Great Grand da da da chief of Yoruba, be
exhumed and studied as the evolutionary link to mankind.
May the prosperity of the nation flourish from the fruits of
my genes.

*THE QUEEN gets up from her throne, walks down her red carpet
and waves to the people goodbye. She has proved her point.
She is THE QUEEN.*

The End.

SOMETHING DARK

Lemn Sissay's Life's Source: An Interview and Commentary

By **Dr Deirdre Osborne**
(Goldsmiths, University of London)

I n 'The Theory of the Parent–Infant Relationship', D. W. Winnicott records the following:

> With 'the care it receives from the mother' each infant is able to have a personal existence, and so begins to build up might what be called a *continuity of being* [...] If maternal care is not good enough then the infant does not really come into existence, since there is no continuity of being; instead the personality becomes built on the basis of reactions to environmental impingement. (Winnicott 1965: 54)

Something Dark is an autobiographical monodrama written and performed by Lemn Sissay that intimately dramatises an odyssey to self-knowledge, to forge a continuity of being. It is a journey that inextricably entwines locating his mother (who had given him up to foster care in the late 1960s), and his own genesis as one of Britain's leading spoken-word poets. The monodrama celebrates his maternal and genealogical reclamation – a journey from near-annihilation, to indisputable validation. As the creator *and* actor, Sissay literally and literarily performs himself into being. He employs trans-generic methodologies – cross-fertilising traditions of spoken-word poetry, solo performance, dramatic monologue and confessional – to produce an experiential aesthetics that testifies to the tenuous and often troubled routes, to self-worth, that confront indigenous black Britons, both socially and culturally.

From the opening, Sissay establishes the birth association – from darkness to light – reminding the audience (sitting in the dark as he, the actor, steps alone into the stage light) of the constant interplay between these two states, so necessary to his chosen medium, theatre. The neuroscientist, Antonio Damasio, reflects upon the anticipation of a performer, waiting in semi-darkness until she or he sees the light and the audience, to chart how 'stepping into the light is also a powerful metaphor for consciousness, for the birth of the knowing mind, for the simple and yet momentous coming of the sense of self into the world of the mental'. (Damasio 2000: 3) *Something Dark* weaves together the development of both an individual and a poetic consciousnessness. Sissay re-inhabits the sensory world of the child, and takes the spectator back to the re-imagined oneness of being inside his mother's womb, 'An island in an island in an island in an island, me. Light.' (330) Although John Donne offered 'no man is an island',[1] Sissay presents himself as marooned from existence, anchored to sanity by writing, until he can be reunited with his life's source, his mother.

Sissay's mother, an Ethiopian national, came to England to attend University. Sissay later learned his father was an Ethiopian Airlines pilot killed in an air crash in 1972. Sissay, who was born as a result of his mother's rape, was given up at birth to a zealous Baptist foster family in Atherton, a Lancashire pit village where he was the only black person. At the age of eleven, the foster parents returned him to Social Services and he lived in a children's home from that point. In his earlier play, *Storm* (2002), and a poem, 'Children's Home' (1999), he voices the tragedies of the young people unwanted and rejected by adults who inhabit such institutions. As though labelled 'return to sender', he writes, '[w]e might well have been all children/But this was no children's home.' *Morning Breaks in the Elevator* (1999: 35)

His deprivation of any sense of origin, which a biological family context offers, produced a sense of disembodiment and insubstantiality, underscored throughout by the repetition of the word 'nobody' during the drama:

Understand? I was the only proof of my own existence, my own echo [...] Nobody but nobody is responsible for me, on my birthdays, at Christmas, when ill, on weekends, on Saturdays or Sundays. No cousins, no sisters no brothers no aunts no uncles
You're lucky

---

1 From *Meditation XVII*, 'No man is an island': No man is an island entire of itself; every man is a piece of the continent, a part of the main; if a clod be washed away by the sea, Europe is the less, as well as if a promontory were, as well as any manner of thy friends or of thine own were; any man's death diminishes me, because I am involved in mankind. And therefore never send to know for whom the bell tolls; it tolls for thee. (John Donne).

> Says a loose friend as he passes me a spliff – families are a pain in
> the arse. And how much would I want that pain, at least if I felt pain
> I would know, I was alive. (338)

With literally nothing to lose, Sissay embarked upon harvesting proof
of his familial lineage, in a journey across decades and continents. He
declared the pertinence to his own quest of James Baldwin's words:
'Go back to where you started, or as far back as you can, examine all
of it, travel your road again and tell the truth about it. Sing or shout
or testify or keep it to yourself: but *know whence you came*' (Baldwin
1985: xix). He testified to the tenacity and all-consuming precision of
his personal fact-finding:

> The narrative of my adult life, ever since leaving the children's homes
> at eighteen years old, has been this: to find my mother, my father,
> my sisters, my brothers, my aunties and uncles; to find out why my
> name was changed as a small child; to find out who did it; to find out
> what happened in the year that I was born. Under what circumstances
> was I taken from a mother who wanted me and fostered for a short
> period of time? How did I find out that fact? All of it has to do with
> going back to where I started. I even know the country that I was
> conceived in. I know the actual hotel where my conception took
> place. [...] I know my mother's footsteps from her age of twenty to
> twenty-two. I was born when she was twenty-one. I know the places
> that she lived. I know where my father died. I searched and travelled
> to where his plane still lies in the Simeon Mountains. It took me two
> days on foot to get there.
>
> My adult life from eighteen to thirty-two has been about finding out
> these three lines: where I started, going back as far as I could, even
> back to where it stops, which is the mother's mind, the father's
> mind, you know, where you can't get anything from that point on.
> I have spent every last dime in searching for them – of emotional
> energy as well as financial. (Personal interview with Deirdre Osborne,
> September 2006)

This was fraught with the frustration of his mother's habitual
elusiveness:

> My mother kept moving. Once I found her in the Gambia – she works
> for the United Nations – she moved from one country to another, to
> another. She didn't tell me, I had to go and find her again. Finally

at thirty years old, I found her in New York, where I spoke to my brother, and then he called his sisters in Senegal and Paris, and then I met them a year later. My sister was the last member of my family to find, because my mother wouldn't tell me who her sons and daughters were – because she wanted them to finish studying – so it took me ten years to find them. Meanwhile I'd found everybody else. (Personal interview with Deirdre Osborne, September 2006)

When asked at which point he decided that he had found out enough, he replied:

I'll tell you exactly when I found enough. Finding I could let them go like you do with any family and see who sticks and also, realising it's not my fault – that was a great thing – it's still a great thing to realise. I think all I needed to do, was know that I wasn't anybody's secret, I wouldn't allow my mother or anybody to define me as a secret. (Personal interview with Deirdre Osborne, September 2006)

Before he located his actual family, the only means of proving his existence to himself was, paradoxically, by literarily materialising his inner world onto the page as poetry. The self-nurturing act of writing became evidence of his validity.

If you have nobody, how do you know that you exist? [...] I wrote, therefore I exist. [...] On the most fundamental, base level, writing proved that I was somebody – it meant that I was alive at any given time. (Personal interview with Deirdre Osborne, September 2006)

The power of the printed word further reinforced his identity when, at eighteen and no longer a ward of the state, he saw his birth certificate for the first time. As the monodrama articulates, it revealed his true name – not Norman Mark Greenwood but Lemn Sissay – and devastatingly, '[l]etters from my mother pleading for me back, writing to a social worker whose name was Norman Goldthorpe. He had named me after himself'. (339) Printed words have thus profoundly affected the course of his life, in ways which evoke the description of Bakhtin and Volosinov: 'In point of fact, *word is a two-sided act*. It is determined equally by whose word it is and for whom it is meant [...] A word is a bridge thrown between myself and another' (Bakhtin/Volosinov 1986: 86)

In repeatedly performing his monodrama *Something Dark*, Sissay's life's performance through live performance makes the writer an actor of his own life – simultaneously the subject of utterance and the subject of enunciation. In writing about performed poetry, Laura Severin refers to how 'elements collide with the spoken text, in the process creating an art form that is in dialogue with itself' (Severin 2004: 4) – so that a dialogic dynamic emerges from a monologic utterance. In *Something Dark*, the result of such a movement is that life performance becomes an integral part of the act. It tests the boundaries of genre

When asked if the term monodrama generically describes *Something Dark,* Sissay affirms: 'Yeah, monodrama's good, I like that a lot. I like it a lot. I've had people say that to me, "oh that's a monologue" – you see it's not, it's more than that –.' (Personal interview with Deirdre Osborne, September 2006) In distinguishing between monodrama and dramatic monologue, A. Dwight Culler argues that the former explores universal and abstract passions, whilst the latter focuses upon the individual and particular. (Culler 1975: 382). Clearly, Sissay's work blurs such distinctions. Moreover, he is right in rejecting *Something Dark* as being a dramatic monologue, read rather than performed, as Elisabeth A. Howe's definition demonstrates:

> The dramatic monologue is spoken by a persona who is not the poet; and the setting up of distance between author and speaker on the one hand, reader and speaker on the other, prevents the reader from identifying with the speaker [...] or from assuming that author and speaker are one. (Howe 1990:2)

In *Something Dark* the speaker is meant to be the writer and this is reinforced by the fact that Sissay is the only person to have performed the piece, to date. Directed by John E. McGrath, the production was jointly staged by Contact Theatre Manchester and Apples & Snakes at the Battersea Arts Centre, London and for over three years, Sissay has performed it around the UK and the world. Patrick Marmion observed that 'Sissay simply uses his art to make something light and portable of something dark and heavy.' (Marmion 2004: 303). The solo (portable) performer, Sissay, is indisputably the conduit for activating the text and the person whose personal experience is being (re)presented. His choice of form is neither poem nor dramatic monologue – as a monodrama, it embraces the attendant conventions of theatre performance. He reinforces this when describing how he approached acting all of the parts:

> My mind is the centre of every piece of work and therefore, you know, you need to give it a rest and communicate. So I sat with a director, who said to me, 'forget everything you've ever known concerning performance poetry, this isn't it' and 'you are going to have to learn to act like an actor', to quote Gil Scott-Heron, 'act like an actor', when he was talking about Ronald Reagan. So I had to act like an actor. I'm blocked, every section of the play is a five-minute block, a ten-minute block or whatever, and every section is thought about, the vocal, the sound, the body, you know. It's great to have access to the skills that an actor has. So I learned that way and then I had to also communicate with the director as an actor [...] so whenever I wanted to change the lines as an actor in rehearsals, the director would say well no, 'the writer wrote it that way and that's the way you do it'. It was wonderful. (Personal interview with Deirdre Osborne, September 2006)

Sissay punctuates his verbal and printed texts with indicators of other voices (which he plays in performance) to evoke the socio-historical and political contexts in which he participated and now recreates. This produces a double dynamic: of the speaker's growing social self-identity in 1980s together with the continually developing narrative/narrated archive, as the audience are positioned as witness/custodians, acquiring increased information about his life. The interplay between implied and actual addressees vocalises cultural and political conditions. Sissay puns and parodies the politics whilst asserting his artistic integrity.

> 'Are you separating – or integrating?'
> Look when I buy food from a black person or go to a hairdressers that's black, I don't do it cause I want to separate from any white person. I do it because they are the people who give me what I want. The hairdresser isn't dressed in khaki stood at the window with an AK47 saying, 'Did you see any white people go past?'. I didn't live in a black area because there was no white people. I live there because there are people who look like me. You can only know how important that is, if it is taken away from you. I integrate and separate every single day of my life. Maybe I should say, 'I just want you to know

I am integrating with you, right now'. No. No. I breathe therefore
I integrate. All I see are people separating from me pointing their
finger at me saying 'Are you integrating or separating or what?'
'Well are you?'
I just write poetry you know – nothing more and nothing less. I do. I
do it for reasons bigger than this. I'm twenty. (340–1)

In reviewing the play, Ian Johns finds characteristics shared with
Sissay's poetry as 'songs of the street, declamatory, imaginative,
hardhitting: about mothers, supermarkets, dreams of Africa, getting
picked up by the police for being black. Most have an upbeat humour
tempered with a dark and serious streak.' (Johns 2004: 23). Without
wishing to impose a totalising white classical tradition upon Sissay's
design (a feature predominant in the ways in which black British
writers' work is frequently configured in English literature – as though
a case has to be made for its inclusion),[2] there is evidence of the
influence of certain canonical discourses in the dynamics of Sissay's
work.[3] His monodrama evokes Plato's and Aristotle's early modes and
multiples of voice and address which *The Dictionary of World Literature*
summarises as:

[a] speaker (poet) may (1) speak in his own person, or (2) assume
the voice of another person or set of persons and speak throughout
in a voice not his own, or (3) produce a mixed speech in which the
basic voice is his own, but other personalities are at times assumed
and their voices introduced, i.e., directly quoted. (Shipley 1943:
616)

2   If the work of Black writers is included in the white-dominated literary and dramatic
canon, a re-coding of the work in terms of authoritative (white-dominated) aesthetic
models has generally occurred. Furthermore, inter-culturalism in theatre and performance
studies has often been a one-way academic street as Rustom Bharucha (1993) identified,
with little opportunity for the non-Western critic to offer reciprocal theorisation about
Western theatre and drama practices.
3   Sissay acknowledges the influences of canonical texts upon his writing, 'I read
T. S. Elliot's *Macavity the Cat* and for various reasons saw Macavity as very similar to
myself, and also my foster father was an English teacher. So what I had with them was a
love of English, which was subconscious. What they did emotionally was terrible, but what
I had was my first eleven years crammed full of stories. You know, whether it's the Bible
or whether it's poetry or whether it's *The Lion, the Witch and the Wardrobe*, or *Famous
Five*, [...] I loved the metaphor and the trying to work out what a story meant.' (Personal
interview Osborne, 2006)

Sissay also employs the rhythm of the confessional – the staged introspection of his thoughts, processing the fragments of the past (into poetic form) for public utterance in the hope of (self) forgiveness, liberation and renewal. The prism of perception through which this is filtered is the underlying tension between revelation and secrecy, forgiveness and blame. The juxtaposition of forgiveness and blame is dramatised as an abusive distortion in Norman Mark Greenwood's treatment at the hands of his zealous foster parents and their church. 'I was never beaten – I was chastised. Chastised with belts, chastised with rulers, chastised with slippers and with canes. Chastised.' (335) yet, the social worker states, 'none of this is your fault' – an unsatisfactory atonement for the system in which he is complicit. The first major revelation closes the 1st Act when Sissay discovers his true name, the next is when he tracks down his mother after two years of searching and finds out he is her secret. As his mother keeps him at arm's length, Sissay is keen to remind the audience that she is doing nothing wrong. He defends her endlessly. Exuding childish enthusiasm he affirms, '[b]ut I could keep a secret. This was the first family secret I had ever been asked to keep.' (345)

However, the joy at a reunion with her becomes a shocking *coup-de-théâtre*, where the audience is potentially misled by the chatty, nostalgic register that precedes her earth-shattering revelation – which is then sealed off – with the repressive necessity for secrecy. Sissay conveys the impossibility of this simultaneity.

> She was twenty-one when she came to England, when I was born. I was twenty-two when I met her, my father would've been twenty-three or so. The last time she saw him he would have looked like me. Her meeting me would have been the first time she had seen him since then. 'Look there was no other way of putting this – I was raped.'

> Who else could she tell? Who could I tell? [...] I scared the living life out of her. I had the life scared out of me. I was the life scored into her, scarred into her. I am an alleged crime, an illegitimate allegation. A crime figure. (344)

After hearing the truth of his conception, he reiterates, '[a]nd no-one was to blame.' (345) The monodrama closes, asserting 'that what is, simply is' (348), the end of his quest, an acceptance of self after a process of revelations. It is an acknowledgement of the self-legitimising power of narrative, exemplifying what Mary Stuart describes:

> There is no rigid self, but a flow between the external and internal, a constant critique, a shuttling back and forth between imagination and perception, between induction and deduction, between 'I' and "me", creating a fragile and multi-faceted self which we represent to the world. (Stuart 1998: 146)

Versions of the truth present themselves as a series of fractured parts that are in a state of moment-by-moment assembly, so that no definitive narrative is possible. The narrative trajectory of *Something Dark* also shares common ground with the self-narrating practice of psychotherapy – throughout Sissay makes wry reference to this, 'my inner child' being one such example – and also the hallmarks of self-strategies for surviving trauma, his self-harming tattoos, the dissociation[4] of going without shoes for a year, even in the snow – signatures and battle scars from being raised in care. Yet, he adamantly demarcates the difference: 'psychotherapy is psychotherapy, this is different'. (Personal interview, Osborne 2006) This suggests what Celia Hunt and Fiona Sampson refer to as the therapeutic benefit of writing (or also, in this case, repeated performing) coming from 'default rather than by design'. Sissay is acting, not acting out.

In delivering the final lines, 'I told them what I believed had happened. And each of them gave me a different truth.' (348), Sissay deconstructs the illusion of absolute truth: 'It's not black, it's not white, not dark, not light'. (348) He implicitly reminds the audience that he is, first and foremost, a poet and that crafting poetry has been integral to his survival. From a summative viewpoint, he has aesthetically displayed his experience as being, what Abbs terms, 'simultaneously formative and "deformative"'. (Abbs 1998: 127)

---

4   Phil Mollon defines dissociation as 'an attempt to deny that an unbearable situation is happening [...] something like a state of self-generated hypnosis, developed to deal with unbearable pain or terror'. (Mollon 1999: 4)

Something Dark

by

Lemn Sissay

Something Dark was first performed at Contact, Manchester, on 12 February 2004. It was produced and commissioned by Apples & Snakes and Contact in association with BAC.

Written and performed by Lemn Sissay

Directed by John E McGrath

1st Act

The stage is bare but for a black backdrop. The play begins with a juxtaposition of light darkness time and events.

From stage left LEMN SISSAY *walks out and across the stage until he notices somebody and centre stage turns to face the audience.. Immediately the lights shuts down plunging the entire stage into darkness.*

LEMN SISSAY:
Dark. In Darkness always comes the question, Where is the light?

The light pours upon him

Light. Light. It begs the question, Why was it dark?

The lights shut down

Dark. Where is the light?

The light pours upon him

Light. Why was it dark?

The light shuts upon him.

Damn. Darkness. Light, light. Light.

In centre stage the light pours upon him as he's trying to tell the story.

The Story. The Child…
    But events get in the way.
    Waiter. Waiter, Waiter, can I get a little service here? A little service, here? I would like your finest light *s'il vous plaît*. I'd like one portion of light with a little light on the side, if that's okay? Is that Okay? Damn. The Question. Darkness. Ofcourse it's okay! LIGHT.
    The Story. The Child…
    Look, I just want a little bit of light here. Is that too much to ask? I mean…in the great scheme of things; in the great who's who of what's what. We've got to fight for the right to light. Light is right. Light power. Friend of mine in New York

329

says 'Hey hey Lemn don't be so heavy. Tune in to Light FM'. Heavy. Light. Heavy. Light. Light. Light. FM. Fuck me. FM…

'Hey. Hey. Hey. No need to swear. No need to use profanities. There are children here.'

No there are not, It clearly says on the poster…

'Hey. Hey. What about my inner child?'

Your inner child?

'Yeah my inner child?'

Look it says on the poster no children and that includes your inner child.

The story. The child. The child inside a woman, the woman inside a bed, the bed inside a ward, the ward inside a hospital inside a city a foreign country inside the sea. Me. An island in an island in an island in an island. Me. Light.

Ladies and gentlemen. Shadies and Mentalmen. Thanks for coming! When I say 'coming' I don't mean 'coming'. It's not like I say that anyway. All I wanna say is, you came and that's good – my God, it's great – I love it that you came, that you wanted to come; that you didn't let other thoughts distract like 'I'm going to… I'm going to…' You simply came, which is after all a good thing.

We are all coming and going. A bus driver on the 73 once said to me where are you going. I said Marble Arch. He said 'No……where are you really going?' I got off the bus quickly, really quickly. Darkness. There I was stood on the Tottenham Court Road. Middle of the night. Darkness. Now there's something critical about being out late at night. If you're a black man – Something Dark. Taxi. Ribbons of yellow light flash past like the eyes of wolves. Light Darkness. Taxi. Taxi. Taxi. The light passes and pisses its yellow stream over me. I'm not pissed – I'm pissed off that the third pisshead passed. Darkness! I didn't see it coming – the darkness. The mental stillness. I just saw the light run away from me. I just needed a lift. It's not heavy. It's Light.

So there I am on another day with a very good friend who you could describe as 'white'. Six taxis go past as I try to catch one. Darkness. Let's look at the odds. I am in my home town – whatever that means. It's two am, I am hailing a cab and…

not one but six drive by, they slow down, they look at me and they carry on. I put the bread knife away.

'I'll prove it', I tell my friend, so I sit behind a wall. My friend hails a cab. The cab stops. We get in. 'I don't believe it', my friend says, 'six cabs go past and don't stop cause my friend he's…'

'I stop for anyone, anyone', barks the driver.

Darkness. I look at my friend talking to the taxi driver and the taxi driver talking to my friend and I'm still behind the wall…folding up my darkness and gently placing it into my inner child's mouth telling him Shut the fuck up! Damn it shut the fuck up – It's only a cab! Listen to your friend, listen to the driver. Everything's okay. Darkness. I hide behind a wall to prove why the taxi is hiding from me – in a mental stillness. Darkness.

The story begins proper:

It's 1968. It's the year of the Enoch Powell speech. The year Martin Luther King was killed and the year that the Beatles released The White Album. And she arrives here from the bright lights of a decolonised Africa – an Africa that had fought for its freedom – an Africa in its 20th-century heyday. She's here…in the dark industrial north of England. Illegitimate. She's pregnant. She's cold incredibly cold. I'm an island inside an island inside an island. And she needs help. She needs light at the end of the tunnel.

Wigan Metropolitan Social Services. The social services offered single fallen women 'The Mother and Baby Home' – This would sort out the problem. This would be the light. This Ethiopian woman wanted her child fostered, wanted good wholesome foster parents while she studied. But there was another agenda, these homes were adoption houses. I am fostered and my mother returns to Oxford. As the kind foster parents lift me up from the cot the social worker tells them – poor child, abandoned by a Negro. As soon as we find her, we'll get her to sign the adoption papers. So they did as their God had instructed them. I was a sign. I was a message from God. I was Norman Mark Greenwood.

For the next eleven years all I hear is that this woman should have her eyes scratched out for not signing the adoption papers. She was an evil woman too selfish to sign.

I spent the eleven years kneeling and praying. I tried praying 'can I have a bike for Christmas', but I would always answer myself 'course you can'. Then I was supposed to determine whether that voice was God or the Devil. I was told and believed that the Devil was inside me and had to be cast out. The Baptists loved a good carpet, for kneeling and the 1970s has never known a more knee-friendly floor covering than the shag-pile carpet. 'Praise be to Baptist friendly unfortunately named shag'. It came in handy for the weekly ritual.

My knees are crushed to the floor and my neck bent like a giraffe. I look up and the tiniest bauble of spit spun from an elder's mouth. It caught the reflections of all four men who encircled me. Their reflections turned as the moving glass at the end of a blowpipe. Finally I saw my own concave reflection wobbling towards my eye. Blink. Blink. Blink. An Elder looked at my Dad, both acknowledged the devil was leaving me through my tears. But I was being spat on.

I took to counting the threads in the shag. The hand firmly planted on the crown of my head took the grip of a basketball player. The church elders were on the attack.

'Cast it out', growled an elder. It felt as if the thin volcanic ground was about to crack open giving way to the pressure of the hand on my head. Was the devil crawling its way from the centre of the earth reaching out its spiny arms from the howling bowels of Babylon wrapping its sinewy hands around my neck my legs…pulling me down.

My father and the elders were on the precipice and above them our burning destroyed house, fire's pouring from the mouth of the mantelpiece, the curtains, the roof all but gone to a fierce red and black sky. The elders held crosses in one hand and my hand in the other – God's wrathful face hung in the congealed sky… Father began quoting the Bible, while mother started to pull her hair and speak in tongues, an unintelligible language that only God knows……

Bugger I thought.

This carpet needs cleaning. I start counting the threads.

One piece of thread two pieces of thread…

The hand's no longer on my head but in it between scalp-skin and skull. Four hands now sinking and seeking rubbing beneath and into my head. Start again.

One piece… One piece of thread two pieces of thread.

As the Devil punched his angry fist into my stomach the threads of the carpet became coils of smoke from the peat fire fields of the highlands.

'Cast the Devil out of this boy'

'In the name of Jesus Be Gone Beast.'

'Seven pieces of thread eight pieces of thread.'

Shit, the Devil's inside me.

Somewhere within this gigantic biblical labyrinth that had been built inside me. Somewhere in there, down one of its corridors was a room within a room that led to a door from which there was a rope bridge which led to a crack in the rock which led to a door and as I opened it there was a little boy giggling and laughing. But the key to the door to the bridge to the door to the room to the room to the corridor to the way out, of the labyrinth was sown into his own skin, in his back, beneath a minute scar that he had never seen. It's known within the hospital industry as a foreign body. But I loved them.

*

They do though don't they families? Not all the time but on occasion, they have The Family Meeting. The family meeting suggests a revelation, an opening, an issue.

'Children, Mummy and Daddy don't like each other any more' or

'Children, Daddy will now be known as Gwendoline.'

There was such a day such a moment such an event. I was told about it a whole 24 hours before and a dangerous excitement blushed inside… I couldn't wait to get home from school. I'm eleven years old. And there it was, the drop-leaf table fully stretched – fully extended.

Maybe Mom was having another baby. But that couldn't be right, she's just had one. She called her an accident which I thought was an unusual name. The alerted senses, the prickle

of excitement, the wonder, the danger, the nature of discovery
is revelation.

The first weird thing was that none of my brothers or
sisters are here, just me. Wait till I tell 'em – just wait. I can't
remember who spoke – I was so excited – I just remember
seeing their mouths move in slow motion and the words settle
into my head once there lips had stilled.

Yes… I said

'You don't love us do you?'

I was still waiting for the actual revelation, for the reason for
the meeting.

'Yes yes yyy'

'Stop', she said. 'We want you to go and spend the next day
thinking about love and what it is, read the scriptures and
return tomorrow and give us your most honest and most
truthful answer. Okay?'

I see. I saw. I was being asked to commune with God and his
work and to dig deep inside my heart and soul where there
should be an answer there which was not instinctive but
instructed from God. Praise him. Tomorrow came.

I had studied the question at home at school at night and day.
If they were asking me whether I loved them or not, and if they
are the ones who taught me what love is, then I musn't love
them, because otherwise they wouldn't ask.

This led me to the miracle of thought that I think they wanted
me to get to.

'I shall ask God for forgiveness and thorough his benevolence
I shall learn, learn to love them and him. His love will shine
through me to them.'

The theology was perfect, the humility unquestionable, and
the timing impeccable and the answer as honest as a sinner
could ever get. How fantastic. This was an opportunity.

'I musn't love you', I said, 'I will ask God for forgiveness…'

'Because Norman, because you don't love us you have
chosen your path.'

Twenty-four, twenty-four hours later my social worker, this
strange man who visited me every month, was waiting in the
car as I said goodbye to my parents. Neither of them would
hug me and not in my wildest predictions would I have known

at the time that I would never see them again. Nor that they wouldn't write. I didn't say goodbye to anyone, to my aunts uncles sisters brothers cousins grandparents uncles. Such was the caesarean secrecy. I just disappeared. On the way to the children's home I said to my social worker:

'I know that this is my fault and I will ask God for forgiveness.'

For him, that was the final straw and the last piece of information that he needed to hear, the car shuddered and he pulled into a layby.

'None of this is your fault', he said, 'none of it'.

Twenty years later he tells me that they had called him a month earlier and said 'Norman wants to leave – he has chosen to leave'.

'None...none of this is your fault.'

I had so effectively been brainwashed that at eleven years old I had been convinced that it was. I was a sinner and the Devil was inside me.

'None of this is your fault.' I was never beaten – I was chastised. Chastised with belts, chastised with rulers, chastised with slippers and with canes. Chastised but never beaten.

And as I got to the massive Victorian children's home I began to ask myself 'what has happened to me'. I hadn't had the rug pulled out from beneath me as much as the entire floor had been taken away. From then till eighteen years old I was in children's homes – the legal property of Wigan parented by the Government. They never called. And I simply folded myself into myself and became everyone's extrovert. Within two days of being in the children's homes I was christened Chalky White, Norman! Chalky White.

Tattoos

And there he is – Chalky tattooed into my hand and there he is barely visible tattooed into my hand NG Norman Greenwood. And there it is on my left hand the tattoo of a cross. So there I am in Starbucks, many many years later served by a beautiful girl – as she holds out her hand to give me the change – I see the dark. It was a Vietnam moment. You were in the war I said. She looked at me suspiciously instinctively pulling down her sleeves to cover her arm. I raise my sleeve. 'Me too.' She smiles and we connect, knowing how similar our secrets and lies. We both remember setting off fire extinguishers, running away in packs in the dead of night. We both understood the viscous smell of industrial bleach and the industrial floor polishing machines, the sounds of children crying in the night. Both knew the survival techniques – damn it and we both look back and say damn it – we were just children. And it wasn't our fault! And what did we do besides slitting our wrists, we punctured our skin with blunt pins and blue Indian ink, bottles of Quink. This is my name, worth nothing to no-one but something to me, see. I even spelt chalky wrong – it came out as chaky. But tattooing a crucifix in my hand. Why do you think we and this girl have tattoos on our left arms – it's because we are right-handed!

I had pin points in each knuckle and even a letter-per-finger LOVE. After a few days of them congealing into scabs I scratched at the skin furiously until they poured with blood and ink. Got to get them out. I tore at them exposing deep welts of flesh. So now they lie beneath my skin barely visible – like ghosts. I was fourteen years old tattooing myself and sniffing Evostick.

I have to tell this story cause there was no-one to put two and two together. I was aware that nobody I knew, knew me for longer than a year. Period. I slowly became aware while in care that the only proof of my existence was me. See, that's what family does – it gives you reference points. This is not defining a good family from a bad family. This is saying that you know what your birthday is by virtue of the fact that someone tells you what your birthday is. A brother a sister an aunt a father a mother a grandparent – it matters to someone and therefore matters to you. Understand? I was the only proof of my own existence, my own echo, tattooing myself into myself.

Barefoot Dread Lock

Darkness. Light. In the children's home I'm being told
'When in Rome do as the Romans do!!'

So what did I do in Rome, I did what Romans didn't.
As a good Jewish friend said:
'When in Rome, you're with the gentiles, do what you like.'
Deepest Lancashire always struck me as more 'spam country'
than 'Klan country'. I didn't hate my town, I hated what it
stood for, it stood for nothing!! The miners had been broken,
the mills were being dismantled and this lone black face of
mine represented everything that everyone feared, tomorrow.

And so there I was the boy who had arrived from nowhere to
become nobody in a town that believed in nothing yet stood
against everything. Hey in this town I was somebody, not just
anybody, I was a nobody – and I knew this cause everyone told
me so! Me and my kind are invisible. How could a girl tell her
father:
'Dad I am going out with nobody, would you like to meet him?'
So I became Somebody! I became everybody's nobody. With the
nickname that nobody would forget: Chalky, Chalky White.
Invisible.

   The after-shock started to hit in. I heard whispers of chips
and shoulders and started to listen to Bob Marley and started
to withdraw from the darkness of being somebody to everybody
and no-one to anyone. I could smell a lie and it just got
stronger – I'm fifteen. And being the smiling village idiot didn't
sit right. I realised that acceptance on someone else's terms
isn't acceptance but thinly-veiled rejection. Maybe all I know
is wrong and my intuition is right. Maybe all I am is nothing.
I even asked myself, Why am I asking these questions? Why!?
Why can't I just laugh anymore. Why can't I? The light at the
end of this tunnel is from my torch, and I look back and it's
just as bad – enough to drive a sane man mad, thinking of the
good times I'd never had. The batteries are going...

   After coming back from holiday, Bognor Regis, with the
children's home, I stopped wearing shoes. I stopped wearing
shoes. Without reason I just stopped wearing shoes. Without
thinking I am going to stop wearing shoes – I just stopped. I go
barefoot and treat it as normal as pie. Proudly I learned to walk
on glass and to stub out a cigarette with my little toe. It was
a silent rebellion an implosion. You may take my identity but

you will never take my feet – if you like. I was barefoot and I was barefoot for a full twelve months. In Lancashire.

If ever we had six senses the feet would be the sixth. There is nothing more gratifying than walking on short soft dew-filled grass. Not many things are as sensual as warm pavement stone. My feet became like hands gripping all the different textures of our world. I was becoming to know the difference between tarmacs and the gentleness of soil or peat or heather. Point being, I was searching my senses. Barefoot dreadlocked.

'Bet you can't do that in the snow' was the most common thing people would say, 'Bet you can't do that in the snow.' Of all the things to say. I could have been told 'get some help'. I could have been asked 'What's wrong'. I could have been pulled over the coals and told 'You cannot do this any more you foolish boy'. Who cared enough! Who cared enough.
'Bet you can't do that in the snow.'

It was dark. It was night time and I watched thousands and thousands of snowflakes sloping from the sky. Little pieces of light peppered the darkness. As a child once said to me in a workshop once 'Night time is like a shoal of black fishes sprinkled with sea salt'. Come morning I put on my scarf and walked outward around the housing estate walking through the virgin snow leaving barefoot prints as I walked. I had to leave this town when I left care, because all this town can offer me is 'I bet you can't do it in the snow'. I'll bet I can...

This blackboy who had been called snowflake more time than he cares to remember. This blackboy, commonly known as chocolate drop and widely known as Chalky otherwise known as Norman Greenwood... When I got back to the children's home I put on my shoes. The footprints had melted and the snow had disappeared leaving bits of road salt, the scattered seasoning of winter's coldest dish. It was as if I had never been there!

I'm 18 I am in the flat that I signed on for. I am alone. Nobody but nobody is responsible for me, on my birthdays, at Christmas, when ill, on weekends, on Saturdays or Sundays. No cousins no sisters no brothers no aunts no uncles.
'You're lucky'

Says a loose friend as he passes me a spliff – families are a pain. And how much would I want that pain, at least if I felt pain I would know, I was alive. Dark.

After moving in my social worker sat me down for our final meeting. My whole life had been punctuated by 'case conferences'.

'Norman'

He said

'Your name isn't Norman.'

See, legally the government was no longer my parent and therefore had to pass over one incredible document and that document was my birth certificate. It had two pieces of information – my name Lemn Sissay and my mother's name Etsegenet Amare. It was a dark afternoon mid winter. But there was so much light in that front room – I was someone! This was a truth: a clear undeniable documented recorded hand written witnessed signed piece of incredible undeniable and absolute TRUTH. And there was more, he passed me letters dated July 1968. She said:

'I want him to be with his own colour, his own people – I don't want him to face discrimination.'

The Reply letter:

'Many thanks for your letter. Lemn is doing well with his foster parents and in good health.

Yours faithfully Norman.'

Letters from my mother pleading for me back, writing to a social worker whose name was Norman Goldthorpe. He had named me after himself.

From that point I reverted to the only truth I knew, my name Lemn Sissay. Immediately I lost all, and I mean all, of my remaining friends in that small town.

Who the bloody hell do I think I was, Lemn?

I had to leave everything I knew, not because of what I didn't want to be, but because of what was to become – most of all, and behind it all, I just wanted to find my family. I had no qualifications. I had no experience. I had a birth certificate and a fist full of poems and I was going to Manchester and there would be no going back......

2nd Act

*LEMN SISSAY races out from stage right into stage centre to light
and music he splays out his arms in celebration.*

Lemn Sissay:
Manchester. Light!! The bright lights – the big city. Friend of
mine said, 'I didn't know I lived in the Ghetto until I read it
in the *News*'. The first time someone spoke patwa I just stood
shocked still and rooted to a rootless spot. But this was Vegas,
it was Lagos, it was Kingston Jamaica. It was Hulme.

I was an outsider going to the inside and was all inside out
going the wrong way up a one-way street with too much weight
on my sleeve. And the food. Chicken and the Chicken Run. It
took me years to realise that 'Waaayooowaaan' was not a name
but a question and shouldn't be followed by 'Waaayooowaaan?'.
The chicken... And the fish, red snapper in onion pepper sauce
and dumplings clouds floating in stew. The fried dumplings
like nuggets of air bubbled gold and salt fish fritters. And akee
and saltfish, curried goat.!!! Rice and peas. I had come to the
land of milk, honey, plantain, yam and sweet pumpkin gunga
peas and banana cake. And I was hungry for it – hungry for it
all. Light Light Light. Light – this was light. First time I went
to the hairdressers, first time I went to a dance, first black
girlfriend. First time I spoke with a rasta. First time I had sat
in a room full of black people. First time I had been on a bus
with black people on it. First time I saw black people behind
counters serving me from the bank. Light. So much light. And
the hairdressers... My first black hairdressers. Raymonds on
Great Western Street, filled with hair products with names
like World of Curls and pictures all over the walls with people
smiling – who looked like me. Like me. Light!

'Are you separating – or integrating?'
Look when I buy food from a black person or go to a
hairdressers that's black, I don't do it cause I want to separate
from any white person. I do it because they are the people who
give me what I want. The hairdresser isn't dressed in khaki
stood at the window with an AK47 saying, 'Did you see any

white people go past?'. I didn't live in a black area because there was no white people. I live there because there are people who look like me. You can only know how important that is, if it is taken away from you. I integrate and separate every single day of my life. Maybe I should say, 'I just want you to know I am integrating with you, right now'. No. No. I breathe therefore I integrate. All I see are people separating from me pointing their finger at me saying 'Are you integrating or separating or what?' 'Well are you?'

I just write poetry you know – nothing more and nothing less. I do. I do it for reasons bigger than this. I'm twenty.

Hairdressers

I just wanted to get my hair cut!

'Wayoooowaaaaan?' Just cut them off I said. And I watched my dreadlocks fall like over-ripe breadfruit around my feet. All that weight swept away from my head. I felt a little lighter. My first book of poetry was being published in London, of poetry. The more I found the more I wrote and again it opened up a vastness. Amongst these fluorescent lights. There was only darkness. A coldness that swept across me like wind across an ice pond. And no matter what I did or whom I knew. Facts still remained frozen. I knew no-one for longer than two years. Christmas was when hell froze over... I could follow the hairline cracks of each birthday razor-sharp to the finger touch. I had to find her. From the address on the letter that the social worker sent me – I started to send them out, across the world – wild guesses and hunches. I'd been sending them out since I was eighteen years old. Letters and poems to people I didn't know.

And there it was, an airmail envelope that lay upon my front room carpet. I couldn't believe it.

'Hello my friend I have searched for your mother. It has taken me two years but I have found her. She works for the UN and is stationed in The Gambia at the UNDP offices...'

Before I knew it this Lancashire lad's palms were gripping the seats of a 747 flying to the Gambia. I'd called her, from

England. But every word from her mouth immediately disappeared. As if I the painter swirled his hand in circles on the wet paint of the moment. I remember saying – do you remember 1967? No sooner had the phone been put down than the plane was landing in The Gambia. Dusk.

It's a small world, the larger my knowledge. It really is. There was a time when my little village in Lancashire was the biggest world, then the city and then this... I meet a muslim man on the plane six foot tall two foot wide – he tells me 'Those people behind, they work at the UN as well'. And they did, everybody knows everybody. There is a black Mercedes waiting for them at the airport... 'We will take you', they say. They will take me.

I can't tell you how my head was in that situation, but I will try and describe – Get two pints of mushy peas and place them in a colander and push the mushy peas downwards in your hands – then imagine that every thought is a person stood on stilts – one stilt is longer than the other, the colander is above them – and they are all trying to catch the squeezy cheesey peas in their mouths without banging into each other. I had jumped off the bungee bridge and forgot to measure the rope. Weyhey.

Light. Between dark and light. I was in the UN black Mercedes speeding through the Gambian dusk, golden wings of dust flying from this black panther. One by one the UN people left. Until there was just me and the driver – he had the most fearsome and kind bloodshot eyes. The black panther halts outside tall manicured hedges. I hear her shuffle behind the hedge. My heart's racing, my palms are sweating – how am I to be? I recite a verse I recite a verse to myself.
Gold from The stone/Oil from the earth/I yearned for my home/from the time of my birth/strength of a mother's whisper shall carry me until/the hand of my lost sister/ joints onto my will.
And I'm hugging her and she's hugging me. And I'm hugging her hugging me.
In the dark the porch light pours out towards us. 'Come in you two come in.'

And she says, 'Please I have a visitor, let's not talk about this'. The Mercedes disappears and the Gambian crickets slice into my head.

'Please – let's not talk about this.' I walked inside. She sat. It was the strangest thing. She sat and I made polite conversation with the visitor.

'Well yes it does rain a lot in Manchester but no more than Paris. Ahhh but we see rainbows.' In my head I'm running around. Everything's okay, listen to the visitor, listen to the woman, stay calm, nothing to see here. Put it away. Put it all away. It's okay. Fuckin Paris. Stop it. Fuckin rain. It's hot. 'Yes…orange juice would be great, thanks.' Fuckin rain in fuckin Manchester. What the fuck am I talking about that for. 'Oh yeah it was a good journey.' Fuckin good journey. Fuck the fuckin journey.

In the defence of the mother, ladies and gentlemen. Ladies and gentlemen I am from the rights for women's rights forum sponsored by the rights for women's rights department of the government and you must see that here she, remember, has done nothing wrong.

She has done nothing wrong. She did everything right in her control. What would you say if a twenty-one-year-old guy knocked on your door and said 'HI MOM I'M HOME'? She could not prepare and it's Christmas and it's Christmas in a couple of weeks and it turns out that I've got brothers and sisters and they're coming back too from international schools in Paris and Belgium. And after two days the brother arrives – I still haven't spoken to the mother in any coherent way. Is she avoiding me, work home. 'I wanna talk to you I say, I've got lots of… things…'

She asks me not to tell my brother who I am, she says, she will tell them all on Christmas day and it is a week and a half to go till Christmas day. Each hot Gambian day lasts a year and in this heat I am dying. I watch my brother play with his mother – she is pleased to see him. I have been demoted to Cousin which seeing as he had never heard of me before is bad, distant, the cleaner's uncle's nephew. I can't tell anyone. I just fold myself into myself. And hide behind a wall to prove… Is my mother hiding from me – darkness. A mental stillness. I have to…to get out.

I've never known secrets. Keep it in the family? No family. What goes on between these four walls is our business?… No four walls and there was no 'our'. But I could keep a secret. This was the first family secret that I had ever been asked to keep. I never told my brother. I sat with him, watched him, laughed with him. One time we played draughts near the local shop and I watched him between moves, the way his mouth worked and his eyes' squint as he concentrated on the game. I never told a soul it was two days before my sisters were arriving. But I am going – I can't take this.

My brother was away with his friends. And she was there alone, with me, alone. Look I just wanna talk… I 'Right,' she said. 'Ask me anything you want.' I couldn't think of anything – I just couldn't. I mean, what do you ask… Ummm. 'There is no other way to put it,' she said. 'I was… ' Now there is only so many ways a child can be conceived. My father's name she couldn't remember… Right. Okay. It's a secret she had held for twenty-two years. The second or third secret that I had been asked to keep. Okay and I had to put it somewhere. She was twenty-one when she came to England, when I was born. I was twenty-two when I met her, my father would've been twenty-three or so. The last time she saw him he would have looked like me. Her meeting me would have been the first time she had seen him since then. 'Look there's no other way of putting this – I was raped.'

Who else could she tell? Who could I tell? I had given her my first book *Tender Fingers in a Clenched Fist*; it was dedicated to her. I scared the living life out of her. I had the life scared out of me. I was the life that was scored into her, scarred into her. I am an alleged crime an illegitimate allegation. A crime figure.

I flew back to England, to Manchester, the place I should never have been, named after someone who never should have named me, fostered to beasts who should never have been allowed to foster. Who could I tell?

'Ladies and gentlemen fresh from Africa where he found his mother please – please give a warm round of applause for Mancunian poet Lemn Sissay.' Thanks very much... First poem I'd like to read is called 'Gold from the Stone' – amazing that I wrote this before I met my mother and before I met my sister.

Gold from the stone oil from earth
I yearned for home from the time of my birth
Strength of a whisper shall carry me until
The hand of my lost sister joins onto my will

Root to the earth blood from the heart
Could never from birth be broken apart
Food from the platter water from the rain
The subject the matter – I'm going home again

You can't sell a leaf to a tree nor the wind to the atmosphere
I know where I'm meant to be and I can't be satisfied here
You can't give light to the moon nor mist to the drifting cloud
I shall be leaving here soon costumed cultured and crowned

Sugar from the cane coal from the wood
Water from the rain life from the blood
Gold from the stone oil from the earth
I yearned for my home ever since my birth

Food from the platter water from the rain
The subject and the matter – I'm going home again...

Manchester becomes as close to home. A good place to die. Jesus I am twenty-one and no-one would call me on my birthday that I had known for longer than two years. I came back to England with I had been told, the face of a rapist and of his victim. And no-one was to blame.

  I tried to keep in touch with her. I did. I did. Really. Tried to ignore newspaper reports of the troubled childhood of a a murderer a mugger. That is not me. That is not me. I smile, I get more books published. And she has gone. It takes me five years to find her again. Five years of believing that my own mother believes that I am stalking her, is protecting her daughters and sons from me. But I am an old hand at this now – and through UN links and hook and crook I find her, I fax her... She never tells me to go away, ever. What's his name then. His name... His name is Berhanu Sissay she said on the telephone. He was a pilot for Ethiopian Airlines. I put the phone down. The camera crew were filming me making the call; the director said, 'Lemn could you pick up the phone and put it down again so we can get a shot of your hand, for a cut-away'.

Nobody knew, not the film crew, not anyone after meeting my father I was going to beat him... We flew to Ethiopia, the camera crew and I, and he's dead. Died in a plane crash in 1973. A pilot for Ethiopian airlines from a wealthy family in Addis Ababa. I travel out with his daughter to where the plane lies beneath the earth in the Simeon Mountains by Gondar. Camera crew in tow... You can learn more about someone once they've passed. 'It's as if he has returned', his family tell me. All the grief of his passing and the joy of my being mixed into fascinating stares...long looks and my face being touched. I was touched. Touched.

But there was one man. One man who wasn't related to me. His sister was married to the Prime Minister in the 70s under Emperor Haile Selassie, he too worked for the government and when Selassie was overthrown this man was put in jail for fifteen years, most of his friends were killed. His wife had to flee the country fifteen years ago – I would've been five. His wife was my mother. Her children were in boarding schools in Paris and Belgium... The dictatorship was overthrown. He was free now. A man who had been separated from his own children – my sisters and brothers – and his wife. He peeled open the wedding folder. 'Come see', he said and I looked at their wedding pictures. I would've been five then. 'I knew about you,' he said. 'She tried to get you back.'

What was it between me and him? Neither had done anything wrong but both had to accept at some time...that what is, simply is. The final puzzle to the jigsaw… 'You know what your name means?' he said. 'Lemn. It means Why!'

I'm thirty-two years old my name means why. I'm a poet. Couldn't have a more apt name. I call my brothers and sisters on my mother's side. They learn more about their own mother through me than through her. One sister she says to me, she says – 'It all fits. I was sixteen. I was sent a rape alarm, ofcourse, she keeps a distance from all of us. Ofcourse she does, ofcourse.'

So now I have a fully dysfunctional family like everyone else. Finding them all – all of them. Reaching out and touching them all. I told them what I believed had happened. And each of them gave me a different truth.

It's not black, it's not white, not dark, not light
Secrets are the stones that sink the boat
Take them out look at them, throw them out and float.

35 CENTS

Slave Trade to Trade Slaves:
Paul Anthony Morris' *35 Cents*

By Dr Robert Beckford
(Oxford Brookes University)

One of the recent advertising campaigns by the Jamaican government was a reworking of Bob Marley's classic reggae track 'One Love.'[1] Contentiously, they omitted Marley's questioning refrain 'I'm pleading to mankind' and replaced it with 'See Jamaican Smiling', and 'See Jamaica laughing'. Trans-coding Marley's radical questioning of the place of love in Jamaican society with minstrel-like descriptions of the Island's people signifies a tension at the heart of contemporary reflections of Jamaica's place in the world: between the critical and the exotic. Critical reflections are diachronic, a careful examination of how a former slave colony has struggled to find its political voice and economic footing. The exotic are synchronic reflections based on sensationalist or melodramatic readings of the Island's urban cultures, particularly its music industry. Paul Anthony Morris' play belongs to the first school – an exploration of the destructive impact of unequal trade relations.

35 Cents

Morris' play inspects the international institutions and structural forces responsible, in part, for the impoverishment of the Island. The scenario is a familiar tale told by those who live the underside of globalisation – a developing country heavily indebted, suffering economically from cheap subsidised imports and an impotent political class in the West's pocket. All of which renders talk of democracy and independence at the impending elections at best a waste of time and money and at worst false consciousness – hence the introduction of the 'No Confidence Movement' (NCM).

Parodying radical student movements of the 1960s and 70s, the narrative circulates around the real and imaginary musings of five friends: Peter, James Madeline, Philip and their leader Ruth. After a

1   *One Love* by Bob Marley (1977): 'One love, one heart/Let's get together and feel all right.'

day of leafleting they return to Ruth's living room feeling the stress of campaigning on an Island that '[does not] like change.' (361) In a moment of inspiration Ruth tables another strategy – a campaign to boycott the elections, transforming the NCM into a 'Don't Vote campaign'. The motive is genuine, to highlight the 'real issues' behind the Island's suffering, that is, 'debt, poverty and trade injustice'. (362) In a sequence of sketches, she and her four colleagues imagine the possible consequences.

They begin by dreaming of Bob Marley returning to the Island as deputy leader to spearhead a people's revolution. Not only does the reggae superstar's resurrection remind the audience of his continued iconic status as a champion of the 'sufferers', it also questions the lack of political imagination present amongst the current crop of popular musicians in Jamaica and its diaspora. Next, they imagine Jamaica's political leaders appearing on a satirical TV quiz show to answer for the ludicrous consequences of the country's debt. At this point we are introduced to the play's title – the stark reality that only thirty-five cents is left in each dollar for domestic spending after Jamaica's international debt has been serviced. But then before we can fully comprehend the staggering consequences of the national coffers being bled dry by overseas creditors, we are taken to a local market. A group of market traders are seen contemplating the effects of the undermining of local agriculture from imported fruit and powdered milk. So not only is the Island being squeezed by its creditors, big business is also impacting upon its ability to feed itself. But it gets worse.

Events become more sinister when they turn to the subject of sweatshop labour. They conjure a picture of a foreign-owned company ruthlessly exploiting its workers to produce clothing, probably for overseas markets. We are exposed to a small degree of the misery and oppression caused by working in cramped conditions to service the West's desire for cheap manufactured goods. But misery does not have the last word. The depressive situation is interrupted by a comic exercising of female sexual power and sisterhood – in the form of subversive co-operation between the workers. This scene sets the stage for the introduction of the intriguing idea of legal action on behalf of the Jamaican poor, for 'psychological suffering' – the ways that workers' stress limits economic productivity. Echoing Malcolm X's desire to take African American tribulations to the United Nations, the students now dream of conspiring to bring to account the IMF and World Bank for the 'psychological suffering' these institutions cause the Jamaican people.

The high point of the group's conjecture, is when they imagine that the NCM's boycott gains sufficient popularity and momentum amongst the people to warrant government intimidation and eradication. With several rallies organised they soon become enemies of the State. To ensure maintenance of the status quo, the American and British governments instigate a smear campaign casting the NCM as left-wing militia and terrorists bent on destruction. At first this may seem like an exaggeration – a group of everyday student activists becoming the public enemies of international powers? But we only need to cast our minds back to the ludicrous reasons given by the Reagan regime for the invasion of another Caribbean Island, Grenada, for a sobering reminder that 'students' affairs' can be an excuse for intervention in America's 'back garden'. The story continues with the dramatic arrest of Ruth. She refuses to be co-opted into the ruling party through a power-sharing agreement and is eventually murdered by the government – but her sudden disappearance is passed off to the public as a mystery. The conjecture ends with the group once again leafleting to nurture change – it was all a dream, everything is still the same.

Slave Trade to Trade Slaves

35 Cents raises important themes about student activism and political morality, but the dominant narrative remains – the political strategy necessary to combat multinationals, labour exploitation and puppet governments in the developing world. For many audiences this central motif will have introduced an alternative reading of the Island's woes. The play moves beyond the populist, neo-colonial, personal behaviouralism, that places the blame for the Island's problems – and much of the developing world – on bad governance and an unruly populace and encourages a structural analysis, to expose the wider political and economic causes of distress. In this case, it is the drastic lack of national income available for a decent mass education, health care and job creation – the product of crippling fiscal policies imposed by international financial institutions.

However, what is lacking within the narrative (although it is difficult to address everything in the couple of hours of the play's performance) is the slightly longer historical backdrop that would help to frame the current malaise. Like many post-colonial societies, Jamaica is currently undergoing its second wave of globalisation. The first wave came in the form of the colonial enterprise – initially with the Spanish and then the British just after the middle of the seventeenth century. Slavery and then colonisation in Jamaica established and indeed normalised harsh working conditions, a near-psychotic drive for cheap produce, unequal social relations and foreign domination of social and political affairs. The latest wave builds on the old – the whips and chains being replaced by financial burdens of equal restriction and brutality. Bob Marley was not far from the truth of the rapacious and avaricious nature of the trinity of global capitalism, the World Bank and IMF when he described modernity's economic practice as a form of bewitchment – a vampire sucking the blood of the 'sufferers'.

A broader history also teaches us that the slaves who struggled to end slavery on the Island had to wage war for their freedom: most, like Sam Sharpe and Paul Bogel, paid with their lives. The twentieth-century struggle for independence from colonial rule, while not a bloody affair, was a counter-hegemonic struggle rooted in a mass movement and political agitation that eventually won political freedom and democratic rights for all Jamaicans. While failing to acknowledge the historical continuities from the colonial to post-colonial world, 35 Cents clearly recognises that the present apathy and ignorance will not do. Radical, engaged political and social struggle is again required to defeat the new leviathan.

Intriguingly, 35 Cents, as a diaspora project – after all, the playwright Paul Anthony Morris lives and works in Britain – indirectly introduces the importance of the role that can be played by those working 'behind enemy lines' to provide meaningful analysis and positive engagement with the real causes of Jamaica's distress. 'One Love.'

35 Cents

by

Paul Anthony Morris

Characters

Main characters...   and their ensemble parts

PETER   PRIME MINISTER   STEPHEN   PATRICIA
               BUSH   OFFICER 2   WINSTON

JAMES   SYMERA   REPORTER 3   DELROY
               JANET   POLICE OFFICER   BLAIR
               US AGENT   OFFICER 1   NEWSREADER
               FIDEL

MADELINE   TRISH JACOBS   SECRETARY 2
               REPORTER 1   PHYLLIS   VANESSA
               CONDOLEEZZA   ALEX

PHILIP   JOHNSON   REPORTER 2   PERKINS
               TREVOR   KAREEM   ANNOUNCER
               CPT POWELL   SIMON

RUTH   SECRETARY 1   REPORTER 4   CLORIS
               ANGEL   JOANNE

35 Cents was first performed in May 2007 at the Blue Elephant Theatre, London, in a Crying in the Wilderness production, with the following cast:

RUTH, Julie Hewlett

MADELINE, Irma Inniss

PHILIP, Vinta Morgan

JAMES, Anthony Ofoegbu

PETER, Mo Sesay

Director Paul Anthony Morris

Set & Costume Design Clary Salandy

Lighting Design Giuseppe Di Lorio

Composer Carol Mae Whittick

SCENE 1

PETER, PHILIP, MADELINE, RUTH and JAMES walk into the centre of the stage wearing white tee-shirts with the words 'The No Confidence Movement' emblazoned across their chests and begin to sing the Jamaican national anthem.

Eternal Father bless our land, Guard us with thy mighty hand, Keep us free from evil powers, Be our light through countless hours, To our leaders great defenders, Grant true wisdom from above, Justice, truth be ours forever. Jamaica land we love, Jamaica, Jamaica, Jamaica land we love.

The Pledge

Before God and all mankind I pledge the love and loyalty of my heart, The wisdom and courage of my mind, The strength and vigour of my body, In the service of my fellow citizens. I promise to stand up for justice and peace, To work diligently and creatively, To think generously and honestly, So that, Jamaica may under God, Increase in beauty, fellowship and prosperity, by playing her part in advancing the welfare of the whole human race.

SCENE 2

Street. PETER, PHILIP, MADELINE, RUTH and JAMES begin canvassing the audience.

PETER: Are you enumerated sir?

JAMES: What about you ma'm?

MADELINE: And the rest of your family sir, would they be interested in signing our petition?

RUTH: What about the future of your grandchildren ma'm, doesn't that concern you?

PHILIP: Our petition aims to make this government defend the interest of *all* our young people.

JAMES: Choosing to do nothing is not an acceptable option ma'm – you must use your vote.

RUTH: It's not anarchy sir. We want the leaders of this Island to listen to the voice of its young people.

PETER: I know it's a difficult decision sir but it's one that the whole Island must face up to.

MADELINE: If you sign up to our petition then we'll be able to put pressure on the government.

PHILIP: I know my father is the leader of the opposition party but I support the No Confidence Movement.

RUTH: I disagree, sir, once a party gets into government they must seek the interest of *all* our citizens.

PHILIP: No sir, a message of *no confidence* in the policies of our government will be the best outcome for our Island.

JAMES: No sir, a message of *no confidence* in the policies of our government will be the best outcome for our Island.

PETER: The best outcome for our Island.

PHILIP: The best outcome for our Island.

MADELINE: The best outcome for our Island.

PETER: No confidence ma'm.

MADELINE: No confidence sir.

JAMES: No confidence.

RUTH: What about you sir, no confidence?

PHILIP: No confidence.

PHILIP / RUTH: No confidence.

PHILIP / RUTH / MADELINE: No confidence.

PHILIP / RUTH / MADELINE / JAMES / PETER: No confidence.

A chant begins.

ALL: No confidence, no confidence, no confidence, no confidence. No Confidence.

SCENE 3

Ruth's living room.

PHILIP: Arrggghh. My feet are killing me.

The STUDENTS sprawl over RUTH's living room floor massaging their aching limbs. RUTH gives her colleagues cushions to sit on.

MADELINE: We must have walked 10,000 miles this week.

PHILIP: I've got a blister, a corn, a bunion and an ingrown toenail all on the same toe.

JAMES: I'll never wear another pair of Nike trainers again – all that money just to make your feet stink.

He takes them off.

ALL: ARGGGHH.

PETER: I just hope some good will come out of all the good *walking* we've been doing.

The room falls into silence.

Look, do you really believe in the success of our petition?

MADELINE: Oh don't start that again.

PETER: Why not? What's the sense in deluding ourselves?

MADELINE: Why do you always have to be so pessimistic?

PETER: Because this is Jamaica and Jamaicans don't like change... I'm sorry.

RUTH: Peter's right.

MADELINE: Ruth! Not you as well.

RUTH: No listen. I've got a confession to make. I... I no longer believe that our petition is going to make a difference.

ALL: What!

MADELINE: How long have you felt like this?

RUTH: A while!

MADELINE: A while! And you never said a word, *why*?

RUTH: Because I thought if I worked hard, the disillusionment would pass.

PHILIP: You still should have told us. Especially as it was your idea to petition the Islanders to vote in the first place.

RUTH: I know and I'm sorry but I just wanted some time by myself, to identify what it was that was brooding in my spirit.

JAMES: And did you?

RUTH: YES! It suddenly came to me.

PETER: What did?

RUTH: How to defeat the government!

ALL: What!

MADELINE: By what means?

RUTH: By leading the Island on a national boycott of the general elections.

MADELINE: I don't believe what I'm hearing. Ruth, it's less than ten days before the elections. How do you intend to pull off this fantastic miracle?

RUTH: By highlighting the *real* issues that are responsible for the economic crisis on our Island.

JAMES: Which are?

RUTH: Debt, poverty and trade injustice.

MADELINE: Ruth this is a grass roots movement, set up to deal with local issues.

RUTH: Yes I know. But the time has come for us to transcend our irrelevance by creating a national forum that can *determine* which one of our parties gets into government.

JAMES: Don't you think we could be going *way* over our heads!

RUTH: Yes we could, but I believe we no longer have a choice. We can either choose *life* by standing up for what is *right* or choose *death* by pretending that the facts don't really exist.

MADELINE: Why does every thing have to come down to *life* and *death* with you?

RUTH: Because until you are ready to *die* for what you truly believe in, *nothing* is going to change! I'm sorry Madeline, forgive me… Peter, Philip, James. I must be tired…friends?

PETER / JAMES / PHILIP: Friends

MADELINE walks towards the door to exit. RUTH stops her.

RUTH: Madeline, I'm sorry. Forgive me. Please.

JAMES quickly intervenes putting his arm around MADELINE and escorting her back into the room. They sit down.

PHILIP: So…where do we go from here?

RUTH: I don't know. When I look around me it all seems so hopeless, but somehow we have to send a strong message to our government that *we* the young people of Jamaica are no longer prepared to tolerate the exploitation of our Island.

PHILIP: What if we *used* the Peace Rally tomorrow night to launch the idea of the boycott?

PETER: That would be ideal. But we'll need to find a nostalgic precedent to capture the imagination of the Island.

JAMES: What about Garvey?

PHILIP: Nkrumah?

MADELINE: Malcolm?

RUTH: Will you guys be serious!

PHILIP: What about Bogle?

JAMES: Nanny?

PHILIP: Gandhi?

MADELINE: Martin?

PETER: No wait, I got it, I got it, I got it.

ALL: What!

PETER: Robert Nesta Marley.

JAMES / PHILIP / MADELINE / PETER: YESsssssssss.

RUTH: I don't believe you guys.

PETER: Can you imagine it the *whole* nation standing on their toes in suspense?

MADELINE: Can you imagine the VIPs?

RUTH: *No I can't.*

MADELINE: Mandela.

PETER: Chavez.

PHILIP: Castro.

JAMES: David Beckham.

RUTH: James!

PETER: There'll be satellite coverage from all the leading networks, which we could download onto our mobile phones.

RUTH: This is insane!

MADELINE: Our national youth choir would be robed in our famous colours, chanting to the pulsating rhythms of 'Get up stand up'.

PHILIP: Did you hear?

MADELINE: 'Stand up for your rights'.

PHILIP: One more time.

MADELINE: 'Get up stand up'.

ALL: 'Don't give up the fight'.

PETER: Can you *imagine* what the next 24 hours would be like?

PHILIP: Pandemonium and mayhem!

JAMES: The Jamaican government would enforce curfews and military road blocks all over the Island.

RUTH: Oh stop it.

PETER: Sporadic shooting would interrupt the incessant looting and burning of foreign businesses and government property.

PHILIP: The CIA would be flown into Jamaica to neutralize our cultural icons.

JAMES: And those who they could not silence would be detained, under illegal house arrest.

MADELINE: Jamaica would become one great big inferno.

PHILIP: Can you imagine our Prime Minister's face?

RUTH: No, I can't.

PETER: Citizens, countrymen and friends!

RUTH: Peter!

The group laughs. PETER removes a green napkin from RUTH's dresser and tucks the end of it into the neck of his tee-shirt to create the impression that he is wearing a tie.

PETER: It is my greatest pleasure...

RUTH: Peter!

PETER: To dutifully inform this great island of ours, that the late great Robert Nesta Marley...

PETER picks up RUTH's dresser drawer and turns it into a makeshift lectern in front of RUTH's window. Two of the STUDENTS part the curtains revealing linen curtains that create the impression of a wide screen TV. PETER begins to address the nation in a televised press conference as the PRIME MINISTER of Jamaica.

PRIME MINISTER: ...is alive and has been sighted on more than forty separate occasions over the past twenty-four hours.

Applause from the actors who are now part of the live political broadcast.

I have here in my possession an official letter of invitation *confirming* Mr Marley's new appointment as Deputy Leader of the *People's Popular Congress.* (*Applause.*) It is my firm expectation that within the next twenty-four hours, Mr Marley will be installed into his new office just in time to spearhead our *general election campaign.* (*Applause.*) And so my fellow countrymen, with less than ten days before the elections, I invite the entire nation to join hands with *Bob* and *I* to secure the future of this island by re-electing this government *back into public service.* (*Applause.*) May God bless Jamaica.

Refrain of last line of National Anthem – 'Jamaica, Jamaica, Jamaica land we love'.

Thank you.

PETER closes the curtains in front of him and reappears from behind them. The STUDENTS burst out laughing.

SCENE 4

RUTH's house.

MADELINE: Mr Symera…

MADELINE continues the fantasy by grabbing a hair brush from RUTH's dresser and then pushing JAMES into the centre of the room. She sticks the hairbrush / microphone under his nose. Realising her intention JAMES grabs a yellow napkin from RUTH's dresser and tucks it into the top of his tee-shirt to create his tie. He then appropriates the Opposition Leader MR SYMERA's personality.

TRISH JACOBS: Mr Symera as leader of the opposition party what is your response to the Prime Minister's latest claims, that the international reggae superstar Robert Nesta Marley has agreed to join his party?

SYMERA: It's scandalous. I have just held *secret* talks with Mr Marley and he has agreed to accept the office of Deputy Leadership from *me*… The *Jamaican National Party.*

TRISH JACOBS: Could you tell our viewers what would drive the Prime Minister into making such an audacious claim, if it were not true?

SYMERA: The up and coming elections of course, this is just another tardy publicity stunt to boost support for his fading campaign. He is hoping that if he can remain in the public's eye long enough they won't forget his name on polling day.

He laughs at his own joke.

TRISH JACOBS: Yes. Could you tell our viewers when you will be unveiling Mr Marley as *your new* deputy leader?

SYMERA: I will be holding a press conference with Bob within the next twenty-four hours to outline my manifesto for the forthcoming election campaign.

TRISH JACOBS: And where will that take place sir?

SYMERA: Um, um, I'm afraid those details will have to remain confidential…due to…public safety concerns. Now, if you will excuse me, I have some urgent business to attend to.

He takes a few steps forward and then returns to TRISH remembering something. He raises his clenched fist.

One Love.

He exits.

TRISH JACOBS: This is Trish Jacobs of the Jamaican Broadcasting Corporation reporting *live* from the headquarters of the Jamaican National Party.

Exit TRISH.

SCENE 5

Enter PRIME MINISTER and SECRETARY 1 from downstage right. The whole scene is located between the offices of the PRIME MINISTER and SYMERA.

SECRETARY 1: Prime Minister we're having trouble locating Mr Marley.

PRIME MINISTER: What do you mean you're having trouble? I told the Island that Bob had accepted my offer. He must be found.

SECRETARY 1 exits. Enter JOHNSON the Defence Secretary.

PRIME MINISTER: Well Johnson?

JOHNSON: He just seems to have disappeared, sir.

PRIME MINISTER: What do you mean disappeared? With Bob as my deputy his *popularity* will guarantee me *victory* at the elections. He must be found now.

Enter SYMERA from upstage left, shouting down his mobile phone. His SECRETARY (2) follows closely behind.

SYMERA: I don't care how long it takes. Do you have any idea what this means? With Bob as my deputy I'll be able to attract the votes of all the young people and win the election by a landslide. He must be found *now*.

SECRETARY 2: This was just delivered sir. It's marked urgent.

SYMERA: Open it, open it.

She begins to read the letter which is a white handkerchief.

SECRETARY 2: Greetings in the name of the Most…

SYMERA: Yes, yes. Skip the religious sentiment.

Enter PRIME MINISTER and SECRETARY 1 from downstage left. She is reading a duplicate copy of the letter (white handkerchief) to the PRIME MINISTER.

SECRETARY 1 / SECRETARY 2: I am unable to accept your invitation as deputy leader as I fully support the boycott of the *No Confidence Movement*. However, I wish you all the best in the up and coming elections. PS, I've gone to *observe* the people…*to see how they're living.*

PRIME MINISTER / SYMERA: What!

The PRIME MINISTER and SYMERA walk up and down in their respective offices in an alternating sequence, firing their lines downstage and returning upstage until their delivery.

PRIME MINISTER: You've got to stop him.

SYMERA: He mustn't meet the people.

PRIME MINISTER: If they find out that Bob supports the No Confidence Movement…

SYMERA: The whole Island will run after them. You've got to stop him.

PRIME MINISTER: I don't care what it takes. Arrest him. Lock him up. Do something.

PRIME MINISTER / SYMERA: Don't just stand there get moving.

The SECRETARIES scurry off leaving the two men continuing their routine.

SYMERA: Call in the police.

PRIME MINISTER: Send out the army.

SYMERA: But don't let him meet the people.

PRIME MINISTER: Oh my heart, my heart, heart!

SYMERA: Water, water, water.

Exit SYMERA. *The* PRIME MINISTER *picks up the dressing table drawer again and turns it into a lectern.*

SCENE 6

TV studio. Political broadcast.

PRIME MINISTER: Citizens of Jamaica.

The STUDENTS *have now become journalists and are recording the public address from the wings on their seats/boxes with their arms outstretched towards the* PRIME MINISTER.

I am pleased to inform you that over the past twenty-four hours, the government has been able to confirm that the identity of our celebrated national icon, Robert Nesta Marley, was illegally appropriated by a lone fugitive called *Dwayne Alexander* who is wanted for questioning by the government of St Kitts for illegal arms dealing in the region. I am therefore, pleased to inform the Island that the government has withdrawn its offer of deputy leadership from Mr Alexander and have issued instead a warrant for his arrest and immediate deportation. Any questions?

The REPORTERS *jump from their seats.* REPORTERS 2 *and* 4 *(*PHILIP *and* RUTH*) are on one side together and* REPORTERS 1 *and* 3 *(*JAMES *and* MADELINE*) are together on the other side.*

REPORTER 3: Prime Minister, could you tell us why this impostor Dwayne Alexander would go to such *extraordinary lengths* to infiltrate the ranks of the government?

PRIME MINISTER: Our evidence shows that Mr Alexander was planning to sabotage our lucrative tourist industry. His grievance against *this* government is based upon the intelligence that we supplied to the Prime Minister of St Kitts which exposed his illegal operations in the Caribbean. Next question.

REPORTER 1: It has been rumoured, Prime Minister, that Mr Alexander may have been supplying arms to an extreme radical left-wing organisation on our Island?

PRIME MINISTER: That is correct. Our inquiries have identified a *link* between the impostor Mr Alexander and the radical

369

left-wing student organisation the *No...Confidence... Movement*.

REPORTER 4: Doesn't your personal attempt, Prime Minister, to accommodate Mr Alexander into the ranks of the leadership of your party, *compromise* the integrity of your government?

PRIME MINISTER: Absolutely not. The government simply expressed the democratic *sentiments* of the people.

REPORTER 2: Won't this scandal, Prime Minister, have an adverse effect on your party's chances at the elections?

PRIME MINISTER: Certainly not. The Popular People's Congress is the People's Popular Party.

REPORTER 1: How are you going to deal with the expectations of the Islanders, having roused them with your announcement that Bob Marley was going to be your deputy leader?

PRIME MINISTER: To preserve the integrity of our electoral process, the government will be imposing a complete ban on all media coverage relating to *Robert Nesta Marley*. Last question.

REPORTER 3: It is rumoured, Prime Minister, that you will be appearing on the controversial Theodore Perkins show, as part of a strategy to remove the apathy that is currently surrounding our general election campaign.

PRIME MINISTER: That is correct. I can confirm that the opposition leader and I will be appearing on the famous Theodore Perkins show to encourage our voters to get involved in our general election campaign. That's all for tonight gentlemen. Goodnight.

The PRIME MINISTER retreats behind the curtains and closes them in front of him.

REPORTERS: Prime Minister, Prime Minister, Prime Minister.

PETER reappears from behind the curtain and the STUDENTS fall into hysterical laughter.

SCENE 7

TV Studio. The laughter is suddenly broken by PHILIP *who sets up the controversial Theodore Perkins Show by using another dresser as his lectern.*

PERKINS: Welcome back to the celebrity episode of the Theodore Perkins Show, the game show that is the *best* because it *tests* your intellect. (*Big laugh.*)

PETER, who is sitting on his box/seat in the wings, throws PHILIP *a red sequined bow tie.* RUTH *and* MADELINE *grab their chairs/boxes and run downstage right and left. They lift up the lids of their boxes and take out colourful pompoms and become the conductors for the audience.*

PERKINS: For those of you who have just joined us during the commercial break, we have cooked up a real special treat tonight for you. So put your hands together for the *stoic* and the *impregnable* Prime Minister, Rufus Maloy...

PETER puts on the PRIME MINISTER's *tie and takes one of the larger dressers and wheels it onto the stage and stands behind it.* RUTH *gets up from her box/seat with her pompoms and leads the audience on her side of the stage into cheering for the* PRIME MINISTER.

RUTH: WWOOOOOOOOO.

PERKINS: And the dishonourable Opposition Leader Mr George Symera..

JAMES puts on SYMERA's *tie and takes one of the other dressers and wheels it onto the stage and stands behind it.* MADELINE *gets up from her box with her pompoms and leads the audience on her side into cheering for* SYMERA.

MADELINE: WWOOOOOOOOO.

PERKINS: Prime Minister, you've made it to the final of the Theodore Perkins show, how does it feel?

PRIME MINISTER: I'm extremely nervous Theodore, extremely nervous.

PAUL ANTHONY MORRIS

PERKINS: I'm sure you are Prime Minister. Mr Symera, what's going through your mind right at this moment?

SYMERA: I'm just thrilled to be in the final Theodore, really thrilled.

PERKINS: Okay gentlemen you both know the rules, it's the best out of three. Who ever gets the most right on the night...

PERKINS / RUTH / MADELINE: Wins the top prize –

PERKINS: – on the Theodore Perkins show. May I take this opportunity to wish both our contestants good luck. Fingers on the buzzer, gentlemen. Question one. Why did the Minister of Finance say this week *that our children will be born into poverty for the next three hundred years*?

The PRIME MINISTER beats SYMERA to the buzzer.

Prime Minister.

PRIME MINISTER: Because our national debt stands at six hundred billion Jamaican dollars.

PERKINS: That's correct. Let's give the Prime Minister a big round of applause.

RUTH stands up waving her pompoms and encourages the audience to cheer for the PRIME MINISTER.

RUTH: WWOOOOOOOOOO.

PERKINS: Question two. Mr Symera, you're already one behind, lose this next question and you're out of the game. Here we go gentlemen. If Jamaica receives one million dollars in financial aid as a loan, by the time the interest is added how much does the government have to pay back?

MR SYMERA beats the PRIME MINISTER to the buzzer.

Mr Symera.

SYMERA: UM,UM,UM.

PERKINS: Um... I'm going to have to rush you.

SYMERA: Seventeen million dollars.

PERKINS: That's correct. Let's give Mr Symera a big round of applause.

MADELINE stands up waving her pompoms and encourages the audience to cheer for SYMERA.

MADELINE: WWOOOOOOOOOOOO.

PERKINS: Okay, gentlemen, it's the final question. Whoever gets this question right, wins our top prize which, is a two-week visa to the *United Kingdom*.

RUTH and MADELINE lead the audience into loud cheering.

RUTH / MADELINE: WWWOOOOOOOOOOOOO.

PERKINS: In a recent CIA survey, what percentage of Jamaicans are now living below the poverty line? Prime Minister.

The PRIME MINISTER is the first to the buzzer.

PERKINS: Prime Minister?

PRIME MINISTER: Seven per cent.

PERKINS: It's wrong.

SYMERA hits his buzzer.

Mr Symera you can steal –

SYMERA: Ten per cent. No fifteen. No make it twenty per cent. Sorry I've changed my mind – ten…and a half.

PERKINS: Is that your final answer?

SYMERA: It is.

PERKINS: Gentlemen, for tonight's top prize the answer is… thirty per cent.

RUTH / MADELINE: AAAAHHHHHHH.

PERKINS: Bad luck guys, bad luck. So with the scores still tied, we now go into Suddennnnnn debt.

The programme's signature theme song is played. PERKINS, the PRIME MINISTER and SYMERA come from behind their boxes and begin to do a little routine together as they sing the song. MADELINE and RUTH run to the side of the stage and pick up two cardboard sheets that have the lyrics of the song written on them. They hold them up while circling their boxes for the audience to join in.

373

ALL: Sudden debt, Sudden debt.

> We are going *into* Sudden debt.
>
> If you get the answer right you'll win the visa for the flight.
>
> We are going into Sudden debt.
>
> Sudden debt, Sudden debt.
>
> We are going into Sudden debt.
>
> When you land at Heathrow, will you get in?
>
> We don't know.
>
> We are going into Sudden debttttttt.

Applause. PERKINS, SYMERA and the PRIME MINISTER return to behind their dressers.

PERKINS: Okay, gentlemen, out of every dollar that our government spends on repaying our Island's national debt, how much is left to invest in housing, health, education, employment, agriculture, business, defence and investment?

SYMERA is the first to the buzzer.

SYMERA: Eighty cents.

PERKINS: You're wrong. Prime Minister?

PRIME MINISTER: Thirty-five cents.

PERKINS: For tonight's top prize on the Theodore Perkins Show the answer is… Thirty-five cents.

RUTH leads her audience into cheering and applauding.

PERKINS: Congratulations Prime Minister, you have just won the top prize on the Theodore Perkins show. Mr Symera, my commiserations, you were a superb contestant. It's been great having you on the show. Well, that's it for tonight folks, we'll be back the same time tomorrow with two new contestants. Goodnight, God bless and…

ALL: Byeeeeeee.

The STUDENTS fall out of their characters, laughing at the absurdity of their fantasy game show as they put RUTH's furniture back in its place however, RUTH takes a shirt from one of her drawers and ties it around her waist to make an

apron. She then assumes the posture of an elderly woman,
CLORIS.

SCENE 8

Farmers' market.

CLORIS: Yes ma'm, can I help you?

The STUDENTS slightly confused, pause to see what RUTH is
doing. RUTH addresses someone in the audience.

The milk is seventy-four dollars, the cheese 180 a pound...

The STUDENTS suddenly realise that RUTH is setting up the
scene for their next role play which is a market scene. They
all begin to assume the characters of market traders.

And the butter 120 dollars an ounce.

CLORIS hands a box to TREVOR which is then passed around
in a choreographed style, from one trader to the next, to sell
and advertise their wares to their customers.

PHYLLIS: The pears are eighty dollars ma'm and the pineapples
are two for fifty-five dollars.

STEPHEN: The sweet potatoes are seventy-five dollars sir. And
the plantain is four for forty-five and the yam, ninety-six a
pound.

CLORIS: What do you mean where does my cheese come from?
Mrs Francis you'll have to come back quickly otherwise the
milk is going to go off.

DELROY: That's ninety-five dollars sir. No ma'm, I can no longer
afford to sell mangoes because they're importing cheaper
brands in the supermarket.

TREVOR: The melons are fifty-two dollars ma'm and the
tomatoes forty-nine a pound. Yes, I heard the news on the
radio this morning. They say there's a complete ban.

CLORIS: Miss Ruby welcome home. How was Hingland? Cold!
You must be glad to be back.

STEPHEN: The dasheen is eighty-four a pound sir and the
breadfruit, seventy-five a quarter.

TREVOR: What I don't understand is, how the government managed to find out that Dwayne Alexander was an impostor so quickly. Sixty-two dollars, ma'm.

DELROY: We have ginger beer, soar sap, cucumber, beetroot, carrot juice, pineapple juice and orange juice. That's forty-five dollars, sir.

PHYLLIS: Mr Campbell is you going to desert me again this week? What have I done to deserve such a horrendous snub? That's sixty-nine dollars, ma'm.

TREVOR: I don't care what they say, Dwayne Alexander may be an impostor, but Bob's spirit is still here with us.

CLORIS: Look, I've already told you, we don't sell imported foods in this market.

DELROY: That's seventy-one dollars, sir.

TREVOR: Eighty-four dollars, ma'm.

STEPHEN: Ninety-eight dollars, sir.

CLORIS: Sixty-seven dollars, ma'm.

PHYLLIS: Thank you Pastor and may God bless you sir.

TREVOR: Do come again ma'm and give my regards to your husband.

STEPHEN: See you next month ma'm and thank you for your support.

DELROY: Take care now.

ALL: BYE.

The FARMERS gather together waving goodbye to the customers. We hear the sound of their vehicles (made by the FARMERS) taking off. The FARMERS begin to pack away their stalls.

TREVOR: What a day, what a day, what a day. I'm exhausted and hot.

CLORIS: Here.

TREVOR: What's that? Oh please Cloris, no.

CLORIS: Come on drink it up. Look at the state of you. You're nothing but a bag of bones.

TREVOR: Warm milk, yuk.

CLORIS: Come on, drink it up.

He drinks in one gulp.

TREVOR: That's disgusting. What are you going to do with the rest?

CLORIS: I'm taking some down to the children's home, what's left will simply be poured down the drain.

Pause.

You know, I'm not sure how much longer I can go on.

TREVOR: Why?

CLORIS: Because I can't keep pouring milk down the drain...my cows think it's ungrateful.

Laughter.

Who would have ever believed, that after twenty-five years of dairy farming, I would be put out of business by evaporated cream and powdered milk?

TREVOR: Don't worry Cloris, when Bob becomes our Prime Minister, he'll put an end to all subsidised imports and then we'll all get together and

STEPHEN / DELROY / PHYLLIS: *Feel alright.*

They laugh, giving TREVOR high fives.

CLORIS: He's banned remember! And stop using his name around here, you'll get us all arrested.

TREVOR: Come on Cloris, lighten up.

CLORIS: That's exactly what's happening to our business, the government is making them lighter.

Having burst their bubble, the farmers return to loading up their boxes. TREVOR removes a sticker from his pocket and conspires with the others to play a trick on CLORIS. He places the sticker on his box with the word 'Florida' on it.

Ahhhh it sure is hot... And sticky.

CLORIS fans herself. PHYLLIS drops the box on TREVOR's toe to attract CLORIS' attention. CLORIS looks in their direction to see what the commotion is all about.

What's that?

TREVOR: What!

CLORIS: That. Excuse me.

TREVOR: It's nothing, just some boxes that I'm...

CLORIS sees the word 'Florida' on the boxes.

CLORIS: FLORIDA?

TREVOR: Damn!

The other FARMERS feign shock.

CLORIS: You've been selling *foreign* oranges in our market. How could you?

TREVOR: A sorry.

The FARMERS feign disgust.

CLORIS: Sorry! Sorry isn't good enough. You've made a mockery out of all of us.

TREVOR: Calm down.

CLORIS: No, I won't calm down. Do you think that I too couldn't also strike up some *shady* deal and pretend to our customers that they were buying home grown foods from my stall? I'm ashamed of you.

TREVOR: I'm not the only one. The others have been doing it as well.

CLORIS: What?

PHYLLIS / DELROY / STEPHEN: Judas.

CLORIS: AHHH.

CLORIS puts her hand over her chest. The farmers break off to their stalls laughing.

TREVOR: Oh stop being so dramatic. That's life.

CLORIS: Help, my chest.

TREVOR: What's wrong now?

CLORIS: I need to sit down I feel...

CLORIS staggers.

TREVOR: Look Cloris it was only a...

CLORIS: My chest...

CLORIS screams and falls to the ground convulsing.

PHYLLIS: Oh my God. Someone run and get the doctor quickly.

STEPHEN and DELROY run off.

Cloris, can you hear me? Cloris, Cloris.

She listens to her heart.

Trevor, she's stopped breathing. There's no pulse, no breath. She's dead. Trevor she's dead.

TREVOR: No Cloris no!

PHYLLIS: Trevor, she's gone.

TREVOR: Cloris. I was only joking. Cloris, wake up, wake up.

PHYLLIS: Trevor.

TREVOR: Cloris, I'm sorry.

PHYLLIS: Trevor.

TREVOR: I'm sorry Cloris.

PHYLLIS: Trevor!

TREVOR: Cloris the boxes were just a joke a silly joke. Wake up Cloris. Cloris, Cloris, Clorissssss... You know I think we would make a *fiiiiinnnne* group of entertainers.

Laughter. PHILIP helps RUTH to her feet and the STUDENTS bring out the cushions to sit on, chuckling over the fantasy.

SCENE 9

RUTH's house.

MADELINE: The only problem is, we wouldn't have anybody to broadcast our material. Can you imagine

our Prime Minister allowing the chief executive of the
Jamaican Broadcasting Corporation to televise 'Kick the
multinationals out of Jamaica'? It would be like asking a
Rabbi to welcome a pig in the synagogue.

The group are in hysterics.

RUTH: All this playing around is fine, but we still need to come
up with an idea for the boycott/campaign.

JAMES: Oh come on Ruth, take it easy and relax na. After you
just had us walking up and down the Island leafleting
the Islanders for nothing, I think we deserve a bit of
recreational entertainment. Amen.

MADELINE / PETER / PHILIP: Amen.

The laughter settles down into silence.

RUTH: Philip, I'm sorry you're caught up in *all* this mess.

PHILIP: It's okay.

JAMES: No it isn't, we sometimes forget…about your father. We
don't mean to be so cruel.

PHILIP: That's okay.

JAMES: We're proud of you man.

RUTH / PETER / MADELINE: Yes.

RUTH: How is he going to respond when he finds out that
you're involved in the boycott?

PHILIP: Like he normally does!

JAMES: Where you been boy? (*Laughter.*) Didn't I tell you to stop
running around with them anarchists? (*Laughter.*)

JAMES / PHILIP: Can't you see I have an election to win?

JAMES: You should be here helping your father instead of
turning…

JAMES / PHILIP: The whole Island against me.

JAMES: Come here. You're not too old to beat.

*JAMES chases PHILIP around the room in pantomime fashion.
The group try to prevent JAMES from catching PHILIP. JAMES*

finally catches up with PHILIP *and begins to beat him with his yellow handkerchief whilst the others retreat to the wings to watch the fun.*

PHILIP: Alright, alright that's enough, that's enough.

PHILIP retreats upstage and JAMES *downstage.* JAMES *puts* SYMERA's *yellow tie on.*

SCENE 10

SYMERA's *house.*

SYMERA: Where have you been boy? What have you been doing? Answer me?

PHILIP: I've been with my friends.

SYMERA: Doing what? Answer me.

PHILIP: Handing out leaflets.

SYMERA: What kind of leaflets were you, my *son* handing out? Is this it? Is this what you've been handing out?

SYMERA takes out a white handkerchief from his pocket and reads it.

SYMERA: *'Mr Symera's opposition party is morally bankrupt, economically challenged and politically naive.'* Do you know what members of my party are saying behind my back?

PHILIP: What about my friends?

SYMERA: I don't care about your *damn* friends. How could you say these things about your own father?

PHILIP: Having a difference of opinion doesn't mean I hate you, Father.

SYMERA: No, but this does and I'm going to put an end to it right now.

PHILIP: You can't stop the boycott Father. We're going to disrupt the elections.

SYMERA: Over my dead body! The Americans will never allow it.

PHILIP: They can't stop it. The No Confidence Movement is determined to make a real difference in this Island.

SYMERA: Do you know the enemies that these friends of yours will create for this Island? The Americans will invade this place just like they did Grenada and you and all your friends will be dead. Dead.

PHILIP: Well, it's just like our leader says, until we are ready to die for what we truly believe in, nothing is going to change.

SYMERA: What kind of nonsense talk is that? Have you become a *fanatic*? Don't you care about what your mother thinks? What if she hears you talking like that?

PHILIP: Dad, you haven't cared about what Mum thinks for over twenty years. At every election campaign, you cart her out like some retired race horse, just to boost your fake public image.

SYMERA: What! That's it. You're going to resign from this No Confidence Movement and support my election campaign.

PHILIP: And I've told you before Father, I'll never betray my friends.

SYMERA: But you'll betray your own father... your own flesh and blood. For that alone I'll beat you.

He throws PHILIP to the floor.

I'm still your father and as long as you are under my roof, you'll do as I say.

SYMERA begins to whip PHILIP with his tie until he is exhausted. He collapses on the floor, with laughter echoing from the others.

JAMES: Oh God Philip, I can't beat you no more. You take a good beating boy. Man you can take licks. Philip, Philip.

PHILIP: ARRRRGH, ARRRRGH, ARGHHHHHHHHHH.

JAMES attempts to raise PHILIP from off the floor but PHILIP pushes him away. He attempts to raise him again but PHILIP pushes him away harder this time. The group suddenly stop

laughing. JAMES looks back at the group who are in shock over
PHILIP's anguish.

JAMES: Philip, it's me James.

PHILIP: Arrggghhhh Arrgghhhhh Arrrrgggghhhhhh.

JAMES: Philip, it's okay, it's me, James. Philip, Philip, Philip.

PETER pulls JAMES – who has now become distressed over
PHILIP's discomfort – away. JAMES attempts to comfort PHILIP
but he is held back by PETER. RUTH walks over to PHILIP and
kneels next to him placing her hand on his shoulder. MADELINE
picks up PHILIP's glasses and carefully hands them to him.
PHILIP takes the glasses and exits.

SCENE 11

Factory. PATRICIA enters the factory carrying her chair/box. She
places it in the middle of the stage. She opens the lid and takes
out her overalls and white cap and begins to put them on. Enter
JANET who follows the same routine as PATRICIA. Dressed, she
swallows several pills and puts the bottle back into her pocket.
She then starts up the generator (making all the sounds) which
feeds power directly to the sewing machines. She then turns
on the power switches on the machines, individually (four)
and then sits at her station directly opposite PATRICIA. They
both release the safety catch on their machines together and
say in a very dry manner.

JANET / PATRICIA: Morning!

In a unified sequence they begin sewing at speed (making all
the noises). They drop each tee-shirt that they have completed,
into their individual baskets beside them, which represent
their quota for the day. After completing three tee-shirts,
VANESSA enters, following the same routine set by PATRICIA
and JANET.

VANESSA: Morning.

JANET / PATRICIA: Morning.

Dressed, VANESSA takes out a large plastic bag from her box
and lays it before PATRICIA and JANET. The two women stop

*sewing and clock what VANESSA is doing. VANESSA folds up the
bag and tucks it into her trousers behind her back. PATRICIA and
JANET stare at each other and then begin sewing very quickly.
VANESSA sits down at her machine next to JANET and joins the
fast rhythm set by the women. Moments later, ANGEL enters
the factory late and flustered. She quickly changes into her
overalls and sits at her station next to PATRICIA and opposite
VANESSA.*

ANGEL: Sorry I'm late.

*ANGEL tries to get into the rhythm set by her colleagues but it
is clear that she is not a competent machinist. She gets herself
in a tizz with the machine and cuts her finger. She jumps up
sucking the blood.*

Blast. I hate these machines. When's he going to get some
new ones?

JANET: Let me have a look.

*JANET leaves her station and walks over to ANGEL and begins
to dress her cut.*

ANGEL: WELL. You're his concubine, you should at least have
some idea.

VANESSA: Jealousy will get you nowhere.

ANGEL: Are you serious? Me jealous?

VANESSA: I see your finger's stopped hurting.

Enter KAREEM dressed in a brown caretaker's coat.

KAREEM: What are you all doing standing around. Haven't you
got work to do? Chop, chop get back to your machines. I've
got deadlines to meet.

*He watches them work. His eyes fall on ANGEL and he gives
her a contemptuous look because of her lack of skill on the
machine. He walks over to VANESSA. His tone turns soft when
addressing her.*

How are you this morning? What are you all looking at?
Get back to work. It's almost break time and I've bought
you something special.

JANET: Mr Kareem, we've finished the last batch of five hundred.

KAREEM: What…already. Let me see. I hope you haven't botched them up. These items are now contraband and are now worth a lot of…

He holds up the imaginary tee-shirt.

That's good, very good. Well done Janet, well done, you did very well. Did you all fulfil your individual quotas?

PATRICIA: Yes of course…

KAREEM: But, but, but, but what? Who was it? Was it Angel? Tell me, tell me, tell me.

VANESSA: It was me…… I broke one of my nails and… Angel had to help me out.

He looks hard at ANGEL.

KAREEM: I'm watching you. Janet.

JANET: Yes sir.

KAREEM: Here's the quota for the new order. Please be careful, it's a very important line from one of the top American clothing companies. If we are able to meet the demand by the summer, we'll secure the contract for their *entire* children's line. Here.

He whispers to VANESSA.

See you later. Work faster.

KAREEM exits.

VANESSA: Well!

ANGEL: Well what?

VANESSA: Aren't you going to thank me?

ANGEL: For what?

VANESSA: For saving you from getting the sack. You were late remember, that's the third time this week. If it wasn't for my…

JANET: Vanessa. Now's not a good time.

VANESSA: But she…

JANET: Not now Vanessa. How is he?

ANGEL: He was up all night crying. I can still hear the ringing in my ears. The doctor says that if the operation isn't performed within three weeks, it will be too late.

JANET: How much are you short?

ANGEL: We still need another five thousand US dollars.

JANET: Jesus!

A horn sounds.

PATRICIA: Thank God it's break time. I'm dying for a drink.

Enter KAREEM humming a song whilst wheeling in a vending machine. He plugs in the cord and switches on the machine.

ANGEL: What's that?

KAREEM: A vending machine.

ANGEL: I know it's…a vending machine but what's it doing here?

KAREEM: The company has a new contract with American Cola.

ANGEL: Where's Winston?

KAREEM: I've disposed of his services. You can't be a supporter of the *No Confidence Movement* and expect to continue to work for me.

ANGEL: Are you saying Mr Kareem that…we can't even have… a political opinion in our *own* Island?

KAREEM: This is not Jamaica. This is an American *free trade zone*. By the way I have decided to cut down on our utility bills by switching off the air conditioning during break times.

ANGEL: You can't do that. How are we supposed to keep cool?

KAREEM: Have a coke.

The phone rings.

How many times must I tell you people no phone calls? Well which one of you is going to answer it?

Nobody moves. KAREEM answers the phone.

Hello…Mrs Stewart.

ANGEL: Damn.

KAREEM: How are you? How's your grandson. Still poorly I'm sorry to hear that. Yes, Angel is here. Hold the line.

ANGEL takes the phone.

ANGEL: Hello Mum. No. Now's not a good time Mum. It's in the cabinet in the kitchen. Bye Mum, bye.

KAREEM: The phone is installed so that I can keep an eye on you it's *not* for your personal…

The phone rings again.

Well aren't you going to answer it Angel?

ANGEL: Kareem Manufacturers, how can I help you? No it's in the cabinet the blue one. Bye Mum bye. Sorry it won't happen again.

KAREEM: It better not. Vanessa.

Exit VANESSA and KAREEM.

ANGEL: Ahhh what does she see in him? He makes my skin crawl.

JANET: Take it easy. Having Vanessa around makes it easier on us.

ANGEL: How can you say that?

JANET: Because it's true. For the next fifteen minutes, we're going to enjoy an unofficial break that the other workers won't have. At lunchtime Vanessa keeps him busy for an extra half hour and at teatime, for an extra twenty minutes. Everybody has their use, even Vanessa.

From offstage we hear KAREEM shouting.

KAREEM: (*Off.*) Hie hie Hieeeeeee.

PATRICIA and JANET burst out laughing.

ANGEL: It's disgusting. How could she sleep with him?

PATRICIA: You just close your eyes and think of Jamaica.

From offstage we hear KAREEM screaming and banging furniture.

KAREEM: (*Off.*) Yes, yes, YESSSSSzzzzzzzzzzzzzzzzzzzzzzzzz.

JANET: That didn't take long. We better get back to our machines. Blast, it's hot and my clothes are soaking.

Enter VANESSA fixing her dress. She walks up to the vending machine and purchases a can. She opens it and drinks. VANESSA burps.

VANESSA: I needed that.

ANGEL: I bet you did.

The phone rings again. ANGEL answers it.

Mum. How is he? Thank God. Listen Mum I forgot to tell you I'm doing overtime tonight. I need the money. Mum if he doesn't have the operation, I'm not shouting. I know it's stressful but we have to manage. Well, what do you want me to do?

JANET: Angel!

ANGEL: Look Mum I've got to go... If I'm caught on the phone I'm sure to be fired, Mum stop crying.

JANET: Angel.

ANGEL: Mum, Mum.

JANET: Angel.

ANGEL: Mum. Damn.

KAREEM: (*Off.*) Who's been...

ANGEL runs to her seat. Enter KAREEM.

On the phone? I've been trying to get through for over twenty minutes. Well who was it?

KAREEM is eyeballing ANGEL. ANGEL is about to stand up when VANESSA stands.

VANESSA: It was me... I was arranging...you know...

KAREEM: What?

VANESSA: You know.

KAREEM is confused.

KAREEM: Oh yes… YES. And.

VANESSA: It's been arranged.

KAREEM: REALLY? I mean… really?

VANESSA: Really, why don't we go into the office and discuss it. I can give you all the details.

KAREEM: Yes why don't we? Work faster.

Exit KAREEM and VANESSA.

ANGEL: I really can't take much more of this.

JANET: Come on dry your eyes. You don't have much choice. What are you going to do, leave the poor child to die?

ANGEL: Yes. Why did God give him to me?

JANET: Because he knows you're the only one who will find a way to save his life. Now wipe those tears.

KAREEM: (*Off.*) Yes, yes yessssssszzzzzzzzzzzzzzzzzzzzzzz.

ANGEL: I can't stand this.

KAREEM: (*Off.*) Mercy Vanessa, mercy darling, mercy ahhhh, aahhh, aahhhhahhhh.

ANGEL: How much longer will we have to put up with this? What is she doing to him in there?

Enter VANESSA without her overalls and hat on carrying the plastic bag that she hid under her clothes and placed behind her back. She quickly lifts up the lid of her box/seat and puts the bag into it.

VANESSA: I need a drink.

She runs to the vending machine, purchases a can and gulps it down. Recognising the distress she is in, JANET forces the can away from VANESSA and begins to calm her down.

Here.

VANESSA hands an envelope to JANET.

JANET: Wow. Is that it?

VANESSA: Yes.

She hands another envelope to PATRICIA.

PATRICIA: Vanessa, we were just about to tell Angel what you *get* up to with Mr Kareem. Remember?

VANESSA: Yes.

ANGEL: Please spare me the gory details. I'm not interested.

VANESSA: Do you think it's disgusting?

ANGEL: Of course it is. The man's married for one and secondly, what you're doing is prostitution.

VANESSA: I agree with you for once, it is disgusting.

ANGEL: So why do you do it? Why do you lower yourself to foreigners and give all of us a bad name?

VANESSA: Because it's liberating.

ANGEL: What's liberating about a man emptying himself inside of you?

VANESSA: I wouldn't know.

ANGEL: Excuse me!

VANESSA: I said I wouldn't know. I don't have sex with Mr Kareem I just beat him.

ANGEL: You're lying.

PATRICIA: It's true.

ANGEL: Janet.

JANET: It's the truth.

ANGEL: You mean to tell me that he bought you the *clothes* the *jewellery* and the *car* because you *spank* him.

VANESSA: That's right. His wife refuses to do it.

ANGEL: What kind of foolishness is that? Are you serious?

VANESSA: Absolutely.

ANGEL: You've never had sex with Mr Kareem?

VANESSA: Never! Cross my legs and hope to die.

ANGEL begins screaming with joy.

ANGEL: Why didn't you tell me?

PATRICIA: We didn't want to spoil the fun. You should have seen what they did to me when I first joined.

ANGEL: I feel like a damn fool. Vanessa please forgive me for all…

VANESSA: Forget it. It should be us apologising.

ANGEL: Listen the next time you're going to spank him could you sneak me in so that I can give him one big slap across his backside?

They laugh.

VANESSA: Here.

VANESSA gives ANGEL an envelope.

ANGEL: What's this?

VANESSA: Open it.

ANGEL: Five thousand dollars?

VANESSA: It's from all of us. Now go and get your son on the first available flight and get his operation done.

ANGEL: I will never forget you, never. Every time I look at my son, I'll remember you all.

VANESSA: Come on and dry your tears. That's better. Now go. We'll finish up here.

ANGEL: What about the sewing?

VANESSA: Go, before we change our minds.

PATRICIA escorts ANGEL off the premises.

JANET: Well!

VANESSA: I propose a toast.

VANESSA purchases two cans from the machine and gives one to JANET.

To Kareem.

JANET: Kareem.

They drink. Enter PATRICIA.

JANET: What now?

VANESSA: We'll have to get rid of his body...starting with his head.

VANESSA opens up the lid on her box/seat and holds up the plastic bag. JANET and PATRICIA look inside the bag and see KAREEM's head. They wince and quickly begin to close down the factory. Finished, they remove their overalls and place their boxes / seats in their original positions. They are now standing with their No Confidence tee-shirts exposed. They begin to sing the last refrain of the national anthem slowly.

MADELINE: Jamaica.

RUTH and PHILIP enter and join them standing by their seats.

JAMES: Jamaica.

JAMES / MADELINE / PETER / PHILIP / RUTH: Jamaica, land we love.

SCENE 12

RUTH's house.

JAMES: You know, I'm seriously considering getting involved in this show business, business. I never knew acting was so easy. It could be my best ticket off the Island.

MADELINE: Er, I don't think so.

JAMES: Madeline what are you saying that I'm not funny? Peter, Philip tell Madeline I'm funny, go on, tell her.

MADELINE hits JAMES with one of the cushions. He retaliates by striking MADELINE with the cushion in his hand. PETER and PHILIP join in and the activity degenerates into a free for all. RUTH is sitting on her seat reading a magazine.

RUTH: THAT'S IT.

The play fighting stops.

MADELINE: Jesus. You nearly gave me a heart attack.

RUTH: You know I've been struggling to come up with a... *concept* for our boycott.

ALL: Yes.

RUTH: Well I think I've got it. Listen to this. Professor Lyndon of the Institute of Psychology in Washington has recently submitted his annual report to the US government on the effects that *stress* is having on the US economy. Professor Lyndon says that *psychological suffering* has cost ordinary Americans more than 400 billion dollars in lost revenue and, that *stress* is the 'number one enemy to the commercial success of the American economy'. We should use this report to calculate the *psychological harm* that the Western governments have been inflicting upon our Island and use it as a basis to galvanise support for our boycott.

JAMES: I don't understand. What do you mean *stress*?

RUTH: If *stress* is undermining the commercial success of the richest country in the world, then imagine the damage that it is causing in poor countries. What kind of *stress* must our farmers be under after having their industry decimated by subsidised imports? Imagine the stress levels of the thousands of Jamaican women that are working in those concentration camps that they call factories, for less than a hundred US dollars a month. And what about the stress levels of our doctors who have to watch innocent children die because of the cutbacks in public spending that have been imposed upon our government? And what about the anxieties that are overwhelming the Island due to the proliferation of guns and drugs that are being imported by foreigners – not to mention the breaking up of our families because our parents are having to find menial work aboard in order to feed their children back home? And what about your anxieties – Madeline, Philip, James, Peter – are they not also burdensome and intolerable?

The group hang their heads.

If we can get our hands on the statistics that prove the
structural adjustment programmes of the World Bank
and the IMF are *still* responsible for the economic crisis
that exists in our Island then we could harangue them for
violating the United Nations charter for human rights.

PHILIP: That's brilliant.

RUTH: Human suffering is detested the world over right.

ALL: Right.

RUTH: Whether it's the carpet factories in Asia, the coffee
plantations in South America, or slavery in the sub-
Sahara – but what about the organisations like the G8 and
the EU who are making billions of dollars out of our human
suffering? Our campaign must clearly link them to the
extreme levels of poverty, crime, disease, unemployment,
poor education, poor trade and poor health that exist in our
Island.

JAMES: How are we going to bring this to the public's attention?

RUTH: We'll organise a press conference at the Peace Rally
tomorrow night and challenge the government to disprove
our allegations.

MADELINE: Which are?

RUTH: That the Western governments are responsible for
creating the *psychological suffering* that is overwhelming
our Island.

PHILIP: I can use my father's contacts to organise the press
conference and get the statistics that you need.

RUTH: Are you sure you want to do this Philip? We can find
another way.

PHILIP: I'm sure. Besides you guys are the only family I now
have.

JAMES: Yes man.

RUTH: At last we'll be able to make a real difference on the
Island.

JAMES: So what do we do now?

RUTH: I suggest you all go home and get some rest so that we can make a fresh start on our campaign first thing tomorrow morning.

The STUDENTS get up to prepare to exit.

PETER: Aren't you forgetting something?

RUTH: Sorry.

PETER: I said aren't *you* forgetting something?

MADELINE: Like what?

PETER: How do you think the government is going react? Do you think that they are just going to sit there and allow us to galvanise the Islanders against them?

JAMES: They won't have a choice. By the time they realise what is happening it will be too late.

PETER: Really!

JAMES: Yes really. Oh come on Peter this is no time for your cynicism. Wake up and smell the coffee. If you're afraid then say so but don't try to stop us off from doing what is right.

PHILIP: That's not fair James. Peter does have a point.

JAMES: Who's talking to you?

MADELINE: Calm down.

JAMES: No I won't calm down.

MADELINE: This is all your fault.

PETER: What did I do?

JAMES: Look this is a chance we have to take.

PETER: No, we won't need to take chances if we stop and think this through.

MADELINE: Why do you always have to be so pessimistic?

PETER: Okay then, what about the innocent people? How are we going to protect them?

JAMES: We won't need to.

PETER: That's reckless James.

JAMES: Who you calling reckless?

PETER: YOU!

The STUDENTS are locked in a bitter argument.

RUTH: Stop it, stop it, stop it, stop it. This is not supposed to be happening to us. We are not the enemy remember? We're friends.

RUTH brings the group together and piles their hands on top of each other.

Friends!

ALL: Friends!

The STUDENTS quickly disperse and retreat to different parts of the room still simmering. RUTH's attempt to reunite them has failed.

RUTH: Peter you're right.

JAMES: Oh God.

JAMES slithers to the floor leaning up against the wall.

RUTH: None of us can truly predict how the government and the Islanders are going to react to our campaign. So why don't you talk about your concerns amongst yourselves? If at the end of it, you decide that we should go ahead with the boycott then we will, but if you decide against it I will never mention the campaign again and we will remain a grass roots movement.

RUTH begins to exit.

JAMES: Where you going?

RUTH: To give you some privacy to talk but if you need me at any time just come and get me. Agreed?

ALL: Agreed!

RUTH exits.

PHILIP: So what do we do now?

JAMES: Don't look at me. Ask Peter he's the one with all the big ideas.

PETER: Look James, what Ruth is asking us to do is *huge*. All I'm simply saying is that we need to be aware of the consequences before we commit ourselves.

JAMES: Consequences! Anything is better than the position that we find ourselves in right now.

PETER: Is it?

JAMES: Yes. We all agreed in the beginning that doing *nothing* was not an acceptable option.

PETER: Are you prepared to die James?

JAMES: WHAT!

PETER: I said are you prepared to give up your life?

JAMES: It won't come to that.

PHILIP: Really? What did Ruth say earlier on?

JAMES: I don't know

PHILIP: What did she say James?... James?

JAMES: She said *unless you are prepared to die for what you truly believe nothing is going to change*...but it won't come to that...isn't that right Philip?... Philip?

PHILIP: Peter's right James. We all know how volatile things can get during the elections. The government's response could be immense.

PETER: And...we also have to discuss whether or not...we can trust Ruth with our lives.

JAMES: What! And how the hell do you propose that we do that eh?

MADELINE stands up.

MADELINE: Why don't we imagine (like we've already been doing) that we are at the Peace Rally and...there are thousands of Jamaicans already in attendance?

397

PHILIP: With media coverage from all over the Island and the whole of the Caribbean.

The STUDENTS begin to transform RUTH's living room.

PETER: We'll need banners, posters and leaflets.

MADELINE: And a stage…

PETER / PHILIP: Yes.

MADELINE: With Ruth as the main…

MADELINE / PETER / PHILIP: Speaker.

They all look at JAMES who is still festering. Unable to escape their glare he rises from the floor and participates in setting up the scene still disgruntled.

JAMES: We could broadcast her speech live on the radio, the TV, and the internet.

PHILIP: And the whole Island would be gripped with excitement and suspense.

PETER: A chant would begin at the front of the stage…

PHILIP: No confidence, no confidence.

PETER: And accelerate right the way through the large crowd setting everyone alight.

PHILIP / MADELINE / JAMES: No confidence, no confidence, no confidence, no confidence.

PETER: Everybody ready?

MADELINE: Roll cameras.

JAMES: 3, 2, 1 and action.

PETER and PHILIP are together on stage right and JAMES is stage left. They are punching the air with their fists as they chant. MADELINE moves down centre stage and once again becomes the reporter TRISH JACOBS reporting live from the demonstration. The chant at various levels continues right the way through the scene.

PHILIP / PETER / JAMES: No confidence, no confidence, no confidence, no confidence.

TRISH JACOBS: The sudden popularity of the No Confidence Movement has become the catalyst for some spectacular events that have recently taken place on the Island. Under world bosses pledged in front of this very large crowd of more than 7,000 young people to put an end to the political intimidation leading up to the general elections.

PETER exits and returns with RUTH. She is led up the platform which has been erected behind the STUDENTS. RUTH is astonished at the large crowd and electric atmosphere.

This was followed by extraordinary scenes never witnessed on the Island before. Gunmen voluntarily surrendered their weapons to Ruth Casey Macdonald, leader of the *No Confidence Movement*, and vowed to support her boycott of all the political parties on the Island. With another four more rallies scheduled to take place over the next ten days it is clear that the campaign of the *No Confidence Movement* to lead the electorate on a national boycott of the general elections is gaining in momentum. Hold on, yes, yes, yes, where going *live* to the broadcast of the *No Confidence Movement* where Ruth Casey Macdonald is about to address the Island.

The chant increases and then lowers as RUTH addresses the crowd.

RUTH: We the students of the *No Confidence Movement* indict the western governments of violating the basic human rights of the citizens of Jamaica. Our research shows that the World Bank, the IMF, the G8, the EU are directly responsible for the psychological suffering that is growing within our Island. We also indict our current government and all previous administrations for not strenuously resisting the imperialist *strongholds* that are responsible for our psychological trauma.

The chant increases again and then lowers.

We therefore urge the citizens of Jamaica to stand up to this injustice by casting a resounding vote of No Confidence against all the political party's on the Island. And to form instead a people's government that will defends the interests of all our citizens. May God strengthen our cause.

The chant increases as the STUDENTS *march up and down waving their fists in the air.* JAMES *runs up the centre aisle to become the voice of a police officer.*

POLICE OFFICER: This is the police. This is an illegal demonstration. I repeat. This is the police. This is an illegal demonstration.

JAMES returns to his place among the STUDENTS *who have been seized with fear by the number of armed police officers that have surrounded them.*

RUTH: Students of Jamaica do not panic. You have nothing to fear. Do not be intimidated.

PHILIP: No confidence…no vote. No confidence…no vote. No confidence.

PETER / MADELINE: No vote.

PHILIP: No confidence.

ALL: No vote.

PHILIP: No confidence.

ALL: No vote.

PHILIP: No confidence.

ALL: No vote.

PHILIP: No confidence.

ALL: No vote.

RUTH runs down from the platform and joins her colleagues shouting at the officers.

RUTH: Officer, officer control your men this is a peaceful demonstration.

MADELINE: Don't run. Stand firm. Stand firm.

The STUDENTS *begin to run around as one unit in different directions on the stage.*

JAMES: Officer the children, mind the children, mind the children.

PHILIP: Move back, move back you're hurting her.

RUTH: Officer, tell your men to retreat, tell them to retreat.

PETER: Get of him, get off him, get off him.

MADELINE: Jesus they're killing him, they're killing him.

RUTH: Officer control your men, control your men.

JAMES runs down the centre aisle again.

POLICE OFFICER: This is your final warning drop your guns and move back. I said drop your guns and move back.

JAMES returns to the group.

RUTH: Guns what guns?

PETER: Hey what are you doing?

MADELINE: The lights I can't see, my eyes, my eyes.

JAMES: No officer, don't shoot, don't shoot. Officer, officer, officer.

A single gun shot is fired.

ALL: Runnnnnnnn.

SCENE 13

The White House.

ANNOUNCER: The President of the United States.

The STUDENTS hum the American national anthem. BUSH steps into the spotlight

PRESIDENT BUSH: Over the past 24 hours our worst fears were realised in the early hours of this morning when news broke of a failed coup attempt on the elected democratic government of Jamaica. Our security forces in the region have informed us of a growing anti-American left-wing militia group called the *No Confidence Movement* who sought to seize control of the Jamaican government. Our response to this act of evil has been swift. The search is now under way to hunt down the leader of this evil regime Ruth Casey Macdonald.

Since September 11th the war against terrorism has been the rallying cry of this administration. This government is determined in its pursuit to secure freedom and democracy for all peoples – it is to this end that we have committed ourselves to resolving this crisis in the tiny Island of Jamaica. Already a number of civilised nations have begun to rally to our call by insisting as we do to stand united against this evil. The international peace envoy for the Middle East, the former British Prime Minister Tony Blair has also made *his* intentions very clear – to *liberate* the peoples of Jamaica. Therefore, we have *not* ruled out the possibility of a pre-emptive strike against the terrorists. Our missiles are ready and our troops are on full alert to hunt down the enemies of *freedom* and *democracy*. May God bless America.

ANNOUNCER: The International Peace Envoy for the Middle East Tony Blair.

The STUDENTS sit down.

TONY BLAIR: I would just like to confirm my support for pre- emptive action against the radical left-wing militia in…Jamaica. Over the past three days our intelligence has secured…*substantial* and *irrefutable* evidence concerning the…capabilities of this terrorist group…on the Island. Our sources confirm *unequivocally* that…this group of *extremists* possess the ability to launch weapons of destruction on…the elected democratic government of Jamaica within the next…forty- five minutes.

SCENE 14

RUTH's living room.

The STUDENTS begin putting RUTH's furniture back as they talk.

MADELINE: Philip do you really believe that Ruth's campaign would actually make the Americans invade our Island?

PHILIP: It's possible. They invaded Grenada in the 80s remember…and everyone knows that they're still active in Haiti.

JAMES: But what about our Prime Minister, wouldn't he have a say in the matter?

PHILIP: No. It's an invasion.

JAMES: Jesus! Peter I'm sorry. I never thought the Americans would get involved.

PETER: Nor did I, it was Philip's idea.

MADELINE: So what do we do now?

PETER: I suggest we continue the discussion from where Philip left off.

MADELINE: And where's that?

PETER / PHILIP: The Americans!

PETER and JAMES spin out of the scene making helicopter noises whilst PHILIP makes the noises of a police siren. MADELINE exits.

SCENE 15

Fields. PETER and JAMES stand on their boxes with torches in their hands circling the auditorium / audience whilst making the sound of a helicopter. PHILIP's police siren which initially accompanied the helicopters fades. Three times PETER and JAMES stand and sit on top of their boxes to search the audience with their lights. Suddenly RUTH runs onto the stage hiding behind one of the boxes. PETER and JAMES rise a fourth time panning the location were RUTH is hiding. RUTH runs over to another place to hide. Instantly MADELINE appears. The helicopters bear down on her with their torches. MADELINE hides behind the box where RUTH first hid. The helicopter lights find her. MADELINE gets up and runs in the direction where RUTH is now hiding. Simultaneously RUTH runs from her position across the stage to hide in another location whilst the helicopter lights are still circling above. The helicopters eventually disappear. MADELINE carefully arises from her hiding place and begins moving into the centre of the stage.

MADELINE: Ruth, Ruth, Ruth.

Not knowing who it is that is following her, RUTH makes a dash for it.

RUTH!

Recognising that it's MADELINE RUTH runs to her.

Thank God! I thought they captured you.

The helicopter lights suddenly appear bearing down on the two women. RUTH and MADELINE retreat to hiding in front of the box that they first hid behind. The helicopter moves away.

RUTH: Where are the others?

MADELINE: I don't know. After the demonstration everyone disappeared and is still in hiding.

RUTH: This is all my fault. I never knew Jamaica had so many men in the army.

MADELINE: They don't. We've been invaded by the Americans.

RUTH: Oh. We'll have to hide out here for a while until things quieten down. I managed to… What's wrong?

MADELINE: The reward that is out for you is…*dead* or *alive*. The government has used the media to turn you into a real anti-hero.

RUTH: What about the campaign?

MADELINE: It's been shut down. All our materials have been confiscated. It's like we never existed.

CAPTAIN POWELL: Don't move. Get down, get down, get down.

Enter CIA AGENT wearing jacket and dark shades with two SOLDIERS. RUTH and MADELINE get down on the floor with their arms spread out before them. The third SOLDIER is standing some yards away on a box with his rifle pointed offering the AMERICAN AGENT and CAPTAIN POWELL cover.

AMERICAN AGENT: Well done Madeline. You can put your hands down now. Your government will reward you richly.

MADELINE: What are you talking about?

AMERICAN AGENT: You've fulfilled your part of the bargain now we must fulfil ours.

RUTH: Madeline!

MADELINE: Ruth I don't know what he's talking about.

AMERICAN AGENT: Sure you do. You can forget the pretence now Madeline, the 50,000 dollar reward is yours.

MADELINE: Don't listen to him Ruth he's lying.

AMERICAN AGENT: Your country owes you a great debt Madeline. I'm sure the Prime Minister will want to honour you personally.

RUTH: Madeline how could you!

MADELINE: He's lying Ruth. They must have followed me here without me knowing. I never told them anything.

RUTH: Madeline you…

RUTH is slapped across the face.

SOLDIER: Shut up!

AMERICAN AGENT: Get her out of here.

RUTH is dragged away.

MADELINE: Ruth. Ruth, Ruth.

AMERICAN AGENT: Pipe down now she's gone. The damage has already been done.

MADELINE: You …

She attempts to slap his face. The AGENT catches her hand. The third OFFICER cocks his gun to shoot. The AGENT holds up his other hand and stops him. The SOLDIER lowers his rifle slightly but maintains his aim.

AMERICAN AGENT: Go home Madeline the movement is dead. We've got what we wanted.

MADELINE: You had us both why didn't you take us?

AMERICAN AGENT: To kill Ruth's spirit. Let's face it Madeline, Ruth's the revolution, not you. We both know I lied. But she believes it and so will the rest of the Island by tomorrow morning.

MADELINE: What do you mean?

AMERICAN AGENT: The morning headlines will feature you, Peter, James and Philip assisting us in the capture of the international terrorist Ruth Casey Macdonald and by tomorrow evening Ruth will be shot dead trying to break out of prison. We've already planted one of our operatives in her cell to lead the mock breakout. You, your friend and your whole goddammed movement will be dead and buried within the next 48 hours.

MADELINE collapses.

Oh shit.

SCENE 16

White House.

ANNOUNCER: The President of the United States.

The anthem is hummed by the STUDENTS. PHILIP has a bomb detector which he runs over the lectern where the PRESIDENT is going to stand to address the nation. JAMES, PHILIP, MADELINE and RUTH have become SECURITY GUARDS scanning the audience during the PRESIDENT's address.

PRESIDENT BUSH: Over the past 24 hours our intelligence as recently confirmed that the terrorist Ruth Casey Macdonald leader of the radical left-wing militia group the No Confidence Movement has been captured by our security forces and detained under the law of international *terrorism*. It is believed that the *terrorist* Ruth Casey Macdonald was recruited from *within* the Island, trained aboard and then sent back to the Caribbean to plot *evil* and *destruction*. Her simple aim was to disguise her regime as a legitimate political alternative whilst waging acts of *evil* and *terror* against innocent women and children. Due to the success of our military campaign we have been able to eliminate this threat and I am pleased to announce to the *world* that the Caribbean island of Jamaica has been *liberated* and her peoples have been *set free* and the elections can now go ahead as originally planned. May God bless America. Now watch this.

BUSH comes from behind the podium. One of the SECURITY GUARDS *gives him a golf club, another sets the tee and the other guard places the ball.* BUSH *makes a swing with the golf club.*

SCENE 17

PRIME MINISTER's office. The PRIME MINISTER *hums the national anthem whilst preparing drinks for him and his guest.*

PRIME MINISTER: To the elections.

CONDOLEEZA: The elections.

The PRIME MINISTER *and* CONDOLEEZZA RICE *clink glasses and drink satisfyingly.*

SYMERA: (*Off.*) Prime Minister, Prime Minister...

Enter SYMERA. *He is hysterical.*

The whole Island is in chaos. There are uprisings everywhere the people are...you didn't tell me she was here.

PRIME MINISTER: You were saying Mr Symera?

SYMERA: There are protests the length and breadth of the Island Prime Minister. The youths are baying for our blood. They're demanding the immediate release of Ruth Casey Macdonald otherwise they say they will seize control of the government.

PRIME MINISTER: I'll send in the army to bring down their resistance.

CONDOLEEZA: That would be a terrible mistake Prime Minister. After what happened in Uzbekistan, our President would find it very difficult to justify your actions.

SYMERA: Then we should do what President Aristide did in Haiti – escape to America until everything has calmed down.

CONDOLEEZA: That would also be another mistake, particularly after what happened to the governments in Ukraine, and Georgia.

PRIME MINISTER: What if the President...

CONDOLEEZA: I'm afraid not Prime Minister. This is a local issue, something that we cannot at this time be seen to be getting involved in. Arresting terrorists that are a threat to international security is one thing, but getting directly involved with the internal affairs of your government is something completely different.

SYMERA: I don't understand. You brought about a regime change in Iraq... Sorry.

PRIME MINISTER: What if we released the prisoner?

CONDOLEEZA: You'd only strengthen the resolve of the mob as they would conclude that you yielded to their pressure. The only way around this problem is to find a way to appease the mob whilst at the same time maintaining the upper hand... I got it, I got it, I got it. Why don't you invite the No Confidence Movement into the coalition?

SYMERA: Are you mad? They'll never accept our terms.

CONDOLEEZA: Exactly. However, you would have appeased the anger of the mob by extending the hand of *inclusion* and *friendship*.

PRIME MINISTER: That's brilliant, brilliant.

CONDOLEEZA: If you make the *terms* of the coalition unacceptable then the No Confidence Movement will be forced into rejecting your invitation.

SYMERA: But what if they accept?

CONDOLEEZA: Then invite only Ruth into the coalition. If she accepts it will be to your advantage as her personal ambition will be greater than her loyalty towards her party and her members. Then go to the electorate and explain that Ruth has *accepted* your invitation to join the coalition which will in turn pacify the anger of the mob and neutralise the No Confidence Movement. You must release her immediately.

SCENE 18

RUTH's living room.

JAMES: So what do you think would happen next? I mean this is all pure conjecture right?

PHILIP: I believe Ruth would never accept their offer of power sharing as it would compromise her ideals.

MADELINE: I don't think that we could ignore this opportunity Philip. Ruth would be no good to us rotting in prison.

PETER: And if she comes out and joins the coalition she would be no good to us at all.

MADELINE: There is a third option.

JAMES: What's that?

MADELINE: That Ruth would reject their offer of power-sharing and the Americans would allow her to come home because they no longer consider her to be a threat. I know it's a bit of a long shot but I believe that this is the option that we should consider. Especially as it would probably be the only way that we could *secure* Ruth's release.

PETER: So what you're saying Madeline is that *we* should persuade Ruth to come out of prison and attend talks to join the government in the *hope* that she rejects their offer.

MADELINE: I'm saying that we should do everything possible to keep Ruth out of prison. Twenty-five years is a long time Peter.

PHILIP: That's unfair Madeline, for Ruth and for us. Suppose our plan backfires and Ruth joins the government because of what *we* have convinced her to do?

MADELINE: Then we will know that we can't trust Ruth with our lives…but at least she'll be free. So…what's Ruth's future going to be – prison or freedom?

JAMES: Freedom.

MADELINE: Peter.

PETER: Freedom.

MADELINE: Philip.

PHILIP: Freedom.

MADELINE: Okay then, now let's see if I can convince her.

SCENE 19

Prison. RUTH is standing in a box with a prison shirt on.

MADELINE: Ruth.

MADELINE steps out of the darkness. PHILIP, PETER and JAMES stand watching the scene unfold from the wings.

RUTH: Madeline!

They embrace. The three men look at each other.

I thought I would never see you again.

MADELINE: So did I.

They embrace a second time.

The Americans set me up Ruth.

RUTH: I know. I... I almost fell for the oldest trick in the book. Any news on the whereabouts of Peter, Philip and James?

MADELINE: They're fine. Philip sends his love especially.

RUTH: Thank God they're alive.

MADELINE: Yes.

Pause.

RUTH: We almost did it Madeline. We were on the verge of bringing about an historic change.

MADELINE: What do you mean *almost*? Haven't you heard?

RUTH: What!

MADELINE: You mean they haven't told you.

RUTH: Told me what?

MADELINE: I can't believe you don't know. Ruth, the Prime Minister has been *forced* to order your immediate release.

RUTH: What do you mean *forced?*

MADELINE: After you were arrested the whole Island went on strike. Everything was at a total standstill. The shops, the banks, the hotels, the airports, nothing moved.

RUTH: No!

MADELINE: Then suddenly thousands of young people from all over the Island began to descend on the Prime Minister's office…

In various parts of the scene PETER, PHILIP and JAMES who are watching the scene chant quietly in the background.

PETER / PHILIP / JAMES: No confidence, no confidence, no confidence, no confidence.

MADELINE: And demanded the immediate inclusion of the No Confidence Movement into the coalition government.

RUTH: I don't believe it.

MADELINE: At first the Prime Minister ignored their threats until he saw that they were about to seize control of the government.

RUTH: UHHH.

'No confidence' chant.

MADELINE: It was amazing Ruth, I wish you were there to see it. Then early this morning I was summoned to the Prime Minister's office and told to organise your immediate release. You're free Ruth free, free, free.

MADELINE takes RUTH's hand and RUTH steps out of the box. They rejoice.

RUTH: That's incredible.

MADELINE: I know. Thanks to the *People* Ruth, we can now transcend our irrelevance and do big things in this Island. It's what you've always talked about and now the opportunity is here. We can't let the *People* down Ruth we can't.

RUTH: What do you mean Madeline?

MADELINE: Ruth haven't you been listening to what I have been saying?

No confidence chant.

The *People* want the No Confidence Movement to be their representative in the coalition. It's like what you said in the beginning about the need for creating a national forum remember? Well now we'll be in a position to *really* determine the policy's of our government.

RUTH: Yes.

MADELINE: I know joining the coalition may at first may seem like a slight detour from your original plan, but now we'll be able to make changes from the inside instead of banging our heads against the wall from outside. Peter, Philip and James think it's worth *trying* and so do I.

A car horn sounds.

That's the car waiting to take us to a meeting with the Prime Minister.

RUTH: What about Peter, Philip and James?

MADELINE: They're going to meet us there.

The car horn sounds again.

Come on Ruth let's get out of here. The *People* are waiting.

They exit.

SCENE 20

RUTH's house. JAMES and PETER pick up their box/seat and sit opposite each other as if they were at the opposite ends of a table. They put on their yellow and green ties and become the PRIME MINISTER and MR SYMERA. MADELINE leads RUTH to the centre of the table and places her in the box again. She then exits and watches the scene with PHILIP from the wings.

PRIME MINISTER: Ruth, our economy is managed from overseas.

RUTH: Yes I know Prime Minister, but unless poverty is fought at the highest level we will never be able to secure a positive future for our children. By 2020 we have to ensure that

all our children possess the ability to finish secondary
education. This initiative would be enhanced by re-directing
25 per cent of the interest payments on our debt back
into the education ministry. We should also endeavour to
divert a further 10 per cent into fighting the HIV epidemic
that is accelerating across the Island. In tandem with this
proposition Prime Minister I propose that we appeal to
Fidel Castro and President Chavez for financial assistance
to help us develop a basic health care programme that will
be free for all our vulnerable citizens. Now with regards to
foreign subsidies…

PRIME MINISTER: Now hold on young lady you're going *way* too
fast. Our economy has been structured and restrained to
servicing our debt.

RUTH: Yes I know but we must now begin to consider new
alternatives for our economy.

PRIME MINISTER: Young lady I admire your passion and your
panache, but your proposals are not practical. We can
not afford to deviate from our repayment programmes.
This would only exasperate our situation and impede all
possibilities for lending in the future.

RUTH: On the contrary sir. Right now Prime Minister, the
whole world is waking up to the gross injustices that
the G8 has been exerting over the developing nations. I
am predicting that *this* global *movement* will make the
scourge of debt so unpopular that many of the Western
governments will be shamed into cancelling our debts.
However, without making the necessary *reforms* to *trade*
we will be plunged right back into debt once again only this
time, instead of cancelling our debt, they could be sold off
as financial packages to private investment companies.

SYMERA: What are you saying?

RUTH: That our debt can be bought by a private consortium in
much the same way as a debt-collecting agency.

SYMERA: That's outrageous!

413

RUTH: What is outrageous Mr Symera is that there are private businesses out there that are specifically buying up the debts owed by poor countries and then turning around and suing these same governments for up to 800 times their original debt. What makes you so certain Mr Symera that our Island won't be next? That right at this very moment, some company isn't planning to sue our government, because of our inability to pay off our debts? Instead of going forwards Prime Minister we're rapidly going backwards.

An uncomfortable silence fills the air.

I'm sorry sir I seem to have rambled on. My excitement seems to have gotten the better of me. You were saying Prime Minister?

PRIME MINISTER: After deep consideration Mr Symera and I thought we'd start you off in the Ministry of *Education and Public Services.*

RUTH: Wow... Wwwwhat departments were you thinking of placing my colleagues?

SYMERA: I'm sorry but we've made no provision for the other members of your organisation. You'll be pleased to know that our invitation extends only as far as *you.*

RUTH: I thought you wanted the No Confidence Movement to make up part of the *coalition?*

PRIME MINISTER: You *are* the *No Confidence Movement* Ruth. You have a *brilliant* mind and a *bright future* ahead of you and *we* want to make sure that you get the right *grooming* and come into contact with the right *people* to *accelerate* your rise up the political ladder.

SYMERA: *We* believe that ten years from now Ruth *you* could make a serious challenge for the leadership of any one of *our* parties *and,* if you're ambitious enough *we* could steer your career towards securing the top seat in government.

PRIME MINISTER: As you rightly stated earlier, it's time this government began to seriously invest in this Island's future.

What greater initiative could there be than investing in our Island's *next female Prime Minister*?

RUTH: That's incredible.

PRIME MINISTER: Yes. We thought you'd be pleased.

RUTH: What about our ideological differences?

PRIME MINISTER: Don't worry about them in time we'll *smooth* them *all* out. Well what do you say, do we have a deal?

RUTH weighs up the offer and is about to step out of the box. The PRIME MINISTER *and* SYMERA *stretch out their hands to assist her.*

RUTH: I acc…

MADELINE / PHILIP: No confidence, no confidence, no confidence, no confidence.

RUTH pauses placing her feet back into the box. She ponders the offer again. With her mind made up she prepares to step out of the box once more. The PRIME MINISTER *and* SYMERA *stretch out their hands to assist her again.*

RUTH: I accep…

MADELINE / PHILIP: No confidence, no confidence, no confidence, no confidence.

RUTH pauses again inside the box. We see her struggling over her dilemma as she weighs up the consequences of her decision. With great difficulty she finally comes to a conclusion.

RUTH: I am… afraid Prime Minister that…the… *No Confidence Movement* finds your terms for the coalition totally unacceptable. *We* would prefer Prime Minister to hold on to our *integrity* and fight over the future of this Island at the ballot box. Good day Prime Minister, Mr Symera.

RUTH is about to step out of the box when she is stopped.

PRIME MINISTER: Ruth.

RUTH: Yes Prime Minister.

PRIME MINISTER: Where are you going?

RUTH: Home.

RUTH steps out of the box and walks down stage. She is emotional.

SCENE 21

RUTH's living room.

ALL: YESSSSSSSS.

PETER, MADELINE, PHILIP and JAMES all jump on RUTH celebrating.

JAMES: Ruth you almost had me there I thought you were going to accept.

MADELINE: I must have died ten times watching you.

PETER: I *never* want to experience something like that again never.

PHILIP: We almost lost you Ruth we almost lost you. Welcome home.

ALL: Yeahhhhhhhhh.

RUTH: What you guys put me through was *really* hard. I almost saw myself going. I could feel the power.

PETER: So what stopped you?

RUTH: All of you. We would no longer be together… And I also figured that if I was asking you to make a serious commitment to me, then I would *first* have to make a serious commitment to you. I know it sounds like a cliché but it's true.

JAMES: Thank God for that.

PHILIP: Here, here.

PHILIP / PETER / JAMES / MADELINE: Hurray.

The laughter dies down.

RUTH: So…have you all come to a decision about the boycott?

PETER, MADELINE, JAMES and PHILIP get into a huddle.

MADELINE: We have. And I'm *sorry* but we have decided to give you our fullest support for the boycott.

RUTH: Yes, yes, yes, yes, yes. At last we'll be able to make…

RUTH / JAMES / PHILIP / MADELINE / PETER: A real difference on the Island.

PETER: Well people it's late and it's time to hit the sack ready for the launch of our *new campaign* tomorrow morning. Thanks for everything Ruth, at least I had a wonderful evening.

JAMES: And next time the entertainment's at my place okay?

PHILIP: As long as it's minus the trainers.

JAMES / MADELINE / PHILIP / PETER: Amen.

MADELINE: See you tomorrow darling.

RUTH: Good night Madeline.

PHILIP: Good night Ruth.

They embrace.

RUTH: Night Philip. You be careful how you get the information from your father.

PHILIP: I will. See you tomorrow.

Having all exited RUTH begins to clear up singing the last refrain of the National Anthem: 'Jamaica, Jamaica, Jamaica land we love'. She discovers PETER's wallet.

RUTH: Oh no Peter's forgot his wallet.

The car drives off.

Never mind he'll get it in the morning.

RUTH continues clearing up. There is a knock at the door. She picks up PETER's wallet.

Hold on Peter I'm coming.

She opens the door. Three SOLDIERS charge in wearing balaclavas with Jamaican, American and British ties tucked into the top of their tee-shirts.

What's going on?

417

CAPTAIN POWELL: Search the house.

RUTH: What for?

CAPTAIN POWELL: Shut up.

The OFFICERS return.

OFFICER 1: Nobody's here.

OFFICER 2: The place is empty sir.

CAPTAIN POWELL: Where are the others, your friends?

RUTH: What have I done?

OFFICER 2: Here you are sir.

RUTH: What's that?

CAPTAIN POWELL: It's a recording of the conspiracy that you have been planning tonight.

RUTH: Conspiracy, what conspiracy?

CAPTAIN POWELL: You are under arrest.

RUTH: What for?

CAPTAIN POWELL: For planning to overthrow the government.

A single gun shot is fired to RUTH's head. She collapses.

SCENE 22

TV Studio.

NEWSREADER: Good evening. Fears over the *disappearance* of Ruth Casey Macdonald (*Picture.*) leader of the students' *No Confidence Movement* continues to grow as the investigation over her mysterious disappearance enters its third day. Chief Superintendent Kernel Davis is appealing to members of the public to come forward with any information no matter how trivial those details may appear. Opposition leader Mr George Symera is expected to convene an emergency meeting with members of the *No Confidence Movement* to express his concerns and sympathy over the sudden disappearance of Ruth Casey Macdonald.

The Inter-Island Caribbean Commission for Economic Development which is to be hosted in Jamaica next month

has invited Sir Bob Geldof (*Picture.*) to an extensive tour
of the Caribbean to highlight the economic conditions of
many of the region's Heavily Indebted Poor Countries. Sir
Bob is expected to arrive in the Caribbean a week before
the conference to meet privately with members of the
Commission to discuss the grievances that are affecting
the economic stability of the region. That's it for now we'll
be back with further updates within the hour. And now...
Twenty years later.

SCENE 23

Street.

Anthem

Eternal Father bless our land, Guard us with thy mighty
hand, Keep us free from evil powers, Be our light through
countless hours, To our leaders great defenders, Grant true
wisdom from above, Justice, truth be ours forever. Jamaica
land we love, Jamaica, Jamaica, Jamaica land we love.

SCENE 24

Street.

WINSTON: Are you enumerated sir?

FIDEL: What about you ma'm?

ALEX: And the rest of your family sir, would they be interested
in signing our petition?

JOANNE: What about the future of your grandchildren ma'm,
doesn't that concern you?

SIMON: Our petition aims to make this government defend the
interest of *all* our young people.

FIDEL: Choosing to do nothing is not an acceptable option
ma'm – you must use your vote.

JOANNE: It's not anarchy sir. We want the leaders of this Island
to listen to the voice of its young people.

WINSTON: I know it's a difficult decision sir but it's one that
the whole Island must face up to.

ALEX: If you sign up to our petition, then we'll be able to put pressure on the government.

JOANNE: I disagree sir, once a party gets into government they must seek the interest of *all* our citizens

SIMON: No sir a message of *no justice* in the policies of our government will be the best outcome for our Island.

FIDEL: No sir a message of *no justice* in the policies of our government will be the best outcome for our Island.

WINSTON: The best outcome for our Island.

SIMON: The best outcome for our Island.

ALEX: The best outcome for our Island.

WINSTON: No justice ma'm.

ALEX: No justice sir.

FIDEL: No justice.

JOANNE: What about you sir, no justice?

SIMON: No justice.

SIMON / JOANNE: No justice.

SIMON / JOANNE / ALEX: No justice.

SIMON / JOANNE / ALEX / FIDEL: No justice.

A chant begins.

SIMON / FIDEL / ALEX / JOANNE / WINSTON: No justice, no justice, no justice, no justice. No justice.

SCENE 25

ALEX's house.

SIMON: Arrggghh my feet are killing me.

FIDEL: We must have walked 10,000 miles this week.

WINSTON: I just hope some good will come out of all the *walking* we've been doing.

JOANNE: Why do you have to be so pessimistic?

WINSTON: Because this is Jamaica and Jamaicans don't like change... I'm sorry.

ALEX: Winston's right.

JOANNE: Alex! Not you as well.

ALEX: We have to be realistic. No grass roots movement has ever overturned the tradition of the electorate. We have to find another precedent to capture the imagination of the Island.

SIMON: What about Garvey.

WINSTON: Malcolm.

FIDEL: Or Nkrumah.

ALEX: Will you guys be serious we can't keep romanticising about the past.

JOANNE: What about Martin.

SIMON: Nanny.

FIDEL: Or Lumumba.

JOANNE: No I've got it, I got it. I got it

ALEX: Will you guys stop?

JOANNE: Ruth Casey Macdonald and the No Confidence Movement.

JOANNE / FIDEL / SIMON / WINSTON: YESSSS.

ALEX: Noooo. We can't keep making the same mistakes.

JOANNA: Can you imagine it, the *whole* Island standing on their toes in suspense?

SIMON: There'd be international coverage from all the leading networks.

ALEX: This is insane.

FIDEL: The government would impose an 18-hour curfew across the Island.

WINSTON: The Americans would invade our Island and infiltrate the ranks of our military.

SIMON: Our politicians would be fighting over each other to make Ruth Deputy Leader of their party.

WINSTON: However, Ruth would resist their offers of Deputy Leadership and find herself on the run from war lords, drug barons and political assassins.

FIDEL: But *Bob*…

ALEX: No.

ALL: YESSSSSSSSS.

FIDEL: Would mysteriously appear…

Bob's silhouette begins to slowly appear.

FIDEL: And rally the youth of Trench Town to come to her rescue.

JOANNA: Can you imagine the streets?

FIDEL: Pandemonium and mayhem.

ALEX: We mustn't do this.

JOANNE: We'd be dancing to the pulsating rhythms of *Get up stand up.*

SIMON: Did you hear?

JOANNE: Stand up for your rights.

SIMON: One more time.

JOANNE: Get up stand up…

ALEX: Listen.

ALL: Don't give up the fight.

Fade slowly to police sirens approaching.

APPENDIX

Writers' Biographies

Lemn Sissay

Lemn Sissay is Artist in Residence at The South Bank Centre, London (2007–8). He has held numerous writer-in-residencies around the world. In January 2008, he was British Council Writer-in-Residence, at The State University of California, Los Angeles. Author of four poetry collections: *Tender Fingers in a Clenched Fist* (1988); *Rebel Without Applause* (1992); *Morning Breaks in the Elevator* (1999) and *The Emperor's Watchmaker* (2000) and the editor of *The Fire People: A Collection of Contemporary Black British Poets* (1998). His work is extensively anthologised and he is a regular contributor to *Poetry Review*. His previous stage plays are *Chaos By Design* (1994) and *Storm* (2003). *Something Dark* toured nationally and internationally, was adapted for Radio 3 and won the RIMA award (2006). His latest play, *The Lost Boys of Africa*, was broadcast on BBC Radio 4 (November 2007) and he has been commissioned by the West Yorkshire Playhouse to write the adaptation of Benjamin Zephaniah's book, *Refugee Boy* (2008). His next collection of poems *Listener* (working title) will be published by Canongate (September 2008) and a new poem will be unveiled – inlaid in a sculpture – in The City of London in the same year.

Mojisola Adebayo

Mojisola Adebayo is a performer, writer, director and teacher. She has an MA in Physical Theatre (University of London) and has undertaken extensive training with Augusto Boal and others. She has worked on various theatre projects all over the world and as a performer in Britain and Ireland, with the Royal Shakespeare Company, Abbey Theatre, Cardboard Citizens/RSC, Creative Origins/Birmingham Rep, Southwark Playhouse, Black Mime Theatre/Nottingham Playhouse, Theatre Resource and London Bubble and various television and radio productions for BBC, Channel 4 and Thames. She plays Nina Udenze in RTÉ's *Fair City*. As well as her dedication to physical performance and political drama, Mojisola is a specialist in Theatre for Social Change. She is currently writing *Theatre for Development: a Handbook* with John Martin (Pan Intercultural Arts) and Manisha Mehta (Vidya, India).

She has directed over thirty productions for various companies, and devised as many scripts. *Moj of the Antarctic* is her first independent production and she is currently developing her latest play, *Muhammad Ali and Me*.

Lennie James

Lennie James was born in 1965 in south London to Trinidadian parents. He wrote his first play *Trial and Error* at seventeen which was published by Faber and Faber. James trained as an actor at the Guildhall School of Music and Drama, graduating in 1988. His television drama, *Storm Damage* which he wrote and starred in, received the 2001 Royal Television Society Award and a BAFTA nomination. His theatrical work includes leading roles in London's major theatres for productions such as: *A Raisin in the Sun*, *This is a Chair*, *Fallout*, *Two Gentleman of Verona*, *Pericles* and *Macbeth*. He has performed in numerous films, including *Sahara*, *Snatch*, *Lucky Break* and *24-Hour Party People*. Lennie's television work includes: *Cold Feet*, *Buried*, *Born with Two Mothers*, *Jericho*, *The State Within*, *Outlaw*. He reprises his stage role of Joe in the televised series of *Fallout* in June 2008.

Courttia Newland

Courttia Newland was born in 1973 and writes novels, short stories and plays. His first novel, *The Scholar* (1997), was soon followed by *Society Within* (1998), *Snakeskin* (2002) and *The Dying Wish* (2006). His short stories appear in many anthologies such as: *Disco 2000*, *Vintage New Writers* (1998), *Afro Beat*, *Playing Sidney Poitier* (1999), *England Calling* (2001) and *'Whose Story'* (*The Times*, 2006). His collection of short stories *Music for the Off-Key* was published in the same year. Courttia has been a Royal Literary Fund Fellow (2003–4), and held writer-in-residencies for the British Council in both Dublin and Washington DC. He wrote many dramas for the Post Office Theatre prior to *B is for Black*, which is included in this volume. Since this, his other plays include: *Whistling Maggie* (2005), *Sweet Yam Kisses* (2006) with Patricia Cumper and *White Open Spaces* (2006). He won the Royal Television Society Award for Education for his documentary *Guns are Cool* and was co-editor with Kadija George of *IC3: An Anthology of Black British Writing* (2000).

Valerie Mason-John

(Honorary Doctor of Letters, University of East London)

Valerie Mason-John is a British Council Visiting Writer – to Sierra Leone in 2007 and on tour to India in 2008 where she will launch her latest book *Broken Voices: 'Untouchable' Women Speak Out*. She is the author of six books and received an honorary Doctorate of Letters from the University of East London 2007, for her lifetime achievements and contributions (through her writing) to the African Diaspora. She has received many awards: amongst these, the Windrush Achievement Award, Arts and Community Pioneer in 2000, and her debut novel *Borrowed Body* won the Mind Book of the Year Award 2006. Known for her hit play *Sin Dykes,* which played sell-out seasons, she has also written *The Adventures of Snow Black and Rose Red*, *You Get Me*, and collaborated on other plays.

Paul Anthony Morris

During the 1980s and 1990s, Paul Anthony Morris worked as an actor in theatre and television. In 1994 he co-founded an independent production company called Trow Out Poe producing the award winning film *Once upon a Time*. He has trained with mentors in the UK, US and Ghana. This culminated with funding from the Arts Council Decibel to workshop his epic play *The Seer* in partnership with West Yorkshire Playhouse. His current company Crying in the Wilderness Productions showcased *35 Cents* at the STEPS Festival and the Tell Tarra Writers Festival. He directed *35 Cents* at the Blue Elephant Theatre and a revised production of a play entitled *Hope in their Eyes* for Amarantha Theatre Company in 2007. He is currently working on two new plays: *Identity* and *Choices*, a commission for the CIA Community Theatre Company. His recent work at St Michael and Angels Academy trained pupils on various aspects of film writing, directing, producing, and technical learning which concluded with the production of five original short stories, screened at the British Film Institute.

Bibliography

References and Further Indicative Critical Studies on Black British Culture and Drama

Abbs, Peter. 'The Creative Word and the Created Life: The Cultural Context for Deep Autobiography'. in Hunt and Sampson, (1998) 117-128

Adebayo, Mojisola. Programme Notes to *Moj of the Antarctic* March, 2007

Alibhai-Brown, Yasmin. 'Black art can be bad, just as art by whites' *The Independent* 5 February, 2005

----- *Who Do We Think We Are?: Imagining the New Britain* London: Penguin Books, 2000, 2001

----- *True Colours: Public Attitudes to Multiculturalism and the Role of the Government* London: IPPR, 1999

Arana, R. Victoria. ed. *'Black' British Aesthetics Today* Newcastle: Cambridge Scholars Publishing, 2007

----- and Ramey, Lauri. eds. *Black British Writing* New York: Palgrave Macmillan, 2004

Aston, Elaine. ed. *Feminist Theatre Voices* Loughborough: Loughborough Theatre Texts, 1997

----- and Harris, Geraldine. eds. *Feminist Futures?: Theatre, Performance, Theory* New York: Palgrave Macmillan, 2006

Bakhtin, M.M./ V.N. Volosinov. *Marxism and the Philosophy of Language* L. Matejka and I.R. Titunik (trans.), Cambridge MA and London: Harvard University Press, 1986

Baldwin, James. *The Price of the Ticket: Collected Non-fiction (1948–1985)* London: Michael Joseph, 1985

Bharucha, Rustom. *Theatre and the World: Performance and the Politics of Culture* London and New York: Routledge, 1993

Bourdieu, Pierre. *Distinction: A Social Critique of the Judgment of Taste* London: Routledge, (1979), 1993

Bromley, Roger. *Narratives for a New Belonging* Edinburgh: Edinburgh University Press, 2000

Butler, Judith. *Bodies that matter: on the discursive limits of 'sex'* New York: Routledge, 1993

----- *Giving An Account of Oneself* New York: Fordham University Press, 2005

Churchill, Caryl. *A Number*. London: Nick Hern Books, 2002

Croft, Susan. *Black and Asian Performance at the Theatre Museum: A User's Guide* Theatre Museum: London, 2002

HIDDEN GEMS

Culler, A. Dwight. 'Monodrama and the Dramatic Monologue' *PMLA* 90, (1975), 366-85

D'Aguiar, Fred. 'Against Black British Literature' in Butcher, Maggie. ed. *Tibisiri: Caribbean Writers and Critics* Sydney: Dangaroo Press, 1989. 106-14

Dabydeen, David, Gilmore, John, and Jones, Cecily. eds. *The Oxford Companion to Black British History* Oxford: Oxford University Press, 2007

Damasio, Antonio. *The Feeling of What Happens: Body, Emotion and the Making of Consciousness* London: Vintage, 2000

Davis, Geoffrey. and Fuchs, Anna. eds. *Staging New Britain: Aspects of Black and Asian British theatre Practice* Oxford: Peter Lang, 2006

Donne, John. *The Works of John Donne Vol. III* ed. Henry Alfred. London: John Parker, 1839. 574-5

Donnell, Alison. ed. *Companion to Contemporary Black British Culture* London and New York: Routledge, 2001

Freud, Sigmund. 'Family Romances', *On Sexuality* Pelican Freud Library, vol. 7. Harmondsworth: Penguin, (1909), 1983. 217-225

Gainor, Ellen J. ed. *Imperialism and Theatre: Essays on World Theatre, Drama and Performance* London: Routledge, 1995

George, Kadija. *Six Plays by Black and Asian Women Writers* London: Aurora Metro, 2005

Goddard, Lynette. *Staging Black Feminisms: Identity, Politics, Performance* Hampshire, GB and New York: Palgrave Macmillan, 2007

Godiwala, Dimple. ed. *Alternatives Within the Mainstream: British Black and Asian Theatre* Cambridge: Cambridge Scholars Press, 2006

Griffin, Gabriele. *Contemporary Black and Asian Women Playwrights in Britain* London: Cambridge University Press, 2003

Grosvenor, Ian. *Assimilating Identities* London: Lawrence and Wishart, 1997

Grabner, Cornelia. 'Is Performance Poetry Dead?' *Poetry Review* Vol.97 No.2 Summer, 2007. 78- 82

Greer, Bonnie. 'The great black hope' *The Guardian* G2 17 May 2006 22-23

Gunning, Dave. 'Anti-Racism, the Nation-State and Contemporary Black British Literature' *The Journal of Commonwealth Literature* Vol.39 No.2 2004. 29-43

Hall, Stuart. 'Race Culture and Communications: Looking Backward and Forward at Cultural Studies' *Rethinking Marxism* 1992 Vol. 5 (1): 10-18

Haraway, Donna J. Modest_Witness@Second_Millenium.FemaleMan©_Meets_OncoMouse™. New York: Routledge, 1997

hooks, bell. *Black Looks: Race and Representation* Boston, MA: South End Press, 1992

Houswitschka, Christoph. 'Introduction' eds. Christoph Houswitschka and Anja Muller-Muth *CDE Contemporary Drama in English* Vol.12 Trier: Wissenschaftlicher Verlag Trier, 2005. 9-24

Howe, Elisabeth A. *Stages of Self: The Dramatic Monologues of Larforgue, Valéry and Mallarmé* Athens: Ohio State Press, 1990

Hunt, Celia. and Sampson, Fiona. *The Self on the Page: Theory and Practice of Creative Writing in Personal Development* London: Jessica Kingsley Publishers, 1998

James, Lennie. 'Who do you think you are' *The Guardian 11* February 2004. 12

Jantjes, Gavin. 'The Long March From 'Ethnic arts' to 'New Internationalism'' in Owusu (2000) 265-70

Johns, Ian. *The Times* 9 April 2004. 23

Kean, Danuta. ed. *Free Verse: Publishing Opportunities for Black and Asian Poets* London: Spread the Word, 2006

King, Bruce. *The Internationalization of English Literature* Oxford: Oxford University Press, 2004

Low, Gail. and Wynne-Davies, Marion. *A black British canon?* Basingstoke: Palgrave Macmillan, 2006

McMillan, Michael. 'Re-baptizing the World in Our Own Terms: Black Theatre and Live Arts in Britain' *Canadian Theatre Review* No.118, Spring 2004. 54-61

McLeod, John. 'Some Problems with 'British' in a 'Black British Canon'' *Wasafiri* Issue 36, Summer 2002. 56-59

Mama, Amina. *Beyond the Masks: Race, Gender and Subjectivity* London and New York: Routledge, 1995

Marmion, Patrick. 'Something Dark' *Time Out London* (10 March 2004) in *Theatre Record*, Issue 5. 2004. 303

Mason-John, Valerie. ed. *Talking Black: Lesbians of African and Asian Descent Speak Out* London: Cassell, 1995

----- *Brown Girl in the Ring: Plays, Prose and Poems* London: Get a Grip, 1999

----- *Sweep It Under the Carpet*. Unpubl. Manuscript. n.d

----- and Khambatta, Ann. eds. *Lesbians Talk: Making Black Waves* London: Scarlet Press, 1993

Mirza, Heidi Safia. ed. *Black British Feminism: A Reader* London and New York: Routledge, 1997

Mollon, Phil. *Multiple Selves, Multiple Voices: Working with Trauma, Violation and Dissociation* Sussex: John Wiley and Sons, 1999

Naoko-Pilgrim, Anita. 'Shall we dance?: Identification through linguistic tropes and performance' in Rapi and Chowdhry 65-77

Nasta, Susheila. 'Editorial' *Wasafiri* Issue 36 Summer 2002. 2-3

Nelson, Hilde Lindemann. *Damaged Identities: Narrative Repair* Ithaca and London: Cornell University Press, 2001

Newland, Courttia. and Sesay, Kadija. eds. *IC3: An Anthology of Black British Writing* London: Penguin Books, 2000

Osborne, Deirdre. 'The State of the Nation: Contemporary Black British Theatre and the Staging of the UK' in Houswitschka and Muller-Muth eds. 2005. 129-149

----- 'Writing Black Back: An Overview of Black Theatre and Performance in Britain' in *Studies in Theatre Performance* Vol.26 No.1, Jan. 2006. 13-31

----- 'Not 'in-yer-face' but what lies beneath: experiential and aesthetic inroads in the drama of debbie tucker green and Dona Daley' in R. Victoria Arana ed. *'Black' British Aesthetics Today* Newcastle-upon-Tyne: Cambridge Scholars Press, 2007. 222-242

----- 'Lemn Sissay's Poetry and Performance' in R. Victoria Arana ed. *Dictionary of Literary Biography: Black British Writing* Sumter, South Carolina: Bruccoli, Clark, and Layman; & Detroit, Michigan: Gale Research Company, 2008

Owusu, Kwesi. ed. *Black British Culture and Society: a Text Reader* London and New York: Routledge, 2000

Pearson, John. 'The Politics of Framing in the Late Nineteenth Century', *Mosaic* 23.1 1990. 15-30

Phillips, Mike. 'Re-writing Black Britain' *Wasafiri* Issue 36, Summer 2002 62-4

Procter, James. *Dwelling Places: Postwar Black British Writing* Manchester: Manchester University Press, 2003

Rahier, Jean Muteba. *Representations of Blackness and the Performance of Identities* Westport, Connecticut: Bergin & Garvey, 1999

Ramey, Lauri. 'Contemporary Black British Writing' in Arana and Ramey eds. (2004). 109-136

Rapi, Nina. and Chowdhry, Maya. eds. *Acts of Passion: Sexuality, Gender and Performance* New York and London: Harrington Park Press, 1998

Reichl, Susanne. *Cultures in the Contact Zone: Ethnic Semiosis in Black British Literature* Trier: WVT Wissenschaftlicher Verlag Trier, 2002

Roberts, Maureen. 'Does the Writer Have a Responsibility to Their Community?' *Wasafiri* No.41, Spring, 2004. 3-7

Rose, Stephen and Rose, Hilary. 'Why We Should Give Up on Race' *The Guardian* 9 April 2005. 21

Sandhu, Sukhdev. *London Calling: How Black and Asian Writers Imagined a City* London: HarperCollins Publishers, 2003

Sesay, Kadija. ed. *Write Black, Write British: From Post Colonial to Black British Literature* Hertford: Hansib, 2005

Severin, Laura. *Poetry Off the Page* Hants, England: Ashgate, 2004

Shange, Ntozake. *Plays One: For colored girls who have considered suicide. . .* London: Methuen Drama, (1974), 1992

Shipley, Joseph T. *Dictionary of World Literature* New York: The Philosophical Library, 1943. 615-616

Sierz, Aleks. 'Sources for the study of contemporary theatre' *Studies in Theatre and Performance* Vol.20. no.3. 196-204

Sinfield, Alan. *Dramatic Monologues* London: Methuen, 1977

Sissay, Lemn. *Morning Breaks in the Elevator* Edinburgh: Payback Press, 1999

----- *Drama on 3: Something Dark,* BBC Radio, 3 September 2004

----- Personal Interview with Deirdre Osborne, September, 2006

Stein, Mark. *Black British Literature: Novels of Transformation* Columbus: The Ohio State University Press, 2004

Stephenson, Heidi. Langridge, Natasha. eds. *Rage and Reason: Women Playwrights on Playwriting* London: Methuen, 1997

Stuart, Mary. 'Writing the Self and the Social Process' in Hunt and Sampson, (1998) 142-152

Tompsett, A. Ruth. ed. *Performing Arts International* Special Issue: 'Black Theatre in Britain'. Vol. 1, Part 2. 1996

Turp, Maggie. *Hidden Self-Harm: Narratives from Psychotherapy* London and Philadelphia: Jessica Kingsley Publishers, 2003

Ugwu, Catherine. ed. *Let's Get It On: The Politics of Black Performance* London: ICA, 1995

Winnicott, D. W. *The Maturational Processes and the Facilitating Environment* London: Hogarth, 1965

Wisker, Gina. *Post-Colonial and African American Women's Writing* London: Macmillan Press, 2000

A Selection of Useful Websites – operative at the time of writing

http://www.applesandsnakes.org
England's leading organisation for performance poetry

'A State of Perpetual Wandering': Diaspora and Black British Writers Bronwyn T Williams http://social.chass.ncsu.edu/jouvert/v3i3/willia.html

http://www.blackartists.org.uk
The site for the longest running black arts organisation in the UK, Black Arts Alliance

http://www.blacknet.co.uk
A cultural events website

http://www.futurehistories.org.uk
National repository of African, Asian and Caribbean Performing Arts in the UK (Nitro, Black Theatre Forum and Moti Roti archives)

http://www.nitro.co.uk
Leading black music theatre

http://www.talawa.com/about/archive.html
Britain's leading black theatre company

http://www.theatremuseum.vam.ac.uk
Victoria and Albert Museum – Black Theatre History archive